Paradigms of Paranoia

Paradigms of Paranoia

The Culture of Conspiracy in Contemporary American Fiction

Samuel Chase Coale

THE UNIVERSITY OF ALABAMA PRESS

Tuscaloosa

Typeface is AGaramond

∞

The paper on which this book is printed meets the minimum requirements of
American National Standard for Information Science-Permanence of Paper for
Printed Library Materials, ANSI Z39.48–1984.

Library of Congress Cataloging-in-Publication Data

Coale, Samuel.
Paradigms of paranoia : the culture of conspiracy in contemporary American
fiction / Samuel Chase Coale.
p. cm.
Includes bibliographical references and index.
ISBN 0-8173-1447-4 (alk. paper)
1. American fiction—20th century—History and criticism. 2. Conspiracies in
literature. 3. Politics and literature—United States—History—20th century.
4. Conspiracies—United States—History—20th century. 5. Political fiction,
American—History and criticism. 6. Paranoia—United States—History—20th
century. 7. Postmodernism (Literature)—United States. 8. Paranoia in literature.
I. Title.
PS374.C594C63 2004
810.9′358—dc22

2004016479

To Gray and Sam
Always Present, Never "Post"

Contents

Acknowledgements

A postmodern trail led to this book on postmodern patterns.

For me it began in 1998 when Jurek Sobieraj asked me to give a keynote address on postmodern ethics (an oxymoron?) at the Polish American Studies Conference in Ustron. That's when I plunged into the maelstrom of research.

This led to teaching a graduate seminar, "The American Phenomenon of Postmodernism," at the European Humanities University in Minsk, Belarus, in 1999. And that culminated in the keynote address on "Sacred Origins and/as Endless Texts," thanks to Laurentiu Constantin, at a conference at Ovidius University in Constanta, Romania, in 2003.

Wheaton College supported me in all of these efforts, but in particular I would like to thank several students who joined with me in assaulting and interrogating postmodernism, paranoia, and conspiracy in fiction, culture, and media: Isaac Barnett, Joe Bedetti, David Casey, Jessica Corn, Alexandra Davis, Scott Kolp, Sasha Pilyavsky, Mike Salb, Josh Serfass, Wendy Thayer, and Charles Upton, to name just a few.

I would also like to thank Dan Waterman at Alabama for his consistent support of and belief in this project, as well as Dawn Hall, who edited the final text, and Joanna Jacobs, also at Alabama. I couldn't have done it without their thorough and persistent assistance.

Of course any mistakes are my own, and the postmodern quest by no means ends here. I remain grateful that my wife Gray and my film-making son Sam continue the journey with me.

Paradigms of Paranoia

I

The Conspiracy of Postmodernism as Suspect and Sublime

Theory has always been problematic, especially since many theorists now seem eager to leap beyond concepts and focus on the particular and the concrete, as if these categories were virtually theory free.[1] It exudes a kind of vampiric quality in its will to power. It establishes a master/slave relationship between the theoretical propositions it posits and the evidence it unearths. It dominates our vision and directs our gaze.

Postmodern theory began to flourish in the United States in the 1960s and 1970s, an era in which, as a result of the Kennedy assassination, the Vietnam War, and Watergate, an antiauthoritarian skepticism grew and exploded. Jonathan Schell describes that state of radical skepticism that such events fostered and that haunts us still:

> The world of *undiscriminating cynicism,* where no one is trusted and nothing is believed, is in many ways a comfortable one. Every citizen enjoys the automatic right to *a sly, knowing, and superior attitude toward all authorities* but has no obligation to do anything about them. What is the use of changing one for another when they are all the same? . . . Everyone grumbles, but it leads to nothing. . . . "They're all crooks," the people say to one another, and go about their business. *This state of mind is new to the United States.* But it is all too familiar to anyone who has spent some time in Eastern Europe or in South America, or in any of the countless other places in the world where people have lost the bold, sometimes innocent spirit of the free and *adopted the easy sophistication of the powerless.* (italics mine, 1989, 204)[2]

It is this "undiscriminating cynicism," this hermeneutics of suspicion that underscores much of the public attitudes toward postmodernism as it evolved in the United States, coupled with the popular perception of deconstruction's meticulous dismantling of texts, seen simplistically as a never-ending attack on all authority and truth. Most critics would agree that the origins of postmodernism in academic circles can be located in Jacques Derrida's lecture, "Structure, Sign and Play in the Discourse of the Human Sciences," delivered at Johns Hopkins University in 1966.[3]

Postmodern theory certainly acquired some of its negative "aura" from our own Calvinist cultural roots with radical indeterminacy standing in for the absent Calvinist god. A literalness in relation to language—the postmodern notion of words as just marks on a page, distinguishable only by their being different from one another and functioning merely as signs within a material system—after all does suggest both present-day Christian fundamentalists and our Calvinist forefathers' iconoclastic attention to the legalisms and logical arguments of pedantic and dogmatic sermons. The postmodern urge, like deconstruction, delights in resisting and dismantling certainly a major part of the Protestant Reformation as its disciples assaulted the sculptures, paintings, and stained-glass windows of Roman Catholic cathedrals.

For me postmodernism in its theoretical manifestations both extends and dismantles modernism. Modernism in literature assaulted the Enlightenment values of rationality, logic, analysis, and conscious control by revealing humanity's more irrational and brutish side and by exposing the human psyche as fragmented, distorted, and driven by unconscious compulsions and motives. Darwin, Freud, Bergson, and Nietzsche, among others, contributed to this assault, which helped shape the literary visions and structures of writers such as Eliot, Faulkner, Proust, and Joyce. And yet this assault was clearly "author"-ized as were the metanarratives of Freud's oedipal and sexual complexes, Marx's class-conscious economics, and Jung's universal archetypes. For instance, no matter how fragmented and scattered Faulkner's *The Sound and the Fury* first appears to be, it does reveal a "bottom line," a basic chronological plot and recognizably distinct characters who can be understood or at least distinguished from one another. Within or beneath Faulkner's linguistic and structural pyrotechnics lies an "author"-ized and recognizable world.

Postmodernism extends that basic assault, following in modernism's footsteps, but at the same time it also dismantles and undermines those authorized concepts. It subverts and questions every form of authority, including that of language itself, thus underscoring Derrida's deconstructive procedures that interrogate the grounds of any and all philosophical and linguistic systems, and, according to some critics, tries to push beyond "reasonable" limits into some vast, querulous, and pulsating realm of aggravated doubt and corrosive skepticism. Everything becomes relational, debatable, elusive, and precarious. Nothing, in theory, is taken for granted, even the theory that authorizes it. The instability of postmodernism, therefore, posits no bottom line. It demolishes any notion of origins, shredding transcendent ideas about anything, except, of course, the telltale text. Negation stacks the deck and undermines all else.

Reality and the self become provisional, contingent, and uncertain. The deification of the Western rational self bites the dust. There are no authorities, no origins, no logos, no center. Everything becomes relational; signs, signifiers, signifieds, and images can only define one another by being different from each other. Beyond them lies only absence, the yawning abyss. Everything is suspect, neither true nor false but "operative" or "inoperative" depending on the context.

Of course there remain many unanswered questions, for which I have no ultimate answers. Has postmodernist theory, in destroying all other metanarratives, become a metanarrative itself? Does it commit the very "sins" it prides itself on exposing? Are we also merely victims of discourse and "the system," whether the "external" one of politics and culture or the more "internal" and psychological one of consciousness and language (postmodernism would decry the separation of these two realms, viewing them as essentially flip sides of the same coin), locked into techno-babble and spectacle that have reduced us, in theory, to allegorical puppets in some contemporary Hieronymus Bosch panorama? Why was the early American appropriation of deconstruction so exhilaratingly negative in its delight to discover distortions, de-facings, and disfigurements virtually everywhere?

Alternatively, psychologists and others inform us that human beings long for a sense of origin, for some kind of conceptual or intuitional unity in their lives. "All that is left of transcendence now is the yearning for it," writes Marxist critic Terry Eagleton (2000, 208), but that may be more than enough. Even Derrida admits "that it's *because* there is no pure presence that I desire it. There would be no desire without it" (Payne and Schad 2003, 9). Eagleton continues: "The quest for the absolute can never be justified. . . . But the hope for it is never entirely eradicated" (2000, 213).

Thus the contemporary human dilemma: the postmodern celebration of radical skepticism clashes with a deeper yearning for unity and wholeness, however it is defined, what Friedrich Schlegel called "that longing for the infinite which is inherent in our being" (quoted in Eagleton 2003, *Sweet Violence*, 6). As Kant suggested, the search for an organic unity may be built into consciousness itself. We can see this in novels by Don DeLillo and Toni Morrison, as their characters strain and grope toward some spiritual vision the fictional structure they inhabit seems determined to undermine.

Such straining, such obsessions, at least in the United States, have led all too often to fundamentalist, right-wing religious groups who freeze ancient texts, like the Bible, and convert them into sacred scripts that underscore present action and policy. They say they read the Bible literally, but of course one person's literalism is another's distortion. And the very nature of language posits multiple meanings, not just one singular interpretation.

Conspiracy, whether actual or theoretical, provides an antidote to postmodernism: everything becomes a sign, a clue, a piece of a larger puzzle. Signs, then, can lead to the general concept of conspiracy, or as George Hartley suggests, effects incarnate the idea of a transcendent design that seems to lie or exist beyond them. However, "We can never reach the horizon, never willfully step outside the field, simply because the horizon is an effect of the field itself" (2003, 202). Yet the reverse is equally true: the concept of conspiracy that permeates our age and has always permeated American culture reduces everything to evidence and predetermined clues. It literalizes experience, seeing connections in coincidence, chance, and accident. It fixes identity, transforms the fluidity of postmodern theory into the foreordained scripts of conspiracy theory. It denies or undercuts the singularity of particular information and interprets it as part of some larger allegorical structure. An object or event thus embodies a secondary meaning as part of a larger intentional plot. Everything becomes a "pasteboard mask" that veils an ultimate conspiracy. In many ways this can become a comfortable notion since the contemporary world becomes explainable and explained, the postmodern malaise rationalized and understood.

Conspiracy and postmodernism, however, both assault the idea of a transcendent, autonomous and individual self. Each self becomes the subject of a particular discourse or the tool of a particular conspiracy. It is when one assigns agency to events that conspiracy "trumps" postmodernism and, as Timothy Melley suggests, incarnates the concept of a hidden design that speaks directly to those made extremely anxious by the postmodern experience of a rootless, disruptive, and wholly disconnected world (2000).

Paranoia fuels the psychology of conspiracy. It lies at the heart of it, producing the compelling need and desire for an overriding concept or structure to explain events and objects in the world rationally and totally, a metanarrative of deceit and deception unmasked. Thus the once positive ideas that Freud—"everything is related to everything"—and E. M. Forster offered—"Only connect"—have become the far more ominous, Thomas Pynchon–stated, "Everything is connected." For Kirk Pillow, if Kant's idea of reflective or aesthetic judgment anticipates "a hidden, purposive unity ordering experience [, then] paranoia would seem to be the pathological extreme of this reflection." Citing Pynchon's *Gravity's Rainbow,* he adds, "This may help to explain why some 'postmodern' works of literature (*which strive to induce the sublime feeling of grasping for meanings and intentions forever beyond reach*), have made paranoid thinking a prominent theme" (italics mine, 2000, 335n16).

The aura of paranoia that follows in the wake of and is generated by conspiracy reflects "the symptomatic condition of post-modernity in contrast to the name for a personal pathological disorder" (2000, 5), as Patrick O'Donnell has described it. For critics of contemporary conspiracy theory, paranoia has transcended its former definition as merely a psychological and clinical condition and becomes a critically creative perspective, what Peter Knight has defined as a "broad sense of suspiciousness" (2002, 17) that participates in and often reflects more conventional interpretive approaches and practices.

This recent concept of paranoia in particular parallels and reflects the more conventional sense of interpretation and critical theory in general in its most abstract and conceptual manner, more in form, perhaps, than in content. It blurs distinctions between psychological and analytical categories, but I still find it valuable to use in my discussion of conspiracy as it appears in fiction. The cultural status of paranoia, also, appears to be very real when fictional characters reveal their conspiratorial anxieties and fears.[4]

For me conspiracy, with its attendant aura of paranoia in contemporary fiction, embodies this sense of epistemological and ontological anxiety that lies at the heart of the postmodern perspective by providing a structure, a fictional plotting of events, that is a product of and reaction to postmodernism. As a product, conspiracy often locates the individual at the center of some massive but ominously anonymous "master plot" or scheme that is solely beyond one's control, thus reproducing the existence of bottomless interpretation and ultimate insolubility that haunts the postmodern experience and point of view. As a reaction, conspiracy as a fictional structure converts a cosmos of contingency and chance into a more rational realm of devious plot and secretive performance, thereby attempting to ground the mysteries and ambiguities of postmodernism in some kind of recognizable framework. It, therefore, underscores a particular narrative pattern and process that writers have employed to grapple with their own doubts and intimations about how the world is run, or not run, and how the individual, acutely aware of his or her personal impotence in the face of labyrinthine bureaucracies and global forces, feels that he or she has become a function or instrument of some invisible, anonymous, but omnipotent and coercive power.

In addition my own interpretation of the sublime supplies an antidote to the negative aspects of postmodernism and to the literal brutalities of conspiracy theory. As Christopher Norris suggests, the sublime reveals "our coming up against awesome, overwhelming, or terrifying kinds of experience . . . that allows thought to transcend the limiting conditions of perceptual or phenomenal experience . . . forcing us sharply—even painfully—up against the limits of adequate representation . . . because the sublime points toward a realm transcending the limits of phenomenal or cognitive grasp" (2000, *Deconstruction,* 16). The sublime always outstrips our ability to categorize and represent it, since it resonates with a sense of ultimate mystery and irrationality beyond our comprehension.

Relying on Pillow's interpretation of Kant's notion of the sublime as "that always partial, indeterminate grasping of contextual wholes through which we make sense of the uncanny particular" (2000, 5), forever seeking an elusive unity but recognizing the open-ended ambiguity of experience and event, I wish to emphasize the boundlessness of certain intuitions, aesthetic feelings, and desires that always lies beyond cognition and conceptual frameworks. The point Pillow makes, akin to Kant's distinction between determinative judgment, which locates a definitive concept from an analytical point of view, and aesthetic or reflective judgment, which anticipates a more indeterminate unity in "moments of uncanny wonder that no fixed concepts can explain or exhaust" (25), I wish to use as underscoring my literary critical approach in opposition to the conceptualized certainty of conspiracy theories, maintaining that there is a distinct difference between the particular fact or event and the wider notion of a universal truth or vision.

Such historical notions of the sublime have always involved terror, as Edmund Burke suggests, as well as astonishment, danger, and a sense of obscurity and infinity, and he recognized the limits of our abilities to imagine and represent such experiences. Kant celebrates these limits as embodying our response to such experiences, aesthetic or natural, that remain excessive, great, and powerful, and both threaten to overwhelm us and giddily exalt our sense of our own abilities to perceive, intuit, and think about them. In confrontation with the sublime, the precarious sense of our own self-preservation is both diminished and expanded, and no amount of representation can ever conceptualize or ground it.

The sublime, thus, exacerbates the limits of all representation, yet we need not be crushed by this knowledge. Sublime moments do engage the observer or participant in a sense of being overwhelmed, reduced, terrorized, and awestruck, but the experience is not only, as Jean-François Lyotard (1984) suggests, an act of pure negation. His is, indeed, a perpetual critique of representation, embodied in the unstable postmodern quest for gaps, indeterminacies, uncertainties, and disconnections, but the unpresentability of the unpresentable is not entirely negative. Lyotard all too swiftly celebrates the sweeping idea that all representation is ultimately impossible. We know that representation can never coincide with the "real world," but that's the very "given" or nature of language and figuration to begin with. It is not so much negative as it is the nature of representation itself.

The postmodern sublime also encourages exhilaration, a sense of wonder, the exaltation of thought thrown back on itself, delighting in itself, sensing as Pillow suggests, "design but no designer . . . *as if* the web of relations [we discern] were designed or intended . . . without any claim that someone is responsible for the meanings 'found' . . . *as if* it were intended to mean, without imputing any underlying agency" (2000, 310).

We need not rely on any "vast conspiracy" to authenticate our experience of sublime understanding. Pillow's definition of sublime reflection underscores my own difficulties with conspiracy as a given, since he views it as "an interpretive and open-ended process of seeking expressive coherence among the diverse attributes of an object and our response to it" (230). Thus I would not reduce the postmodern sublime either to Joseph Tabbi's description of it as a fascination with and fear of technology or to Fredric Jameson's incarnation of it as a reflection of the conditions of late capitalism and multinational corporations, though both of these visions certainly play their part in the postmodern experience.

I would like to suggest that the more radical postmodern philosophies that emphasize total negation allow no room for other possibilities, for texts when conceived of as open territories and fields of language can suggest as much presence as they do absence.[5] Texts also help create the subjectivity and responses of the self that reads them, thus constituting a self and a text that mutually dominate each other, participating in an overlapping domain of events and an ongoing and open-ended pursuit toward multiple and ambiguous meanings. The matrix of self and sign establishes its own sense of origins, forever more process than product.

Recognizing this, I want to argue in favor of "sublime" mystery and ambiguity as opposed to, for example, Marx's notion of mystification. There is genuine mystery in the way each and every one of us is conscious of our sense of self, of our society, and of the world around us, as are the characters, for instance, in the novels of DeLillo and Morrison. This is no mere mystification, no mere mask for some dark sinister social forces that are out there predicting or predicating our every move. This is not to deny those forces but to suggest that they may act differently on and uniquely for every individual. I cannot prove this. It is probably a novelist's keenest sense, but I do feel that ambiguity is a legitimate point of view and that it is more than likely to come closest to our sense of experience and possibly truth than any absolutist theory, he says absolutely. Of course, as a postmodernist I have got to state that a belief in ambiguity and open-ended encounters, replete with its sense of mystery and despair, elation and terror, is itself a theoretical speculation that I offer as a possible glimpse of truth, not *the* truth. I remain fascinated by the enigma that we all aspire to pursue, corral, try to understand, and explicate, and it does not rest exclusively or solely on a theory that pretends to close the gap and solve the mystery.

What I want to avoid and resist at all costs can be summarized in a line from Fredric Jameson, when, after scrutinizing his students' fascination with literature and other media, he declared self-righteously, "Nothing can be more satisfying to a Marxist teacher than to 'break' this fascination for students" (1991, 155). It is precisely this fascination with and in fiction, what Wendy Steiner has called "enlightened beguilement" (1995, 156), that I wish to acknowledge and explore.

Such concepts as postmodern theory, conspiracy theory, and the postmodern sublime engage with one another in a continuously fluid dialectic that I hope to keep intact and open-ended in my exploration of the work of several contemporary American writers. Each can be viewed as an antidote to the other. At the same time each feeds on and reflects the other. Hence conspiracy theory can approach the sublime when it remains fluid and open-ended. At the same time my notion of the postmodern sublime as the basis for an aesthetic and critical approach to literature continues to undermine specific conspiracies and conspiracy theories in fiction. Postmodernism can also seem conspiratorial since it assaults and subverts the American faith in the autonomous self and views that self as a perpetual victim of discourse, culture, political policies, and paranoia. None of these perspectives stands alone or exists in isolation from the others. Each infiltrates, influences, and infects the other.

Writers such as Pynchon and Joan Didion, in responding to the postmodern sublime, structure their novels in the form of and create plots that reflect various conspiracies, as well as a conspiratorial or paranoid outlook, whether initiated by World War II industrialists, movers and shakers during the Vietnam War, or government bureaucrats amid the coils of the Iran-Contra scandal. Conspiracy in all its structural and narrative complexities and possibilities represents for them the postmodern malaise or zeitgeist. Amid epistemological doubt and insoluble ambiguities, the mind driven back on itself persists in looking for signs of some mammoth cabal, convinced that the final missing piece will complete the puzzle and reveal the true conspirators.

There is a very significant difference between the postmodern sublime, fictionalized by these writers as an open-ended and vast conspiracy and as an assault on such conspiratorial visions and patterns, and the romantic sublime that involves the conception and experience of the autonomous self. Take, for example, Captain Ahab in Melville's *Moby-Dick*. Here looms hate incarnate, a fanatic who believes that when we push against and resist the world, in that very action some "reasoning thing" pushes back (1956, 139). The action produces a counter-action, which, in effect, produces or reveals an opponent who can reason. Of course that "reasoning thing" mirrors Ahab's own paranoid quest, but in his terms it possesses apocalyptic powers that lead to an ultimate battle for control of the cosmos. In a similar manner, the act of projecting a conspiracy out into the world "produces" the conspiring agent or principal who must fight back. That act produces its own negation and resistance and pits the individual reasoning self against a presence or an absence, which must itself be reasoning as well. Beyond appearances, beyond the pasteboard masks of the world that we can see, lies either an ultimate demonic force or a void. In both cases world and word are reduced to mere masks, disconnected from the "thing" as the disguise is disconnected from the true evil one who wears it. Ahab's ego rushes to fill that void, creating his own demonic god, but in his madness, it is the demonic god, either using the whale or incarnated completely in the whale, who is rushing to destroy him.

Ahab becomes Descartes's *cogito,* that subjective self that must exist above and beyond all other forms of existence in order to register, to create, to think up his cosmic conspiracy. He apprehends his own existence because of the world's resistance to it, and by reducing the visible world to a series of mere masks, he projects himself beyond language into the transcendent realm of his mad imagination that blinds him to the very language he uses to create it. The reader recognizes Ahab's madness but also that Ahab's self must exist, "the ungodly, Godlike man," in order to discern, decode, and decipher the cosmic demonic conspiratorial design that surrounds and consumes him. Ahab's obsession infects all he sees and feels. Like Poe's several mad narrators, he begins to see himself as demonically possessed and pursued by a strange and threatening universe.

In postmodern theory the self becomes more or less a shell, a product of social, political, cultural, and sexual forces that inhabit, infiltrate, and ultimately incarnate it. As David Hume believed, in opposition to Descartes's view of the sacrosanct and "intact" ego, and as quoted by Stuart Sim, the self represents nothing more than "a bundle or collection of different perceptions, which succeed each other with an inconceivable rapidity, and are in perpetual flux and movement" (1992, 24). Such radical skepticism underlies the postmodern vision and may haunt the conspiracy theorist's unconscious to such a degree that he or she must posit a system or cabal "out there" in order to justify and strengthen the sense of disconnection, disruption, and victimization that he or she feels. In fact the search defines the searcher.

The postmodern victim, like Thomas Pynchon's caricatures, Don De-Lillo's diffuse and anxious characters, Joan Didion's troubled and drifting women, and Paul Auster's self-eviscerating men, is loose in a world that has become so mediated, dispersed, intricate, and coded that one cannot possibly fathom it and feels only that bitter sense of absence, loss, and impotence. No self could ever stand up against the conspiratorial cabal, technology, multinational corporations, and the system or the federal government, but we must pursue whatever signs we can find in order, at the very least, to keep our head above water and the enemy in our line of fire. This may be the only sublime the conspiracy theorist can ever allow.

From this perspective I want to scrutinize the works of Pynchon, De-Lillo, Didion, Morrison, and others. How do they achieve this complex vision in their fiction? How do they create and complicate this specter of conspiracy that also pervades contemporary American culture? Do they buy into it as a reaction to postmodern times? Do they subvert it as a product of those times? Are they so submerged in such a conspiratorial outlook that they cannot separate themselves from its long shadow?

Language, of course, also contributes to and literally creates this atmosphere and discovery of conspiracy, similar in our culture to the American background in apocalyptic faiths and creeds. The biblical apocalypse may, in fact, be the first conspiracy, embedded in our culture's religious roots, one that for true believers ends well. Contemporary conspiracies and conspiracy theory, therefore, may be the more secular embodiment of our apocalyptic and Calvinist past. I mean to keep this relationship between conspiracy and apocalypse distinctly loose and fluid, only to suggest that the former may owe much to the latter, given the religious background of American literature in general.

It is not surprising that the only apocalypses that have ever taken place (apocalypse as the ultimate ancient conspiracy of a supernatural universe, in which believers ascend to their salvation, and the faithless perish) have occurred in texts both modern and ancient. Apocalypse is, in fact, a textual phenomenon, a product of a visionary's musings or poetic incursions into the future. These apocalyptic texts, types of earlier and ultimate conspiracies at the heart of the cosmos, such as those found in the Bible, have influenced American literature from the earliest days of the Calvinists' attempts to found a city on the hill. American fiction arose with apocalypse in the very marrow of its narrative bones. The essentially linguistic nature of apocalypse is, therefore, a kind of cultural and historical forerunner to the present fascination with conspiracy as an incarnation of postmodern incongruities, and does suggest the rhetorical vision that language in all its spellbinding, image-erupting power can create.

For instance as an example, think of Robert Frost's poem "Design." Here the narrator comes upon an unusual incident in the natural world, a white spider on a white heal-all (a common New England flower that is normally blue), holding up the carcass of a white moth. The spider suggests not danger but the "dimpled . . . fat" characteristics of a baby. And yet once the moth's whiteness suggests an image "of rigid satin cloth," that metaphor generates others as if under its own spellbinding power, and the poet is off and running toward the creation of an imminently dark and conspiratorial design that overtakes and exposes the entire cosmos. In this, "Design" parallels Ahab's consuming madness in *Moby-Dick*. The satin cloth immediately suggests the interior of a coffin, which, with its sepulchral overtones conveys an atmosphere of "death and blight," within which these "assorted characters" are trapped. The images escalate in their power and significance. They become characters "mixed ready to begin the morning right;" the line, which if read aloud and not seen on the page, could also be understood to suggest "mourning rite." The flower becomes a "froth," the moth, "dead wings carried like a paper kite" (both a child's toy and a vulture), and the verb "carried" suddenly introduces the idea that something or someone may have brought these creatures together.

In the next five lines of the second verse, which provide the full six lines of a carefully crafted sonnet (the form itself underscores the inevitability of this design, since it is a very rigid poetic form), the narrator launches into several broad epistemological questions, as does the narrator in William Blake's "Tyger, tyger, burning bright." The questions carry their own ominous appeal and escalating sense of anxiety, since they can never be answered. How dare that heal-all be white, the color of innocence, enlightenment, and the dominant race in Western culture? "What brought the kindred spider to that height?" Aha, now the spider is personally involved, kin to this widening plot. The moth had been "steered," and the horror, of course, took place "in the night," before the morning could reveal the death and devastation that have resulted. Frost is now beguiled utterly by this metaphorical vision that has mesmerized him: "What but design of darkness to appall?" He pulls back, however, not because the design is so dark but because it has been constructed out of the associative logic of metaphors that have escalated almost beyond his control. He undercuts this vision, swiftly and decisively: "If design govern in a thing so small." He has not succumbed to the cosmic conspiracy his very language has conjured up but has abruptly pulled the rug out from under it. It is as if up to a point the language has seduced him—a process that we will also discover in many of the texts we look at it—without his pulling away from the conspiracy or prophecy that has been created until the abrupt final line.

Writers such as DeLillo and Morrison, for instance, employ language in a more ambiguous manner, both exposing and exploring postmodern disconnections and disruptions in their fiction and in American culture. At the same time they struggle, or seem to struggle, for some larger vision of reconciliation and unity.

As Linda Hutcheon argues, the postmodernist critic does not seek synthesis but interrogates texts and contexts, knowing full well that she is complicit in the dominant ideology of liberal humanism. Hence, postmodernism is not a radical change: "It may be an enabling first stage in its enacting of the contradictions inherent in any transitional moment" (1988, 73). "It sits on the fence; it literally becomes a point of interrogation. Its ironies implicate and yet critique. It falls into (or chooses) neither compromise nor dialectic . . . postmodernism remains questioning" (191).

This is the open-ended postmodernism that I favor, especially when it comes to interrogating the fictional texts of Pynchon, DeLillo, Didion, and others. It masks no conspiratorial agenda, nor is it conspiratorial, despite its associations in our culture with Vietnam and Watergate. As Wendy Steiner suggests, art represents, it does not advocate, and in the problematization of representation lies, for me, the true powers of a postmodernist critique.

This essential recognition and terror lodged within the entire postmodernist and deconstructionist program and my sense of the postmodern sublime may be exactly what right-wing politicians and religious fundamentalists are reacting against. The conspiracies they envision make more rational and comfortable the new worlds they are loathe to understand. The impasse at the heart of postmodernism contributes to the hunger for revelation, certainty, and a new logos, a new metanarrative, and because of that intellectually difficult and ambiguous revelation, conspiracy-minded visionaries must assault, eradicate, and deconstruct it in order to try and position themselves in a place of assurance and belief.

If at times I continue to find postmodern theory problematic, I still find it immensely useful in terms of my own sense of the postmodern sublime, especially in dealing with writers like Pynchon, DeLillo, and others. The fiction conjures up the very vision I see beyond and within the various texts I wish to examine, an ongoing task for those of us who cannot conceive of a world without literature.

2

Conspiracy and Apocalypse in Popular Culture

"We're all conspiracy theorists now," Peter Knight explains.[1] "A self-conscious and self-reflexive entertainment culture of conspiracy has become thoroughly mainstream" (2000, 6). Michael Janeway (1999) acknowledges that the assassination of John F. Kennedy initiated "the launching of a feverish American conspiracy-theory industry" (31), which still haunts us as seen in ABC television's documentary on November 20, 2003, that offered "irrefutable" evidence that Oswald alone shot JFK, and in Keith Reddin's play "Frame 312" (playing in New York until early 2004), that dismisses the lone-gunman theory and suggests that the Zapruder film of Kennedy's murder had been doctored. It is almost as if visions of conspiracy have become the conventional explanation of events in our democracy.

Joan Didion, Don DeLillo, Thomas Pynchon, Toni Morrison, and others write in a historical era saturated with conspiracy theories, inflated by the rising influence of the media, spawned by very vocal and public opponents of postmodernism and deconstruction in academe, and since the Reagan "Restoration" of the 1980s, promoted in part by the Religious Right in American politics.[2] If postmodernism helped to underwrite writers' different visions of these tumultuous times and contributed to their exploration of the postmodern sublime as an antidote to and complicit with conspiracy in general, then conspiracy theory helped to structure and ground many of their novels, as they succumbed to its seductive lure as a way of coming to terms with their age and at the same time attempted to deconstruct or subvert it.

By the 1990s conspiracy had become a critical subject in its own right, although at times it was often difficult distinguishing criticism of conspiracy from a parallel vision of conspiracy. Several writers have suggested why conspiracy appeals so strongly to contemporary American minds.[3] For example, Knight believes that it is the result of "a generalized suspicion about conspiring forces . . . an infinite regress of suspicion [that creates] permanent uncertainty" (2000, 4). Timothy Melley sees agency panic, the feeling of the loss of self-control that leads to the suspicion that we are being controlled by someone or something else (2000, 12). Agency, disconnected from the individual self, is then imaginatively transferred to an omnipotent elite or bureaucracy, which may be directed by specific individual agents, exercising their own conspiratorial agendas, a way of keeping the liberal faith in personal agency alive. Thus external agents manipulate and dominate the contemporary self, whose own sense of personal agency vanishes. John A. McClure suggests that conspiracy theory constitutes "a form of quasi-religious conviction [as] a means of mapping the world without disenchanting it, robbing it of its mystery . . . by positing the existence of hidden forces which permeate and transcend the realm of ordinary life" (1994, 8, 103). Others see conspiracy as the new metanarrative for the postmodern era, still others as a spectator sport, a commodity in the form of television series such as *The X-Files.*

This is nothing new in American society. Fear of the Bavarian Illuminati and the French Revolution permeated our political culture at the end of the eighteenth century, just as fear of Catholics, Mormons, and immigrants permeated the latter half of the nineteenth. Our sense of a national identity has often been based on demonizing others, viewing ourselves in confrontation with "aliens" and subversive "outsiders," whether religious, racial, or otherwise.

Alexis de Tocqueville viewed the ideas that percolate within conspiracy theory as part and parcel of the American democratic experience; the rush to connection and cabal by the general public replaced the aristocratic classes in Europe: "The craving to discover general laws in everything [peculiar to American democracy], to include a great number of objects under the same formula, and to explain a mass of facts by a single cause becomes an ardent and sometimes an undiscerning passion in the human mind" (1945, 16).

Our Calvinist roots also contributed early on to conspiracy theories. The famous passage in John Winthrop's journal reveals not merely a battle between a mouse and a snake but an ongoing battle between God and the Devil. The snake, of course, fits very nicely into the mythology, and the mouse, being meeker and less "evil," ultimately triumphs. The extremely tortuous logic of Puritan sermons buttresses such a vision, grounding it in labyrinthine and meticulously filigreed arguments. The greater the powers of the enemy, the more malicious and evil, the more the chosen people must be on their guard against him.

Stripped to their bare bones, all conspiracies have certain things in common. An elite operates behind the scenes in total secrecy, driven by a relentless Nietzschean will to power to control historical and social forces—government, the economy, cultural conventions—and manipulate the public. In fact it often creates these forces so that the public finds itself powerless and impotent. It sponsors a specific agenda depending on what needs to be accomplished: create a New World Order, take over all banking systems, control the minds of the public through the mass media, or recruit others to carry out its policies.

Of course, as we shall see, certain authors thrive on this vision of conspiracy in many different ways. It can emerge from a writer's very language as in the mad narrators of Edgar Allan Poe's stories, convinced that they are both obsessed and possessed by dark internal and external forces. For instance, they try to convince the reader that ghosts, black cats, houses, and tarns are victimizing them, whereas the reader can also see such ravings as the product of a diseased sensibility or mind. Poe's genius resides not in choosing either side but in setting up dialectically dynamic ambiguities that point in both directions at once, both undercutting and sustaining each other, thus creating a kind of postmodern sublime that in this case can be viewed as a dark night of a tortured soul.

Dramatizing a conspiracy-driven point of view can also open the enticingly seductive Pandora's box of conspiracy without end. Take, for instance, the success of the television series *The X-Files,* which consistently reinterprets each episode at a later date and widens conspiracy into an endless maze of open-ended plots. Have aliens come to Earth intending to conquer it? Are they in league with a certain elite cabal of old rich white men? Has the federal government been trying to breed aliens and humans? Has the federal government created the alien menace in order to cover up their own sinister medical experiments, which are a holdover from what German doctors tried to accomplish in Nazi concentration camps? Which is it? One? The other? Neither? Which is the cover-up and which the real historical conspiracy? If government agencies are so riddled with conspirators, anti-conspirators, and co-conspirators from within, who is who? The boundlessness of conspiracies within conspiracies suggests the postmodern sublime at its most labyrinthine and pop-cultural level. Trust no one, even though "the truth is out there."

Certain *X-Files* episodes, such as "The Great Mutato," also partake of postmodernism's self-conscious, self-reflexive intertextuality, none of which weakens the conspiratorial vision but adds to its infiltration into popular culture. "The Great Mutato" opens as a comic book, ends as a comic book, and includes the comic book "The Great Mutato" in its narrative. Tabloid television, such as the Jerry Springer show and the music of the pop singer Cher, permeates the small southern town of the tale, so much so that Scully, Mulder's skeptical and more scientific sidekick, discusses the culture of tabloid TV and its obsession with self-dramatization. The patrons at J. J.'s Diner at first welcome Mulder into their midst when the local paper anoints him as a believer in the monster that supposedly haunts their town, but once Mulder admits that it's a hoax, they reject him outright. The "mad scientist" in the episode is named Polidori, the doctor who suggested that he, Lord Byron, and Mary Shelley concoct ghost stories, which led to Shelley's creation of *Frankenstein*. The "monster"-adolescent raised by Polidori in his basement watches *Mask*, the film in which Cher plays the mother of a "monster"-son. Mulder worries how the story will turn out, since there's no bride (as in the film *The Bride of Frankenstein*) and quips, "Where's the writer?" The episode is even shot in black and white and sets up scenes similar to the original Frankenstein movie. All of this tongue-in-cheek, postmodern pastiche still conjures up the brooding landscape, the isolated town, and the moaning monster in the woods, staples of the gothic-conspiratorial genre. And since we never learn who the father of the monster-adolescent is, the postmodern assault on ontological reality, in addition to its epistemological sleights of hand, remains intact.

The success of the *Matrix* film trilogy also speaks directly to the scope and power of conspiracy theory in pop culture. The traces of and references to the Christian myth; Jean Baudrillard's idea of spectacle and simulacra; classical figures such as Morpheus, Persephone, Plato, and oracles; the Buddhist notion of illusion and initiation; Gnostic visions of the world as prison; Descartes's radical skepticism about what we can and cannot know about our immediate world; political allegories of revolution; and the dualistic vision inherent in many philosophical positions are scattered throughout the film in the manner of what many critics see as postmodern pastiche, hinting at perhaps some wider, more sublime vision but eventually exposed as mere ornamentation and self-reflective décor.

The Matrix trilogy reveals Thomas Anderson's and the audience's initiation into the knowledge that the world of our five senses is nothing more than a matrix, run by machines and fed by human bodies used as batteries and confined in tubes. This "real world" is, therefore, a projection of an entire machine-coordinated conspiracy, and the people within it, the subjects of it, are really subjected to the machines' computerized system. When Anderson breaks free from this world of illusion, thanks to the ministrations of Morpheus, he discovers that the real world beyond it is a grim wasteland, in which the surviving humans are living underground in the grungy city of—more resonant mythic signs—Zion. As in *The X-Files,* the world we think we know is just one more vast conspiracy.

The disappointing conclusion to *The Matrix* comes down to a final shootout between Neo (the "One" to save the world, the savior that Anderson becomes by dying and by being resurrected by Trinity's—of course— kiss) and Agent Smith, the virus within the Matrix who is multiplying and taking over. Neo tells the Head Machine that Smith is a virus, the Machine plugs Neo back into the Matrix to take on Agent Smith, and when Smith touches Neo, the Machine reads his program and destroys him and all his duplications. Thus Neo does not destroy but modifies the Matrix, which is still run by the machines. It becomes a "softer, gentler" world, but the denouement is nothing more than a temporary peace, as if the Matrix used Neo to cleanse itself, just another savior in the seventh cycle of such self-cleansing: send a virus (Neo) to destroy a virus (Smith).

What emerges, finally, is the romance of the quest narrative, the initiated Good Guy versus the villainous Bad Guy, a Hollywood genre as old as film itself. The undigested mix of static monologues, in which the myth of the Matrix is more or less explained by oracles, architects, and Merovingians, with superbly choreographed action scenes in the second film in the trilogy, *The Matrix Reloaded,* produces a lumpy concoction that, in the third film, jettisons the postmodern signposts for "pure" confrontation.

Style overwhelms substance in *The Matrix* trilogy (substance reduced to postmodern pastiche), the films celebrate sculpted bodies and balletic violence, and the result produces a series of emotionlessly masked characters confined to a world of video-game sterility. The directors, the Wachowski brothers, turn out to be as mechanically programmatic as the architect of the Matrix, and a final showdown between Neo and Smith marks the simplistic conclusion. In any case the vision of a total, worldwide conspiracy, with all its postmodern excrescences and ornaments, dominates the entire trilogy and adds to pop culture's conspiratorial view of the world in general.

This yearning for a kind of indiscriminate and constantly shifting conspiracy plagues and excites many of the characters in the novels of Pynchon, Didion, and DeLillo. In trying to discern the contemporary zeitgeist or in surrendering to it, they both exploit and subvert postmodernist views and conspiracy theories.

As I suggested earlier, conspiracy theories in America mimic the American apocalyptic tradition.[4] They may not emerge directly from that tradition, but they often participate within it. The apocalyptic tradition is as old as human language, and its Americanization through Calvinist doctrine and others occurred within the very fabric of the founding of the United States. As Michael Barzun commented in 1983, amid the Reagan Restoration, "Far from suffering terminal exhaustion, apocalyptic literature is more popular in America now than at any time since the early nineteenth century" (quoted in Boyer 1992, 11). Apocalyptic patterns and expectations involve the end of history, its predestined finale and the belief that evil will be justified and eventually explained at that time, as essence replaces enigma.[5] Apocalypse in its purest form will reveal ultimate gain in place of loss, a divine and healing presence (for true believers only) in place of absence, and the completion of a divinely driven narrative in place of elusive endings and forever distant possibilities. Both conspiracy theory and apocalyptic beliefs share their full quota of fatalism and despair, but in each eventually there will be conclusion, and the true believers who are aware of the process and the vision now are the only ones who will be triumphant and saved. Faith will eviscerate skepticism, and skeptics will be crushed.

The dominant fundamentalist doctrine of American apocalypse rests on a premillennialist vision, traces of which can be found in the fictions of Pynchon and DeLillo. Premillennialists believe that seven years of turmoil and tribulation will precede the Second Coming of Christ. Believers will be saved during the Rapture, when Christ will appear presumably in the heavens and lift them up into his arms. Others will die and suffer.

Christ will then battle Satan at Armageddon, and his thousand-year reign will emerge from all the blood and thunder. A final battle between God and Satan will occur after that thousand-year period, and then redemption and salvation, for true believers, will last forever.

This essentially pessimistic faith, which denies the possibility of human intervention for good works in the world, opposes the postmillennialists' vision, which suggests that Christ's coming again will gradually emerge from our own human reforms and policies. Postmillennialism has always been the more "liberal" and optimistic of these two dispensational creeds with its belief in the efficacy of human effort and the inevitability of human progress. Premillennialists have no faith in the human condition. Only supernatural intervention will rescue humanity. Once again we can see the similarities between this view and Jim Marrs's (2000) cosmic conspiracy in which aliens bring civilization to humanity, since humans are incapable of accomplishing such things themselves. The political consequences support a general passivity, wherein the faithful await the Rapture but offer nothing in return, except their own faith.

In this strange new American world after the attack on the World Trade Center towers on September 11, 2001, apocalypse is everywhere and has, of course, already created a cultural atmosphere within which to frame the horror. Terrorism becomes an apocalyptic tool in the hands of fundamentalists and contemporary mythologists, as well as writers such as Don DeLillo in *Mao II*. As Baudrillard suggests, and his idea chills the blood since September 11:

> What, indeed, is terrorism, if not this effort to conjure up, in its own way, the end of history? It attempts to entrap the powers that be by an immediate, total act. Without awaiting the final term of the process, it sets itself at the ecstatic endpoint, hoping to bring about the conditions of the Last Judgment, an illusory challenge, of course, but one that always fascinates, since, deep down, neither time nor history has ever been accepted. (Strozier and Flynn 1997, 254)

These perspectives, rooted in postmodernism, fundamentalism, and apocalypticism, feed upon one another, refueling the attitude, the tone, and the anti-authoritarian rage. In the 1990s the coming of the new millennium further enflamed such visions, a narrative that seized everyone from theologians and philosophers to popular commentators and TV evangelists.

The quintessential text that reveals the ultimate vision of conspiracy of the era is Marrs's paranoid epic, *Rule By Secrecy: The Hidden History That Connects the Trilateral Commission, the Freemasons, and The Great Pyramids.* As a narrative Marrs's ingenious tome is often breathtaking, particularly in its scope and detail, for it includes and connects every conspiracy theory I have stumbled across in the past several years. This is the Bible of conspiracy. Quoth Marrs, "The key to an evil conspiracy is the intent of the secrecy" (2000, 5), and he will expose these intentions, beginning in the present and burrowing back into the past to the pyramids and beyond. He acknowledges only two choices, thus setting up that bipolar dualism that underscores all conspiracy theory, the kind that deconstructionists and postmodernists love and labor to dismantle. Only two views of history can possibly exist: "accidental or conspiratorial" (6). Of course accidents occur, but conspiracy theory rests solidly on the logical basis of cause and effect (as accidents do also, though conspiracists fail to note this). The media, academia, and governments resist conspiracy theories, according to Marrs, because they are precisely the ones who have created them. Thus the people—the readers of this volume, the to-be-initiated—will see through those elitists' denials and strategies of deception. "A handful of men [and we should always note the gender] . . . an oligarchy" (10) runs the world. Marrs cannot unearth absolute proof because of all the secrecy that surrounds this cabal, so "researchers often must look for patterns of behavior and personal links between people and organizations" (17). The pattern replaces the absolute proof, which is impossible to find. Trace the social and institutional networks, as viewed within the scrim of conspiracy, and all will be revealed. Oedipa Maas, as we shall see, in Pynchon's *The Crying of Lot 49* attempts to unearth a similar pattern.

Assumptions, accompanied by enormous leaps of faith, structure Marrs's argument. The Illuminati, for instance, "can be traced back through history to the earliest sects" (2000, 235), but he traces nothing. He insinuates but presents no actual traces. A man named Kolmer, described as "the most mysterious of all the mystery men" (236), who, as "suspected by some researchers," may have also been Altota, a man who knew the French court magician and revolutionary Cagliostro and had also imbibed the secrets of Egypt and Persia, influenced Adam Weishaupt, the professor of Canon Law at Ingolstadt University in Bavaria and founder of the cult. Kolmer "reportedly" met Cagliostro on Malta. What proof does Marrs offer to support this? He offers John Robison's *Proofs of a Conspiracy against All the Religions and Governments of Europe Carried On in the Secret Meetings of the Free Masons, Illuminati, and Reading Societies* (1797)! Even reading becomes part of the conspiracy! One other reference, which was at first difficult to track down, since Marrs first refers to it on page 153 and does not identify it until page 222, is Nesta H. Webster, author of *Secret Societies and Subversive Movements*. The title itself reveals a kindred soul.

Marrs tells us that when the Bavarian government cracked down on Weishaupt's group in 1783, members fled and founded secret splinter groups in other parts of Europe. He offers no proof whatsoever, since these groups remain secret. Thomas Jefferson praised Weishaupt's ideas, many of which he had used in the Declaration of Independence: "Either Jefferson lacked knowledge of the inner Illuminati teachings or, as was charged in his time, he himself was a secret member" (2000, 230). Jefferson was charged as being a secret infidel—by his Federalist opponents who used slander and libel not as a scalpel but as a machete, as Jefferson's own party did as well.

Thus Marrs weaves his web of guilt by association. Kolmer influenced Weishaupt—how? when? in what way? Webster authorized that point in 1924 in her particularly conspiratorial manner, since Kolmer was "the most mysterious of all the mystery men." Mystery becomes personalized, a particular man, a villain who exists in the shadows, the phantom behind the arras, the origin and source of Egyptian and Persian lore. Gnosticism, that ancient cult of secret and inner wisdom, mirrored Manichaeism, that Persian heresy of the third century, which had used the word "Illuminated" prior to the third century (2000, 236). Weishaupt had studied to become a Jesuit and "may have taken the name 'Illuminati' from a secret splinter group [is there any other kind?] called the 'Alumbrados' (enlightened or illuminated of Spain)" (236). Ignatius Loyola, founder of the Jesuits, also founded Alumbrados, which taught "a form of Gnosticism." Perhaps the Illuminati originated in the Muslim Ismaili sect, which was closely allied with the Knights Templar and was known as a cult of infamous assassins who smoked hashish, "a harbinger of the 1960s" (237). In fact Weishaupt's philosophy "has been used with terrible results down through the years by

Hitler . . . the end justifies the means" (237). All this Marrs tells us in two pages.

As we meticulously unravel the elaborate and demonic tapestry of this epic exposé, we finally arrive at ancient Sumer. "All Roads Lead to Sumer," Marrs assures us. The end has clearly justified the means. Every sect, cult, organization, club, and governmental cabal "can be traced directly to earlier secret organizations, *forming a conspiratorial chain throughout history. They appear to be following a plan* formulated and articulated many years ago" (italics mine, 2000, 109), and that plan directs us to Sumerian civilization, which "seemed to appear from nowhere" (374). The Sumerians produced cuneiform, an early form of writing, as well as the zodiac, ziggurats, medical science, and other civilized wonders. How could they have possibly created such things on their own? After all, they were merely human. They had to have had help. Human beings could not possibly have created such a rich civilization and culture. They are too primitive, too stupid. Some smarter, more civilized creatures must have brought civilization to them.

Marrs reports that the Sumerians claimed that the gods brought them culture. Their myths reveal as much. What if those myths were not really myths but literally true? Like a fundamentalist worshipping the literalness of the Bible, clasping the icon to his breast, Marrs accepts the theory of one Zecharia Sitchin, a Russian, educated in Palestine, who received a degree in economic history from the University of London, who launched himself on "a lifetime quest for the truth behind the inconsistencies and puzzles of the ancient texts" (2000, 379). The Sumerians referred to their gods as the Anunnaki, which, as translated by Sitchin, means "Those Who Came To Earth from Heaven" (378). And so they must have. Extraterrestrials from another planet, Nibiru actually, must have descended upon Sumeria. This cosmic vision "requires," Marrs suggests, "only a slight shift in mindset" (378). "Why not also consider their written history as reality?" After all, like Sitchin we should be able to take "the attitude that . . . history as they [the Sumerians] understood it [transcends] mere myths." And how do we arrive at this mindset? By "using Sitchin's translations as a springboard . . . " (379). As Sitchin advised, "Why not take the [Sumerian] epic at face value?" From there to the planet Nibiru requires only a minor narrative shift: "Truly amazing is the fact that. . . . Interestingly enough, this theory could explain [the] comets . . . " (380).

Zecharia Sitchin turns out to be the author of a series of popular books called *The Earth Chronicles*. These include *The Twelfth Planet* (1976), *The Stairway to Heaven* (1980), *When Time Began* (1993), and the latest in the series, volume six, *The Cosmic Code* (1998), which includes below the title on the cover the phrase, "The incredible truth about the Anunnaki who divulged cosmic secrets to mankind."[6] Like all true conspiracists, Sitchin attempts to fuse fact and speculation, muddying the distinctions between actual archaeological sites, in the case of *The Cosmic Code,* and his vision of extraterrestrial beings. It makes for fascinating reading with its mythic maneuverings, numerological certainties, and prophetic musings and would make a stunningly epic film directed by Steven Spielberg, but the vision works only if the reader can make the ontological and seismic shifts that Sitchin makes.

For instance, *The Cosmic Code* begins with lucid and evocative descriptions of the astronomical purposes of Stonehenge and a Near Eastern Stonehenge discovered in the Golan Heights after the Six Day War of 1967. Sitchin concludes that both were used as astronomical observatories, particularly in terms of determining the solstices. He then raises the question of who might have constructed such a site and, since it was discovered by Israelis, states, "It was therefore perhaps unavoidable that Israeli researchers turned to the Bible for an answer . . . " (1998, 12).

Sitchin goes on to locate passages in the books of Numbers, Joshua, and Deuteronomy that describe a kingdom ruled by Og in the Gilead mountains whose sixty towns were "fortified with high walls and gates and barriers, apart from a great number of unwalled towns." For Sitchin that general description of many ancient kingdoms suggests the particular "features of the enigmatic Golan site" (1998, 12). According to the Bible, Og was a big man: "this giant size, the Bible *hints,* was due to his being a descendent of the Repha'im, a giantlike race of demigods who had once dwelt in the land" (italics mine, 12). We have jumped from one ontological reality to another, from the actual existence of the Golan Stonehenge to ancient and biblical myth, and Sitchin literalizes that myth as though it were actual fact without acknowledging the shift. This is a typical conspiracist's method, the leap from the literal to the metaphysical, from actual landscape to visionary realm. He next pursues biblical genealogy, for instance identifying Abraham's father (assuming, of course, that Abraham was a single individual), Terah, as an oracle priest (*Tirhu*) from Sumer. His people, the *Ibri* (Hebrew), "suggests to us that they considered themselves to be Nippurians—people from the city Nippur that in Sumerian was rendered NI.IBRU" (27). The sleight of hand delights but remains spurious, as does the concluding sentence to his first chapter: "And, as we shall see, that is just the beginning of *intricate and interwound associations*" (italics mine, 18).

Marrs concludes his epic yarn by insisting that there now exists "the wealth of data . . . that supports this incredible narrative. . . . And none of the authors and researchers studying this subject feel they have all the facts [so certainly some of this is] bound to be somewhat distorted" (2000, 403). Then he retreats to the kind of fundamentalist faith that underscores such scenarios. None of this denies the existence of the One God who must have created the Anunnaki "because, as we all know, there is more to life than this material plane of existence" (405). Aliens taught humanity its civilized manners and methods: this is the Secret of Secrets, the ultimate solution, the core of the cosmic conspiracy, the answer to all X-Files. "It just makes more sense [and is] not only internally consistent but well supported by evidence from all around the world . . . " (405). Maybe they are still among us . . .

Yet Marrs holds out hope. The very fact that we are reading his book demonstrates that "the centuries-old plot to control human destiny has not yet achieved total success" (2000, 408). We have been initiated into his cult of revelation. Our crisis conversions shimmer with the truth that he has given us. We can prevent the cosmic plot from succeeding by keeping our eyes open, looking for further signs, warning our family and friends. Our new cult of believers will combat and expose this historical cult, and only then will we be saved. "Each individual makes his or her own destiny" (410), Marrs insists, in effect undermining all that he has written, which has just asserted exactly the opposite. There is the "out." If we choose to believe, we shall be saved. If not, only certain oblivion awaits us.

Marrs's literal and often apocalyptic interpretations of ancient myths in particular reflect the fundamentalist vision of the Bible and history in general. Most critics agree that the belief in the literal truth of the Bible lies at the heart of the fundamentalist faith, the historical backdrop of much conspiracy theory in the United States, accentuated in contemporary times by its opposition to that fierce bugaboo, "secular humanism," itself insidiously aligned in the public mind with or the result of postmodernism and other academic evils. Literal interpretation (all of which is, of course, selectively literal, the very term "literal interpretation" being an oxymoron) becomes the ultimate metanarrative, the counterpoint to the postmodernist's lack of faith in such things. Not only that but such literal interpretation always corresponds to historical events, either in the actual past or in prophecies for the future.

From 1970 until the mid-1980s, Hal Lindsey's *The Late Great Planet Earth,* which rings changes on all these conspiratorial fears and apocalyptic visions, outsold all other books, and by 1990 twenty-eight million copies remained in print. Like good fundamentalists everywhere, Lindsey took biblical images as coded messages for historical events. The scriptures literally predicted the future, and he interpreted them literally, except when he interpreted them figuratively. He omitted, ignored, or quashed those images or interpretations that did not fit his premillennialist paradigm, pretending at times that those images and scenarios he chose to focus on literally interpreted themselves. Like a good conspiracy theorist, he found no coincidences, no accidents in his biblical treatise and insisted that only by personal conversion to his way of thinking could anyone escape certain and final destruction.

Lindsey eventually proclaims the essence of his premillennialist fantasy near the end of the book: "We are 'premillennialists' in viewpoint. The real issue . . . is whether prophecy should be interpreted literally or allegorically. As it has been demonstrated many times in this book, *all prophecy about past events has been fulfilled literally,* particularly the predictions regarding the first coming of Christ. The words of prophecy were demonstrated as *being literal,* that is, having the *normal meaning* understood by the people of the time in which it was written" (italics mine, 1970, 164–65). At the same time he categorically dismisses the postmillennialist position: "There *used to be* a group called 'postmillennialists.' . . . These people rejected much of the Scripture as being literal and believed in the inherent goodness of man. . . . *No self-respecting scholar* who looks at the world conditions and *the accelerating decline* of Christian influence today is a 'postmillennialist'" (italics mine, 164).

Lindsey craftily connects the scriptures he quotes to contemporary times and then subtly shifts his position to prove that in seeing these connections, we cannot fail to understand that these things must come to pass. We must fulfill the roles that scripture has ordained for us. Escalation is inevitable toward the denouement, and the real horror lies with our not doing the things we should be doing in order to be saved. Lindsey creates an epic narrative in ordinary understandable language that sweeps the reader along, creating its own spellbinding trajectory. Such a story must obviously derail the niggardly, skeptical ramblings and doubts of critics. "Has the academic community found the answers?" Lindsey posits, sidestepping the fact that perhaps the truth of education lies in the process of raising certain questions and possibilities rather than answering them. "There are many students who are dissatisfied with being told that the sole purpose of education is to *develop inquiring minds.* They want to find some . . . solid answers, a certain direction" (italics mine, 1970, vii). Obviously continuous inquiry can only muddle and detract from the "solid answers," a conspiracy theorist's and fundamentalist's salvation.

Carefully, Lindsey lays the groundwork for his vision of catastrophe: "The Bible contains clear and unmistakable prophetic signs. . . . History verifies the accuracy of these prophecies. . . . Biblical symbolism is established in historical fact" (1970, 7, 37, 8). Postmodernists and deconstructionists rush in where angels fear to tread. Whose history verifies these prophecies? What underlies the dualism of biblical prophecy and history? Why are they seemingly at odds? Who chooses the facts to support the prophecies? And as in any text, what is being excluded, what is being included, and what is the nature of the approach that justifies these actions? Lindsey marches blithely onward: "When the *plain sense* of Scripture makes *common sense,* seek no other sense; therefore, take every word at its *primary, ordinary, usual, literal* meaning . . . " (italics mine, 40). These are loaded words, populist paradigms at work here—plain, common, ordinary, usual. What of translation, historical and cultural context, the idea that "common sense" is as contrived a philosophical outlook as the most metaphysical of speculations?

Ezekiel, to take one example, prophesied that the nation of Israel would be restored in the future. Jesus spoke of this generation's experiencing his second coming, and since for Lindsey a generation lasts about forty years, and since the nation of Israel was restored in 1948, this generation, the one from 1948 onward, will clearly experience Christ's return: "We are living in the times which Ezekiel predicted in chapters 38 and 39." Lindsey interprets his selected excerpts literally, provided that we can accept the connections he makes between Ezekiel's time and our own. "How could

Ezekiel 2,600 years ago have forecast so accurately the rise of Russia" (1970, 55), Lindsey asks after laying out a tortuously labyrinthine logic on which to rest his case. "This king of the North I *conceive to be* the autocrat of Russia" (italics mine, 52), intoned Dr. John Cumming in 1864, whom Lindsey quotes to shore up his fragments against certain ruin. "Ezekiel once again 'passes the test of a prophet,'" Lindsey continues. "He was guided by the Spirit of the Living God." And just to be on the safe side, he adds, "But know this first of all, that no prophecy of Scripture is a matter of one's own interpretation" (55).

"There is a cohesiveness to the Scriptures that is fascinating" (1970, 81), Lindsey maintains, and the fascination lies in the fact that nothing remains coincidental or accidental. "The divine hand from somewhere" manipulates the prophetic drama, as the Anunnaki manipulated the Sumerians. Things just fall into place, as he places them. The Old Testament truthfully predicted the events of the New Testament, so the Bible must be thoroughly reliable on all counts. Again the critic would suggest that the four gospels were written by men who specifically wanted to view Christ as the New Testament incarnation of Old Testament prophecies and thereby prove him to be the Messiah who was foreseen. For Lindsey the text itself—plain, common, ordinary, and primary—creates its own origins and, therefore, is identical with them, an idea postmodernists and deconstructionists would find incredibly hard to swallow. Even texts can send mixed messages and undermine themselves, as language slips and slides through many generations and many interpretations. The very form of the Old Testament, historically a text of bits and pieces, "may insist on meanings and relations which the treatise denies or confutes" (Kermode 1967, 137).

As in conspiracy and fundamentalist faiths, consistency always overrules coincidence in such matters. For Lindsey because the Hebrews handed down such scrupulous and meticulously detailed prophecies, "they had to be revelations from God, otherwise they would not have been preserved in such a consistent manner" (1970, 23). It is perhaps this very ogre of consistency that novelists such as Didion, Pynchon, and DeLillo feel the need to assault and dismantle, like the best deconstructionist at the top of her game.

Lindsey goes on to insist that the third Jewish Temple will be rebuilt. Prophecy tells us as much. Of these images and prophecies, "Do we *dare allegorize away* the meaning of these?" (italics mine, 1970, 31). But certainly this is precisely what Lindsey does within his premillennialist framework. Prophecies "can be pieced together to make a coherent picture, even though the pieces are scattered in small bits throughout the Old and New Testaments" (33). Yet the very one who is doing the piecing claims that the puzzle comes together on its own. Such a perspective suggests the power of the icon to mesmerize and spellbind in a way that defies our ability to try and piece together a powerful description of or allegory out of it. Literalness shimmers with certain unbeatable truths: "We are not playing *a game of Biblical hopscotch* when we turn from one prophet to another. If there was not *a strong recurring theme* in all the prophets, this book would have no validity" (italics mine, 108). Methinks he doth protest too much and in doing so gives the game away. "*We are not attempting* to read into today's happenings any events to prove some vague thesis," Lindsey continues. "This is not necessary. All we need to do is know the Scriptures *in their proper context* and then *watch* with awe while men and countries, movements and nations, *fulfill the roles* that God's prophets said they would" (italics mine, 65–66). This belaboring of my point serves, I hope, to expose the assumptions on which conspiracists and fundamentalists predict the impending catastrophe.

In the apocalyptic yarn the Antichrist must come from and rule Rome. Lindsey defines Rome "in its revived form" (1970, 84), which becomes the European Union. If the United States is still around at that critical time, it will exercise no power whatsoever. "If you follow this Scripture [about the Antichrist] from Revelation, *without being bothered by the figures of speech which are used,* you will see that the Bible explains the meaning" (italics mine, 92). Language, of course, bristles with figures of speech and derives its texture from them. One does not need to buy Paul de Man's radical argument that rhetoric forever precedes logic and that logic is nothing more than a series of figures of speech craftily woven together to recognize the elisions and evasions of Lindsey's interpretive approach.

In explaining the meaning of particular passages, Lindsey employs the passive voice and in doing so elides his own active creation in forcing images to appear as literal facts. Fire and brimstone, of course, conjure up nuclear war. A bear represents the Media-Persian Empire, because it "was very strong and powerful" (1970, 94). Pliny's Scythians become "a principal part of the people who make up modern Russia" (53), so that Lindsey's

Russian scenario will fit. The Antichrist will demand his throne: "This means world government" (95), that New World Order that frightens fundamentalists as much as it does conspiracy theorists. When Christ returns "accompanied with 'the clouds of heaven,' we believe that the clouds refer to the myriads of believers who return in white robes with Jesus" (162).

To show how terrible the present world has become, Lindsey describes and recoils from a week dedicated to Arab culture on a college campus as a conspiracy. The fact that money may be handled electronically in the future also clearly reveals the Antichrist's power and conspiratorial designs. Since God destroyed the Tower of Babel, no one-world government could possibly be good. Astrology, drugs, witchcraft are everywhere. "There's a bunch of us up at Big Sur," a young man comments, "who worship idols and stuff" (1970, 113). This is more than enough to send Lindsey over the edge. "A major television station had a potpourri of news and showed the great interest high school students have in witches" (115). Interest automatically indicates worship and devotion.

Lindsey's final message praises passivity: "God doesn't want us to try and clean up our own lives, but rather to be available to His Spirit who now lives personally within us" (1970, 175). Forgo institutional churches, "believe in the final authority of the Bible" (172) as interpreted by Hal Lindsey, and convert quickly. Lindsey's other books shift historical data to remain true to his premillennialist vision, but the message remains the same. It proclaims the faith in the cult, the cabal, the apocalyptic vision, and the fearless leader, aspects of conspiracy that suggest a version of the postmodern sublime in its open-ended and virtually infinite infiltration of all things, all of which DeLillo, Pynchon, Didion, Morrison, and others continue to wrestle with, indict, emulate, and re-enact.

3
Conspiracy in Fiction
From Da Vinci to Damascus

The literary critic Tony Tanner recognized early on that, "The possible nightmare of being totally controlled by unseen agencies and powers is never far away in contemporary American fiction" (Melley 2000, 8). Titles of recent books on this explosion of "conspiracy consciousness" cover everything from enemies within to empires of conspiracy, from American extremists to postmodern apocalyptic revelations, from paranoid politics to cultures of conspiracy. In poll after poll the American public has responded to this barrage by seeing conspiracy everywhere as a kind of ultimate knee-jerk response to contemporary experience. If, as Edward J. Ingebretsen has maintained, ours is "a culture authorized by Revelation" (2001, xix), then surely such an atmosphere will inevitably and in many different guises permeate contemporary American fiction.

Such fictions raise several questions: Do these texts undermine or contribute to the conspiratorial vision? Do they reflect their times in this regard, or do they seek to subvert and overcome them? Are such novels in league with the darker powers and visions that conspiracy theory has helped to generate, or do they attempt to refute them? Can a postmodern reading of several postmodern texts help us see more clearly the roots of contemporary paranoia, a facile fundamentalism, the continued lure of apocalyptic prophecies, and festering millennial anxieties? Do such darker fictions mimic the very conspiratorial culture they decry?

In more formulaic popular fiction, conspiracies, as an antidote to postmodern uncertainty, are clearly identified, isolated, and resolved. The bipolar world of good and evil in all its Manichean simplicities emerges in such novels, where moral good inevitably triumphs over manipulative and evil monsters. Conspiracies consist of distinct and separate cabals, exceptions to the rule of law, isolated cultlike groups that harbor violent agendas. The plot usually involves a character or characters eager to track down the conspiracy, discover and/or infiltrate it, and then dismember and destroy it. Once this has been accomplished, as in all conservative visions of the world, "normalcy" triumphs, and the conventional social order celebrates its victory.

Susan Isaacs' *Red, White and Blue* easily fits this particular category. The first half of the novel, *Becoming American,* traces the various families that have sprung from the loins of thirty-six-year-old Herschel Blaustein and fifteen-year-old, already pregnant Dora Schottland who meet on the boat to Ellis Island from Poland in 1899. They turn out to be the great-great-grandparents of the main characters in the second half, *The Americans,* in which straight-shooter, FBI agent, Wyoming-bred thirty-four-year-old Charles Bryant Blair meets Lauren Ruth Miller, twenty-seven, a New Yorker and reporter for the *Jewish News.* Blair infiltrates Wrath, a white supremacist and anti-Semitic group in Bride, Wyoming, led by Vernon Ostergard, who may or may not have tried to blow up a Jewish-owned video store—the bomb fizzled and was discovered near a videotape of *Schindler's List*—and/or have blown up a film director's local ranch with his housekeeper inside. Miller comes to Wyoming to cover the story.

Isaacs makes it perfectly clear that Ostergard and his thickheaded compatriots are not real Americans: "They isolate themselves. . . . All they hear—all they allow themselves to hear—is conspiracy" (1998, 350). "Monster manipulators" run the country and the world, since "history did not unfold naturally but was controlled by malignant, unseen forces" (258). They are clearly marginal, psychologically dysfunctional, sociopathic, and opportunistic.

Of course not only will Charlie Blair successfully deter this pernicious pod, but he will also go on to wed Lauren Miller. In an article she writes for the *Los Angeles Times Magazine* in the novel's "Afterwords," Miller trumpets the real American creed: "What holds us together? What do all of us have in common? . . . the one quality we share is optimism . . . we believe in happy endings. We root for the underdog" (401–2). As for Ostergard and his ilk, clinging to their "recycled nightmares of destruction and vengeance, . . . they are not Americans" (Isaacs 1998, 402).

"*Everyone loves a conspiracy,*" writes Dan Brown in his enormously popular novel, *The Da Vinci Code,* "And the conspiracies kept coming" (2003, 169). His fascination with codes within codes approaches the postmodern sublime in its sense of open-ended awe and wonder until, as in most popular fiction, an actual conspiracy is exposed, thereby revealing a "self-authorizing language" (205) that defies postmodernism's assault on all authority and reduces ultimate wonder to recognized cabal.

Brown's brilliance as a writer is to have employed "real" conspiracy theories, as opposed to actual, provable conspiracies, in his novel. Several theorists have imagined that Christ married Mary Magdalene, that they produced heirs linked to the French Merovingian royal family, and that the Catholic Church, in the guise of Opus Dei, has suppressed such early Christian truths in its determination to legitimize itself and turn early pre-Christian faiths "from matriarchal paganism to patriarchal Christianity" (2003, 124). Support for the latter view has surfaced in the Gnostic gospels as popularly described by such analysts of early religion as Elaine Pagels. Much is at stake here as Brown's hero, Harvard symbologist Robert Langdon, recognizes: "Every faith . . . is based on fabrication. That is the definition of faith. . . . Metaphors are a way to help our minds process the unprocessible. The problems arise when we begin to believe literally in our own metaphors" (341–42). This proves to be ironic in that it is precisely Brown's faith in the literalness of language, metaphor, and the parameters of an actual conspiracy that underscores his ontological thriller.

Brown's sense of conspiracy mirrors Marrs's *Rules by Secrecy,* Lindsey's more apocalyptic *The Late Great Planet Earth,* and the source of much of Brown's yarn, *The Templar Revelation: Secret Guardians of the True Identity of Christ* by Lynn Picknett and Clive Prince who insist that "we were struck by the pervasive feeling here that something much more significant lay just under the surface. And it was precisely that submerged, *subterranean* vein of meaning that we were determined to uncover" (1997, 59). The vein, as expected, lurks in "the shadowy group with their own agenda [that] existed behind Jesus and his known followers" (241). Even when different theories strike Picknett and Prince as outrageous, such as the Merovingian cover story, they push on to declare "that *many* have concluded that they *must conceal* a deeper, secret message" (italics mine, 193). This plays directly into what could be described as the main thrust of Brown's novel: "People love a quest—a search for something that is tantalizingly elusive, but perhaps still almost within reach" (2003, 361), a proposition that suggests the postmodern sublime.

Brown manipulates history as others have before him: the pope's creation of the Knights Templar in 1118 at some time merged with the Priory of Sion, founded in 1099 during the First Crusade, and later with the Free

Masons who, according to the Catholic writer Abbe Barruel, in 1797 instigated the French Revolution. Jacques Saunière, who is found murdered in the Louvre at the beginning of *The Da Vinci Code,* shares his surname with Francois Berenger Saunière (1852–1917), who built a citadel filled with Templar and other enigmatic symbols in Rennes-le-Château and had written over the door, "Terribilis est locus iste": "This is a terrible place." Picknett and Prince connect the historical Saunières to John the Baptist and Mary Magdalene, the Black Madonna, the Gnostic Cathars in Languedoc, and the pope's massacring of 100,000 of them; to Isis, to the Knights Templar, etc. Thus Brown's novel is a fictional rendition of a "real" conspiracy with its secrets hidden in Da Vinci's painting *The Last Supper* and elsewhere.

Popular culture has enshrined *The Da Vinci Code* and the questions it raises in its conspiracy-haunted temples. The *New York Times* on November 3, 2003, published Virginia Heffernan's article "The Volatile Notion of a Married Jesus: A novel becomes a news special, riling some clergy members," and even though Heffernan debunks the ABC pseudo-documentary "Jesus, Mary, and da Vinci," the connections to Brown's novel are explicit. *Newsweek's* front cover of December 8 proclaimed, "Mary Magdalene: Decoding *The Da Vinci Code,*" and even though the article debunks most of Brown's logic—a married Christ, Mary Magdalene seated at Christ's right in *The Last Supper,* Da Vinci hiding other church secrets in his paintings—it does make the case that Mary was not a prostitute, that early church fathers did cover up the role of women in the church, and that the discovery of the Gnostic gospels does lead to the credibility of Brown's overall vision, thus establishing the context if not the content of Brown's fictional conspiracy (2003, 64). Not to be left out of the loop, *Time* on December 22, 2003, declared, "Gnosticism! At a Theater Near You!" and reported that *The Da Vinci Code* suggests that the Catholic Church in its earlier incarnation had suppressed at least eighty gospels. The article goes on to link these with *The Matrix* trilogy, describing its Gnostic vision as built on the notion that "the world we know is neither good nor real but the creation of a malign power" (56). Conspiracy theory helps underwrite such pronouncements.

In the more hard-boiled novels, where cynicism struts its stuff as a kind of callous sentimentality and hard-nosed "realism," conspiracy consumes the world completely. Everything's crooked, fixed, wiretapped, scammed, conned, spied on, and slept with. In James Ellroy's *American Tabloid,* for instance, con artists, politicians, mobsters, hit men, wheeler dealers, snitches, CIA and FBI agents—each is an absolute reflection and reproduction of the other—perform in conspiracies so elaborate and labyrinthine that you need a scorecard to try and keep everything straight.

Ellroy conjures up the testosterone tactics of his omnivorous underworld by placing them in the years 1959–63 that lead directly to Kennedy's assassination, for most people the origins of our contemporary fascination with and belief in multiple conspiracies. The CIA and the Mob are in cahoots to kill Castro, so that the mobsters can get their casinos back in Havana, and the various CIA and FBI underlings can run drugs, create slush funds, skim the take from the gambling halls, and lead the high life with easy sex and easier money. As one character intones, "Those we understand are those we control" (1995, 273). This grimly Darwinian landscape operates solely in terms of domination and submission with death as the only alternative.

Ellroy's style bristles with the brutality of short, abrupt, abrasive sentences. Each line reads like an insider's corrosive view of the inner workings of people in high and low places. These maliciously cold and cruel potshots power the entire novel, a supra-macho domain of play or be played, kill or be killed, deal or be dealt with. Ellroy underscores this "realistic" unveiling of the corrupt sources of real power by dividing his novel into five parts—SHAKEDOWNS, COLLUSION, PIGS (as in Bay of), HEROIN, and CONTRACT—in yet another take on the Kennedy assassination and then adding place names and dates at the head of each chapter to lend authenticity and legitimacy. He emulates the sarcastic style of *Hush-Hush,* the tabloid rag that appears throughout the novel, and tosses in "Document Inserts" that read like court testimony and wiretapped phone conversations. For good measure the likes of J. Edgar Hoover, Jimmy Hoffa, Jack Ruby, and a host of other real people make guest appearances. Conspiracy provides the very lifeblood and purpose for each and every one of them, as they play off one agency, group, and/or individual against another for their own personal profit.

Popular gothic fiction also thrives on conspiracy. In fact the gothic formula itself sounds like the kind of cosmic conspiracy, with its apocalyptic underpinnings and aura, that metastasizes in the worldviews of David Koresh, Timothy McVeigh, and Kenneth Starr. Richard Hofstadter, in his discussion of the paranoid vision, described it as believing that "History *is* a conspiracy, set in motion by demonic forces of almost transcendent power" (*Paranoid Style,* 1963, 29). No writer of popular gothic fictions would disagree, concerned as he or she is with the presence and construction of evil as a demonic, psychic, malevolent, supernatural, and/or cosmic power or force that compels and drives characters to accomplish certain predetermined designs, lending the popular genre its sense of inevitability and doom, its essentially tragic path. The formula, focused as it is on the power relations between masters and slaves, as well as villains and victims, plays to the objects and designs of conspiracy. "You cannot have Gothic without a cruel hero-villain," Mark Edmundson suggests, "without a cringing victim; and without a terrible place . . . hidden from public view" (1997, 130). What better hero-villains than Satan, the Trilateral Commission, Bill Clinton, or extraterrestrials? What better cringing victim than all of humanity, victims of rape, characters pursued and haunted by ghosts, curses, and their own past actions? As for terrible places "hidden from public view," what but Armageddon, moldering mansions, and the human psyche? As Edmundson himself rightfully concludes, "The gothic idiom has slipped over from fiction and begun to shape and regulate our perception of reality" (22). Seen any tabloid TV lately?

We readers know what to expect from a popular, gaudily packaged gothic novel. The formulaic text shapes our responses, organizes and creates our sense of fear and anxiety. The narrative formula, in fact, becomes the authoritative text in this manner as do certain scriptural passages for fundamentalists and such forgeries as *The Protocols of the Elders of Zion* for diehard conspiracists. The text embodies the anxiety, shapes the distinctive narrative that seduces, persuades, and convinces in terms of the sheer power of the tale and narrative themselves. Usually the gothic yarn, as Teresa Goddu informs us, is "spun out of a secret and consists of a series of narratives rather than a single story." No matter what we finally learn and discover, in the best gothic narratives "the excessive explanation cannot completely cover the gap of doubt that always remains" (1997, 36, 88). That is as it should be: the nightmarish reality still shimmers in shadow as we submit to our initiation, through the act of reading, into its wider realms of ambiguity, uncertainty, and doubt.

Apocalyptic prophecies, conspiracy scenarios, and popular gothic novels all rely on prosopopoeia, the act of personifying an abstract, disembodied Other within a narrative. This both comforts and disturbs—comforts because narrative form surrounds and encapsulates the Other in placing it within a particular plot and fictional boundaries; disturbs because such a presence can also threaten that form, as it becomes incarnated in ghosts, secret cabals, and satanic rituals. Such usually overheated rhetoric unleashes the repressed, splinters the everyday self into various confrontational and psychic fragments, pitting characters against unearthly visitors or demonic forces, entombing readers and characters in a claustrophobic world. We are all buried alive in individual delusions, rantings, hauntings, and sightings. The nightmarish realm that gothic writers conjure up achieves a similar fate, whether we are being pursued by the Antichrist, extraterrestrials, demented psychopaths, or prophetic dreams. Thus apocalyptic yearnings, conspiratorial urgings and the popular gothic novel feed off of and upon one another to produce a dark popular literature that shows no sign of abating.

The case of John Saul, a prolific and popular gothic writer, reveals the multiple connections in contemporary culture among conspiratorial visions, apocalyptic imaginings, and the basic gothic formulas of such fictions. Saul speaks directly to the power of the gothic formula in contemporary fiction: "I think people love a roller-coaster ride, and they love to scare themselves half to death, but they also love to know that if it gets too scary, they can put it down and walk away. That's why it's much more fun to go on a roller coaster than it is to tumble down the face of a cliff. In the roller coaster someone is in charge and taking care of you, and you're not actually going to get killed, although you may think you are for a second or two. And I think it's the same thing with gothic novels."[1] Although Saul explains that he "can't deal with scary movies. I've got way too vivid an imagination," he pounced on the appeal of gothic fiction, a very perilous if often contrived balance between fear and control, the latter helping to shape the former, a "conspiracy" of a kind in which the author creates and manipulates the entire frightening terrain and sets up horror after horror in order for the roller-coaster ride to occur: "It's great fun to sit in the middle of the night and shiver and shake and scare yourself half to death—for some people. For me it's not. . . . I can't even write this stuff in the middle of the night. It's got to be nice, bright, and sunny."

Suffer the Children, Saul's first novel, and other novels of its kind remind one of Richard Chase's comment on the dark American romances of Hawthorne and Faulkner: "The discourse of conspiracy was itself a version of 'American romance'" (R. Levine 1989, 12). One can make the same statement about gothic novels, which chart a virtual unveiling of dark, usually supernatural forces that control characters and plots and slowly reveal themselves as the text proceeds, so that the reader can discover their inevitable power.

The gothic formula itself becomes a conspiracy, a narrative as fundamentalist in its views as the most right-wing conspirator. Port Arbello, the New England village in Saul's novel, lies off the beaten track and becomes the dark domain wherein the conspiracy operates and at the end of the novel continues to operate, hidden from public view. In *Suffer the Children* Saul claims his own gothic territory, however formulated by outside market forces: the demonization of the child (an old faithful Calvinist belief that precedes our contemporary romanticized vision of childhood innocence and purity), the dysfunctional family that underscores and practically initiates the psychic demonization, the curse of a violent past, the haunted mansion (which appears in greater detail in later Saul novels), the sudden shocking scenes of confrontation and butchery, the well-oiled (some would add "formulaic") plot, and the child as a spectator whom no one believes. Conspiracy theory and development are alive and well in the pop gothic novel.

In *Nathaniel* (1984), *Shadows* (1992), *Nightshade* (2000), *The Manhattan Social Club* (2001), and *Midnight Voices* (2002), among others, Saul creates particular conspiracies, contrived by specific villains with specific agendas. The formula is by no means finished. In the prologue to *Nathaniel*, for instance, on one "dark and stormy night" a young girl is confronted by a father's fury and a mother's terror, complete with a raging cyclone, a dead baby, the father's remonstrances against God's retribution, her dazed brother's wandering off onto the prairie and vanishing, and her own vow to remain forever silent. In the prologue to *Shadows* Saul experiments successfully with the hypnotic potential of language in its repetition of dark images and one young boy's terror in short brisk sentences:

Shadows.
Timmy Evans woke up in shadows.
Shadows so deep he saw nothing.
Shadows that surrounded Timmy, wrapping him in a blackness so

dense that he wondered if the vague memory of light that hovered on the edges of his memory was perhaps only a dream.

Yet Timmy was certain that it was not merely a dream, that there was such a thing as light; that somewhere, far beyond the shadows in which he found himself, there was another world. (1992, 1)

Notice the stylistic repetition of shadows, light, dream, "so deep" and "so dense." Language supplies the dark enchantment, the hypnotic pull with its roots clearly in Edgar Allan Poe's vision of terror, that of being buried alive, both by circumstances within the plot and by the litany of language that tries to gain a foothold and perspective in a realm so dark, light registers as only a distant memory. Is this a nightmare? Is it more than that? Is it something else? Time and space collapse into each other, a black hole of consciousness imprisoned in darkness visible. It is that dark domain where even the lineaments of conspiracy vanish momentarily, and only a sense of claustrophobic interment remains intact.

In Tim O'Brien's conjuring up of a strange and sinister realm through an incantatory, self-canceling prose at the heart of *In the Lake of the Woods,* we come upon a more postmodern but still gothic scene that is ontologically uncertain in its very being and suggests an ultimately ambiguous world of near negation, a realm of the postmodern sublime, that threatens any epistemological attempt to try and comprehend it:

And in the deep unbroken solitude, age to age, Lake of the Woods gazes back on itself like a great liquid eye. Nothing adds or subtracts. Everything is present, everything is missing. . . . Growth becomes rot, which becomes growth again, and repetition itself is in the nature of the angle. (1994, 289–90)

Here is a place beyond human comprehension, beyond language's ability to make it rationally or logically signify, a place in opposition to any understanding of human history and culture. It is a vast and distant place like the interior of a lost soul. Here enigma reigns, riddles dissolve, characters lose themselves in a mesmeric landscape of unreadable signs, so inscrutable that even its author shares the same doom as one of his missing characters: "Not quite present, not quite gone, she swims in the blending twilight of in between" (1994, 291).

The northern wilderness remains "all one thing, like a great curving mirror, infinitely blue and beautiful, always the same" (1994, 1). Such a world produces "sub-memories. Images from a place beneath the waking world, deeper than dream, a place where logic dissolved. It was beyond remembering. It was knowing" (134). Such a place remains "a puzzle world, where surfaces were like masks, where the most ordinary objects seemed fiercely alive with their own sorrows and desires." Here "we live in our own souls as in an unmapped region" where one submits to "that magnificent giving over to pure and absolute Mystery" (170, 193, 245–46). This is what has always attracted O'Brien: "Mystery everywhere—permeating mystery —even in the most ordinary objects of the world . . . infinite and inexplicable. Anything was possible" (1991, 176). Here, unlike the more positive of American myths, the wilderness swallows and eviscerates the self, and nothing remains but "the solitude bent back on itself."

John Wade, the boy-magician turned politician in *In the Lake of the Woods,* is nicknamed "Sorcerer," which is the perfect name for such a character. He does it with smoke and mirrors: "The secrets would remain secret—the things he'd seen, the things he'd done. He would repair what he could, he would endure, he would go from year to year without letting on that there were tricks." O'Brien quotes Robert Parrish of *The Magician's Handbook:* "We should prefer to make things happen in the more direct way in which savage people imagine them to happen, through our own invocation" (1994, 46, 96). O'Brien himself admits to loving magic tricks as a child: "I liked the aloneness, as God and other miracle makers must also like it. . . . I liked shaping the universe around me. I liked the power" (1991, 175). It strikes a genuine American chord: the American hero as escape artist and confidence man, a kind of cross between Huck Finn and P. T. Barnum: now you see him, now you don't.

Wade crosses the line into genuine conspiracy when he removes his name from Army records, thus hoping to eradicate his past once and for all. His fellow soldiers knew him in the field only as "Sorcerer," so that he believes he can never be found out. By obliterating his name in the records, he conspires to make his past vanish and create the spotless charismatic politician's image in its wake.

Of course such a self will self-destruct when history catches up with it. When Wade loses the primary election for the U.S. Senate after the press has discovered his role in the My Lai Massacre, along with Lt. Calley, at

Thuan Yen in March 1968, his political career is finished as is the Sorcerer's ability to keep pulling the rabbits out of the hat: "Wade felt an estrangement from the actuality of the world, its basic nowness, and in the end all he could conjure up was an image of illusion itself, a head full of mirrors." No wonder O'Brien quotes Hawthorne's description of Wakefield near the very end of the novel: "He had happened to dissever himself from the world—to vanish—to give up his place and privilege with living men, without being admitted among the dead" (1994, 281, 297). Implicit in the very notion of the American myth of self-creation is its disconnection from the rest of humanity and the world and its imminent self-destruction. Wade's alcoholic father who hangs himself in the garage, Wade's spying on his wife-to-be at the university, her abortion to keep his career going at full tilt, her affair with a dentist, and of course Wade's murdering an old man with a hoe and the bloodthirsty PFC Weatherby at Thuan Yen: all these actual experiences return to destroy him.

In *In the Lake of the Woods* history does not just correct Wade's image of himself as Sorcerer and successful politician; it annihilates and obliterates it. The wilderness swallows him whole, and he vanishes, as has his wife Kathy before him. O'Brien suggests that the Vietnam experience has been so awful and so extraordinarily different from other wars that its effects continue to destroy and eradicate rather than to heal and reconcile. Vietnam has changed the way we think and perceive, and therefore, as Philip D. Beidler explains, O'Brien's fiction produces "a sustained meditation not only on the experience of the war but also on the very idea of sense-making itself . . . quite literally inventing its own context of vision." O'Brien's postmodern open-endedness, the fractured and fragmented structure of *In the Lake of the Woods,* and its complex epistemological and ontological ambiguities reflect that "dimension of consciousness where a complex awareness of this process has been . . . a central thematic preoccupation. . . ." (1982, 100, 26). The novel conspires to undermine Wade's conspiracy of secrecy as much as the experience in Vietnam undermines the traditional linear narrative.

O'Brien directly links postmodernism as vision, style, and form to the Vietnam fiasco. Frederick Karl is correct when, in writing about those American writers who have tackled the Vietnam War, he explains that they "have converted it into an ahistorical aberration. . . . By handling it in this way, they make the war more nightmarish: that is, so removed from anything familiar in time or space that it hangs there, itself a fantasy life of sorts" (1983, 115). "For me," O'Brien has said, "Vietnam wasn't an unreal experience; it wasn't absurd. It was a cold-blooded, calculated war. . . . There is a sense of evil out there that one's trying to battle against, but always with a sense of futility" (1992, 138, 139).

In *In the Lake of the Woods* we enter a more mysterious realm of specu-lation, uncertainty, the collapse of the conventional sense of cause and effect, and come upon unexplainable and "absolute Mystery." This is pre-cisely what fascinates O'Brien: "Writing fiction involves a desire to en-ter the mystery of things: that human craving to know what cannot be known . . . a set of 'mysteries' [is] inherent in the process of writing fiction . . . good storytelling involves, in a substantive sense, a plunge into mys-tery of the grandest order" (1991, 176, 179). The text reflects the wilderness into which both Kathy and John Wade vanish, becomes very problematic for those who seek the social and historical attributes of the more tradi-tional novel, and attempts almost impossibly to focus on its own radical absence of final proof and solution, devastating loss, ultimate enigma, and unsolvable riddle. Such a text suggests a kind of poetic incantation or trance in the face of the unknown: "The writer often enters a trancelike state of his own. Certainly this is my own experience. . . . The Kiowa sha-man achieves a similar effect by inducing in his tribe a trancelike state, summoning a collective dream with the language of incantation and nar-rative drama" (1991, 178).

As in most postmodern texts, origins remain blurred and uncertain. Repetition—of important scenes, emblematic encounters, iconic objects, and certain lethal epiphanies—provides the key as the text swallows itself like the serpent swallowing its own tail. Hence O'Brien's reliance on so many different narrative strategies in one book, each of which threatens the other, and each of which helps to undermine and cancel out or sub-due the other. The novel becomes an epistemological nightmare before it disappears into an ontological abyss, the near-perfect realm of the post-modern sublime.

In such a textual space, O'Brien seems to be trying to re-create a primal sense of mystery and enigma that can be neither captured nor completely explained. In doing so he seems to want to return us "to a primal state of undifferentiated possibility . . . [allowing] us to participate in the making of moral signification." Such a state, as described by Richard Brodhead,

produces a "landscape of pure icon . . . [the] stark embodiments of ultimate mysteries, or of experience pressed toward the purity of ultimate
states . . . " (1986, 193, 185). "The mystery of otherness," O'Brien has explained, "seems permanent and binding, a law of the universe, and yet
because it is a mystery, because it binds, we find ourselves clawing at the
darkness of human nature in an effort to know what cannot be known"
(1991, 181).

In such an enigmatic textual space the reader becomes a participant,
entangled in its contradictions and dialectics, a postmodern fiction, which,
according to Edgar A. Dryden, makes "the experience of reading explicit
in a way that disturbs and blurs the distinction between creative and interpretive acts and raises the question of its own relationship to history and
tradition" (1988, 212). As O'Brien has suggested, "The more I write and
the more I dream, the more I accept this notion of the writer as a medium
between two planes of being—the ordinary and the extraordinary . . . a
medium of sorts between two different worlds—the world of ordinary
reality and the extraordinary world of the imagination" (1991, 179, 178).

O'Brien grapples with these issues within the different strands of his
narrative, as he has done before in *Going After Cacciato* (1980), most
specifically in his elongated footnotes where he can speak out directly as
the mystified and troubled narrative voice that disconnects itself from the
story he is writing and comments on it. The other strategies include the
chapters that deal directly and "objectively" with the events that occur at
the lake from September 20 to October 26, 1988, and begin with "How,"
"What," "Where," for example, Chapter 8, "How the Night Passed," and
Chapter 11, "What He Did Next"; the chapters entitled "Evidence," which
include both actual quotes from memoirs, history books, Lt. Calley's testimony in his court-martial, and other novelists, as well as comments from
O'Brien's own characters who knew both John and Kathy Wade; the chapters entitled "Hypothesis" where O'Brien speculates about what could
have happened to both Kathy and John, including the horrific scene in
which John boils his wife in bed with hot water and dumps her body into
the lake; the chapters which begin, "The Nature of . . . ," and explore such
wider issues as marriage, love, the beast (Vietnam), the spirit (what to do
about Vietnam), love, and loss; and O'Brien's footnotes. Each of these
supports, contradicts, undermines, and often cancels out the others.

O'Brien is totally aware of what he is up to and reveals his own dilemma in the footnotes: "Moreover, there are certain mysteries that weave through life itself, human motive and human desire. Even much of what might appear to be fact in this narrative—action, word, thought—must ultimately be viewed as a diligent but still imaginative reconstruction of events." The impossibility of ultimately knowing anything about human motive and desire builds throughout the footnotes: "The man's soul remains for me an absolute and impenetrable unknown. . . . We are fascinated, all of us, by the implacable otherness of others . . . they are all beyond us." Perhaps his justification lies in the necessity "to bear witness to the mystery of evil." Perhaps the book exists "to remind me. To give me back my vanished life." Or perhaps he's mesmerized by "our love of enigma. . . . No answers, yet mystery itself carries me on" (1980, 30, 103, 203, 301, 269). Ultimately

> there is no end. . . . Nothing is fixed, nothing is solved. . . . Mystery finally claims us. . . . One way or another, it seems, we all perform vanishing tricks, effacing history, locking up our lives and slipping day by day into the graying shadows. Our whereabouts are uncertain. All secrets lead to the dark, and beyond the dark there is only maybe. (304)

"Maybes" beyond the dark provide the postmodern sublime, with its force and seductive power, as if the "maybes" generate a metanarrative in a new fractured, disrupted form, a process of tortured thought rather than the product of analytical and rational resolution. The postmodern weaves its own linguistic conspiracies, luring the reader into the web and pointing to the ultimately unknowable, which resides as ever in the human heart itself:

> Writing fiction . . . display[s] in concrete terms the actions and reactions of human beings contesting problems of the heart. . . . The heart is dark. We gape into the tangle of this man's soul, which has the quality of a huge black hole, ever widening, ever mysterious, its gravity sucking us back into the book itself. . . . To reach into one's own heart, down into that place where the stories are, bringing up the mystery of oneself. (1991, 176, 182, 183)

In his book *Structuring the Void,* Jerome Klinkowitz describes the fiction writer's methods of structuring the void at the heart of such a vision. The postmodern writer must create "a systematic web of relationships that is sustained not by what it captures or spans but rather by its own network of constructions." O'Brien fits into this category easily, concerned as he is with "the presence of the writer/narrator's own endless network of possibilities, which as a self-contained system is created and sustained by the novel's own act of making fiction." Since, according to Klinkowitz, "all such descriptions depend upon difference rather than identity, one recalls that understanding is therefore an ongoing process, a never ending succession of contrasts rather than definitions." I would argue that this is precisely what postmodernist fiction and the postmodern sublime are all about and that, therefore, they must dispense with "linear time [and] empirical observation" (1992, 12, 25, 140), predictability, logic, and the sense that everything is ultimately comprehensible.

For this reason many of the critics who at first reviewed *In the Lake of the Woods* for the popular media, perhaps expecting a straightforward novel, described the book as botched, thin, wanly speculative, and not as viscerally or realistically detailed as *Going After Cacciato.* In this book O'Brien comments, "The essential substances that had once constituted his daily being had been transformed into something vaporous and infinitely mutable"; "Maybe in *Lake of the Woods* . . . all is repetition. . . ." The book does bear the impossible burden of describing the unseen, a radical absence, the dark void after all. When O'Brien describes the massacre at Thuan Yen, he does employ his fantastic and visceral imagery; the writing is more "real," more colorful, more specific, as when Wade shoots an old man and the hoe he is carrying is seen "suddenly sailing up high and doing its quick twinkling spin and coming down uncaught." But O'Brien is trying to grapple with the mysteries of the human heart "where memory dissolves" (1994, 242, 257, 111, 291), and where language, character, deed, and meaning cannot go. The book vanishes or self-destructs in much the same way as Poe's *The Narrative of A. Gordon Pym.* We are left with absolute mystery, strange facts, quotations, descriptions, hypotheses, and character witnesses to try and fathom exactly what happened and why.

In *Going After Cacciato,* O'Brien imagined and re-created a miraculous escape from Vietnam. Again Karl puts it most succinctly. Cacciato's platoon corners him on a mountain: "They expect his surrender and encounter his escape. That is the last known fact. The rest is fantasy . . . " (1983, 115). It is almost impossible to pin down the exact moment when Paul Berlin's imagination takes over, since O'Brien has covered his tracks so successfully and seamlessly. The novel reveals the details and experiences of the Vietnam War, along with such characters as Oscar Johnson, Doc Peret, Lt. Corson, and Stink Harris. It grapples with the very real issues of the war—the lack of knowledge about the Vietnamese people and culture, the strange "plotless" structure of the encounters and battles, the rightness or wrongness of the war, the muddle of American intentions and the "emotion squandered on ignorance. They did not know good from evil"— and recognizes that "the war itself has an identity separate from perception" (1980, 190).

It also focuses on the uncertain border between "reality" and dream, between history and fiction, and memory and imagination in the troubled perceptions and thoughts of Paul Berlin. Thus in the novel, "elements of surreal fantasy are more authoritatively interfused with a sense of close realistic observation . . . " (1980, 53–55). For him "it was a matter of hard observation. Separating illusion from reality," but that also requires "inward-looking, a study of the very machinery of observation—the mirrors and filters and wiring and circuits of the observing instrument . . . [and] a fierce concentration on the process itself" (198). In *Cacciato* it is embodied within the text. In *In the Lake* it has become the text; the former focuses on the experience of Vietnam, the latter on the long-lasting and often distorting effects of that war. Both involve the complex interrelationship between memory and imagination that fascinates O'Brien: "One of the important themes of the book is how one's memory and imagination interpenetrate, interlock. . . . In that sense it's about how one goes about writing fiction, the fictional process" (1992, 128, 135). O'Brien has appropriated Berlin's imaginative journey and made it the center of human perception. In slipping out of himself, he has opened up the precarious and contemporary fascination with fact and fiction, the experiential and the perceptual, deep within the uncertain core or process of the postmodern.

The text of *Going After Cacciato* "breaks" when it crosses from history or experience into Paul Berlin's imagination or the perceptual, but it is not a clean break. Gaps remain. From the confrontation with Cacciato on the mountain, O'Brien skips to "The Observation Post" chapter in which the events occur many weeks later. When he returns to Chapter 3, "The Road to Paris," Berlin's imagination is already at work. His every step "was an event of imagination." We are told about it, but these phrases don't become more significant until the end of the book, and even there O'Brien leaves a gap. The dream ends with the line, "He shivered and wondered what had gone wrong," a sudden space in the text appears, and then Doc is heard murmuring, "It's okay. . . . All over, all over. Fine now." There is even a hint that Berlin may have killed Cacciato: "The enormous noise, shaken by his own weapon, the way he'd squeezed to keep it from jerking away from him. Simple folly, that was all" (1980, 38, 313, 316). All we know for certain, however, is that Cacciato will be reported missing in action.

By the time we arrive at *In the Lake of the Woods*, escape is no longer possible, or if it is, it leads only to death and disappearance. O'Brien has conjured up, once again in American fiction, the dark domain of the postmodern American novel where all solutions vanish, and all remains enigma, as in that "twilight zone" where Beloved haunts the central characters of Toni Morrison's novel. O'Brien's dark domain may be the most apocalyptic of all because of his vision of how the Vietnam War continues to torment us. It places him squarely in the postmodern tradition and in the pursuit of the postmodern sublime, where such a domain "gazes back on itself like a great liquid eye . . . [and] where the vanished things go" (1980, 290, 243).

How better to create a postmodernist text, within which the author appears as one of the characters begged by another to join him in trying to unravel the conspiracy that may involve the Peter Stillmans and the elder's wife Virginia, than to begin to write a formulaic mystery, with all its traditional linearity and ultimate solution, and then undermine it? While O'Brien subverts his novel in the running commentary of his footnotes among other devices, Paul Auster subverts *City of Glass* from within. While O'Brien links the process of his various perspectives to the effects of the Vietnam War on contemporary American experience, Auster links his tale to other stories, mining the intertextual relationships that postmodernism in fiction celebrates and affirms. In both cases texts are foregrounded so that we are aware of their functioning often as reflections of other texts and other perspectives. Both grapple with the mysteries of identity, that fractured, disconnected vision of the postmodern self, and in both, the major characters, John Wade and Daniel Quinn, eventually disappear without a trace. We are left confronting re-enactments of Hume's skeptical self as a "bundle or collection of different perceptions, which succeed each other with an inconceivable rapidity, and are in perpetual flux and movement," which becomes even more radical when selves vanish.

Don DeLillo, a friend of Auster's, once described Auster's work: "Paul's accomplishment is building a traditional storytelling architecture with sharply modern interiors" (Begley n.d., 12). I would describe those interiors as "postmodern," but DeLillo's assessment hits the target. As *City of Glass* begins the narrator muses, "The question is the story itself, and whether or not it means something is not for the story to tell" (1985, 7). Daniel Quinn writes mysteries, and while he writes, he exists. When he stops writing, Auster's novel virtually ends. Quinn uses the pen name William Wilson, which is the pseudonym of the narrator of Poe's story, "William Wilson," who never, in fact, reveals his real name. To Quinn, Wilson appears to lead an independent life, different from Quinn's own. Quinn writes to escape this essential isolation; his wife and son have died. He also reduces himself "to a seeing eye," wandering aimlessly within the "inexhaustible space, a labyrinth of endless steps" that embodies his New York. Wilson's private-eye narrator in his mysteries is Max Work, and so disconnected is Quinn from himself that "Wilson served as a kind of ventriloquist, Quinn himself was the dummy, and Work was the animated voice that gave purpose to the enterprise." Thus at the very beginning of *City of Glass* we are introduced to a character who exists as a series of reflective mirrors, doubled and redoubled in a treacherous and elusive world where "nothing was real except chance" (8, 12, 7).

Quinn loves reading mystery stories and views his own work in terms of other texts. The formulaic patterns of the mystery appeal to him: "Everything becomes essence; the center of the book shifts with each event that propels it forward. The center, then, is everywhere and no circumference can be drawn until the book has come to its end" (1985, 15). Thus Quinn's sense of mystery mirrors Aristotle's description of God, the deity become a literary formula, the modernist notion of a divine presence reduced to the shape of a text that reveals only the deity's eternal absence. The text takes on ultimate authority, at the same time it can only reflect and mirror other texts that have come before it in an endless regression that leads back to Quinn's disturbing sense of his own isolation and alienated consciousness.

Auster plays with luminous refractions of language that reflect Quinn's relentlessly self-receding world. For Quinn's private eye, the Max Work that he as Wilson has created, the letter "i" not only stands for "investigator," but "it was [also] 'I' in the upper case, the tiny life-bud buried in the body of the breathing self. At the same time it was also the physical eye of the writer, the eye of the man who looks out from himself into the world and demands that the world reveal itself to him" (1985, 15–16). The letter "i" suggests the "I" of the self and the eye of the writer: mirrors reflecting mirrors, puns creating puns in that postmodern sense of simulacra reproducing other simulacra with only blankness and emptiness within or beyond.

Of course the doubling and re-doubling does not stop there. Quinn pretends he is Paul Auster when someone dials a wrong number and asks for the Auster Detective Agency. He then pretends to be Auster and ventures forth to meet Peter Stillman who looks like his own dead son and fears the return of his father, also named Peter Stillman. Two Stillmans emerge at Grand Central Station, and Quinn chooses to follow the poor dazed fellow as opposed to the rich shrewd one. Later in the novel Quinn presents himself to Stillman as himself, as Henry Dark, as Stillman's son Peter, and then Stillman himself vanishes.

When Quinn finally goes to see "Paul Auster," he admires Auster's son, who looks like his own and has the same first name, Daniel. Auster happens to be writing an essay on *Don Quixote,* whose initials mirror Quinn's own. Cervantes pretended that his great novel was actually written in Arabic by Cid Hamete Benengeli, "because the book after all is an attack on the dangers of the make-believe," but Quixote, according to "Auster," only pretended to be mad, wanting to test the gullibility of others. Cervantes may in fact have hired "Quixote to decipher the story of Don Quixote himself" (1985, 154), thus reproducing the mirrored images of Quinn's own life and identities. Later Quinn comes across Mookie Wilson, a centerfielder for the New York Mets, whose real name is Wilson, in order to try and keep track of his own reality while holed up, naked, writing in his red notebook, in Stillman's abandoned apartment. Got that?

Peter Stillman Jr., the man Quinn meets, reveals his past life as "the puppet boy," a child locked for nine years in a dark room by his father, disconnected from all outside influences. Quinn ends up in a similar manner. Peter Jr.'s incarceration depended on his father's plan to see if "a baby might speak [God's language] if the baby saw no people." That language depends on total isolation; word and deed become isolated phenomena. It also depends on the elder Stillman's impossible quest to reconnect words to things. "The world is in fragments, sir," he tells Quinn. "And it's my job to put it back together again" (1985, 36, 33, 119).

The Garden and the Tower: Early Visions of the New World, the book written by the elder Stillman, who taught religion at Columbia before his mad scheme with his son was exposed because of a fire, describes language as fallen and scattered, particularly since God destroyed the Tower of Babel, enraged by "the latent power of a united mankind." Henry Dark, a Boston clergyman in the seventeenth century and former private secretary to John Milton, proposed in his pamphlet, *The New Babel,* that paradise exists within man, that man should seek original language within himself and thereby regain the lost stage of innocence, that America was part of that eternal quest, and that the Tower of Babel would be rebuilt in 1960, allowing everyone to enter one of its rooms and restore God's language once and for all. In 1960 Peter the elder confines his son Peter to the dark locked room. He later admits that he invented Henry Dark whose initials he swiped from Humpty Dumpty, "the purest embodiment of the human condition" (1985, 72, 127).

Postmodernism and conspiracy join hands and run riot here. The yearning for the restoration of origins (a lost cause but a very human compulsion); the revelation of "a neverland of fragments, a place of wordless things and thingless words" (1985, 113); the sense that fate and outside forces are directing all things and everyone's lives; the blurring of events, memory, and experience; the doubling and re-doubling of names in such an obsessive manner that it is practically impossible to discover who is who without some kind of scorecard; the elder Stillman's brutal conspiracy to lock his son away from the rest of the world; the obsessive fascination with the relationship between words and deeds, language, and the things of this world; Quinn's own quest that replicates Stillman's, "Auster's," and Auster's; the Baudelairian conundrum "that I will always be happy in the place where I am not. . . . Wherever I am not is the place where I am myself" (168); the image of Manhattan as a prism, a city of glass that reflects the aimless self; Quinn's confinement to the Stillman apartment where he finally vanishes, leaving his red notebook behind; Quinn's awareness that his following Stillman and discerning various patterns "usurp the sovereignty of inwardness. . . . Wandering, therefore, was a kind of mindlessness" (98), and his recognition that "he had come to the end of himself" (191): all of these things create in *City of Glass* a kind of ur-text of the postmodern condition, both in terms of textual reflections and personal experience. The novel eviscerates itself and "ends" open-ended as the narrator, who may be Auster but yet refers to "Auster's" conversations with him about the disappearance of Quinn, discovers the last sentence in Quinn's notebook, which "Auster" has given to him: "What will happen when there are no more pages in the red notebook?" (201). Exactly what happens in *City of Glass:* there is no resolution, only absence and silence, hallmarks of the postmodern sublime, even when the narrator explains that Quinn "will be with me always. And wherever he may have disappeared to, I wish him luck" (203).

The subversion of the mystery formula preserves the sense of ultimate mystery intact. No text can explain it. What remains at the novel's end are "Auster," the character and writer; the nameless narrator (Can it be Quinn? Can it be a Stillman? Is it William Wilson?); Quinn's red notebook that has been left in the empty room (where someone has sent food to him); and New York City, the city of glass with its myriad of reflections, refractions, wayward patterns, and chance. What if Quinn had followed the "other" Peter Stillman at Grand Central Station? Why is it that Poe's detective Dupin celebrates "an identification of the reasoner's intellect with that of his opponent" (1985, 65)? Melville's long last years were spent in New York where his character Bartleby stared at blank walls and preferred not to. Quinn thinks Stillman's walks have spelled out "THE TOWER OF BABEL," and he is instantly reminded "of the strange hieroglyphs on the inner wall of the chasm in Poe's *A. Gordon Pym.*" Quinn often sat in the very spot where Poe gazed out at the Hudson in 1843 and 1844. And Peter Stillman admires Lewis Carroll's *Through the Looking Glass.*

The writing process embodies the postmodern self, which exists only as long as the writing and the reading of it do. At the end there is nothing except questions and speculations. God's language, if there can be such a thing, remains as absent and elusive as those in quest of it. Quinn has passed his obsessions on to "Auster" and the narrator, but his quest remains unfulfilled, unless, of course, the quest mirrors the act of writing and reading. These incarnations in a fallen world provide postmodern humanity's only true quest: we become the very journeys we set out on.

City of Glass mirrors Salman Rushdie's recent description of Thomas

Pynchon's definition of paranoia, "usefully seen as the crazy-making but utterly sane realization that our times have secret meanings, that those meanings are dreadful, immoral, and corrupt beyond our wildest imaginings, and that the surface of things is a fraud, an artifact designed to hide the awful truth from us ordinary deluded suckers." One can choose "to become obsessed investigators of the world's secret meanings . . . accept their impotence and fall into one of a familiar selection of futile, addled, entropic hazes; or to explode into the kind of rage that wants to blow things up" (2002, 318–19). Auster's elegantly contrived and resonant "entropic haze" carries the day.

"Robert Stone has always been good at locating the shadow region where paranoia meets reasonable fear" (1998, 76), suggests Daphne Merkin. As one of the characters in *Dog Soldiers* muses, "[Fear] was the medium through which he perceived his own soul, the formula through which he could confirm his own existence. I am afraid . . . therefore I am" (42). Fear and paranoia permeate Stone's Gnostic and Manichean cosmos, a prison house within which individual spirits remain trapped and doomed, haunted by conspiracy and betrayal, a demonic realm filled with corrupt souls. "It was too dangerous to probe one's inward places," Stone writes in *Children of Light.* "The chemistry was volatile, fires might start and burn out of control" (1986, 185). Human consciousness and the world, obsession and possession mirror each other, and even though one's quest yearns to disentangle oneself from the duplicities of such a dark world, it is impossible to do so. "One had always to wander through vapors among phantoms, one was always just out in it and it never stopped. Illusion compounding illusion—desires, fears, dread shadows, and petty lights, one's own delirium and everyone else's. It was what kept you going. It kept you going until your heart burst" (347).

In *Children of Light*, Grimes expresses his religious compulsions and yearnings as if the yearning for religion itself, consistently rejecting any dogmatic incarnation of it, were religion enough. It was

an attitude which he publicly pretended to share—but which he had not experienced for years and never thoroughly understood. It was the attitude in which people acted on coherent ethical apprehensions that seemed real to them. He had observed that people in the grip of this attitude did things which were quite as confused and ultimately ineffectual as the things other people did; nevertheless he held them in a certain—perhaps merely superstitious—esteem. (261)

According to Stone one of the most momentous moments in his life was his loss of faith at the age of seventeen, which may help to explain his sense of infinite ambiguities and his radical skepticism in league with his yearning after a belief he can never apprehend, another incarnation of the postmodern sublime. His is a faith in the postmodern absence of God, in that gnawing, yawning absence that feels as lethal as a towering presence. As he spells it out at the end of *Damascus Gate*, "A thing is never truly perceived, appreciated or defined except in longing. A land in exile, a God in his absconding, a love in its loss . . . everyone loses everything in the end" (1998, 499–500). This vision of ultimate conspiracy lurks at the heart of things, built into the cosmos and human consciousness, generating conspiracies within conspiracies until the last breath. It also coincides with his own fear of or disgust with an entirely secularized world order that inadvertently or intentionally undercuts any human longing for spiritual independence from or within it.

In *Damascus Gate*, Stone's complex vision materializes at its most religiously intense. "He has been loaded for Leviathan," Jonathan Rosen suggests, "writing with Melvillean chutzpah, his harpoon aimed at the heart of a apocalyptic America" (1998, 14). Jerusalem remains one of the most apocalyptic of cities, the place where three major religions clash and collide, "where earth touches heaven," where the Jerusalem Syndrome attacks and assaults the mind, generating a mad parade of would-be prophets, "a crazed congress of wonders." Metaphors and language shrivel in the wake of such apocalyptic blasts, "every sultry breeze infested with prayer, every crossroads laboring under its own curse" (434, 176, 135). John Barger, in fact, has created a thirty-five-page Web site in which he documents all the references to religious, mythic, and ancient lore that Stone explores, anchoring his text to his religious pilgrims' progress.

In many ways *Damascus Gate* reflects other modernist literary texts. Beneath all the religious paraphernalia, personal prophecies, and visions lies the definite bottom line of a political plot. A political conspiracy exists to secure Avram Lind's return to power in the Israeli cabinet and discredit certain religious fanatics and faiths. The Lind forces consciously pit one religious conspiracy against another, using them to disguise their own distinctive motives. Religion masks the starker, more realistic and political conspiracy. In this Stone writes novels that are closer to Didion's way of viewing the world than to DeLillo's or Pynchon's.

And yet Stone explores so many alternative ways of viewing the cosmos with their roots stretching back and down to ancient cults and ceremonies that they evoke a postmodernist panorama of absence and the forever unknowable. Despite the political conspiracy, the visions of Stone's several religion-hungry characters still haunt and harrow in their own right, outlasting the basic "simplicity" of hardball politics at its dirtiest.

The layers of conspiracy, both cosmic and political, that Stone provides stun the reader, as we try to make our way through everything from Mossad and Shabak to various rumors, groups, interconnections, and "deluded masters." The extraordinarily large cast of characters at first appalls as it passes dizzyingly before us in its "rage for ultimates" (1998, 389,180). For instance Nuala Rice, a pro-Palestinian communist, ships drugs into Gaza in order to trade them for weapons for the Palestinians. She uses Sonia Barnes, who happens to be involved with the novel's major character, Christopher Lucas, and sings at Mister Stanley's Tel Aviv nightclub—he's also involved in drugs with Nuala—as her "beard," using her and her UN vehicle for the run into the Gaza Strip. The Reverend Earl Ericksen, head of the House of the Galilean, a Christian-Zionist fundamentalist organization, may have committed suicide or been murdered because he unearthed the bomb plot that lies at the center of the political conspiracy. His divorced wife, the former lover of Pinchas Obermann, who has been working on a book on the Jerusalem Syndrome and involves Lucas in his speculations (he also introduced Lucas to Sonia), becomes Janusz Zimmer's lover, the well connected Polish journalist and secret agent who is in fact involved with Ian Fotheringill's attempts to flush out and expose the various fundamentalist cults, the links between the Zionists and the American fundamentalists, in order to restore Avram Lind to power.

The major conspiracy builds on the fundamentalist faith that the Muslim mosques atop the Temple Mount must be destroyed in order to make room for the building of the third Jewish Temple. Only then can the apocalypse take place. Only then can the premillennialists "be rapted, like cosmic chipmunks in the talons of their savior, drawn irresistibly heavenward into the Everlasting Arm" (1998, 188). Ralph Arhur "Raziel" Melkier, the musician, former junkie, and cult aficionado, has become the disciple of Adam DeKuff, the former Jansenist solitary, now a Catholic on lithium to control his bipolar disorder, who begins prophesying in the Muslim quarter at the Bethesda pool, later leading a retreat into Galilee, which Sonia and Lucas join. Zimmer and Fotheringill encourage the plot in order to discredit it as a political victory for the politically outcast Avram Lind. Stone very craftily creates his major conspiracy as the mirror image of actual, premillennialist, fundamentalist notions.

Lucas remains Stone's participant-observer, eying the faiths of others, wishing for some restoration of his own, and knowing that no restoration is possible. Upon his own ambiguous but heartfelt yearnings he rests his faith in an absconded God: "the idea of a great absconded Creator must reflect, had to reflect, some actual state of things" (1998, 180). He feels his own isolation, like another of Stone's characters in *A Flag at Sunrise,* "hovering insect-like about the edge of some complex ancient society which he could never hope to penetrate. That was his relationship with the world . . . a bastard of no family origin, no blood or folk. A man from another planet forever inquiring of helpful strangers the nature of their bonds with another" (150). Yet he often envisions a god of punishment, of wrath and blood, as if he, too, were transfixed by apocalyptic fervor. He loves, finally, a sense of ambiguous mystery, the postmodern sublime that stretches on into the infinite, undogmatic, perpetually seductive, and forever beyond his comprehension. He would concur with Obermann's analysis: "First, real things are actually happening, so you have reality. Second, people's perceptions are profoundly conditioned, so you have psychology. Third, you have the intersection of these things. . . . Possibly other dimensions. Mysteries" (47).

Stone's vision finally outruns and transcends the more limited political victory, even as he acknowledges that the political conspirators as double and often triple agents have carefully manipulated the cosmic cults and rabid fanatics that surround them. Yet there are deeper darker fissures in his characters' lives that remain as divided and conflicted as the human heart itself. The ancient Sabazios cult may have created the initial beginnings of all religions with its links to Isis, Zeus, Gnosticism, and Christianity, a revelation that occurs in the dark tortuous tunnels beneath the Temple Mount. In this ultimate labyrinth where the various fundamentalist and political plots come together and expose each other, Stone accomplishes the closing of the circle, thereby re-creating that ancient symbol of wisdom, the serpent with its tail in its mouth, the ouroboros, "the resolution of the noosphere [where] things themselves come to consciousness" (395).

Several critics have suggested that Stone's use of the ouroboros in *Damascus Gate* reveals his participation in the pagan idea that things occur over and over again in cyclical time as opposed to the more linear, Judeo-Christian faith in a history that ultimately produces a Messiah. Such a vision suggests an anti-historical perspective or at least an ahistorical position that at once not only releases one from a final apocalyptic eruption but also incarcerates one within the never-ending cosmos of repetitive, pagan cycles. This would reflect the Gnostic, Manichean view of the cosmos I first suggested in regard to Stone's view. Stone's characters do remain trapped and doomed in his text that in many ways prefigures the premillennial, apocalyptic, and paranoid fantasies and conspiracies of America in the 1990s, but the "circular darkness" (1998, 222) that he conjures up also suggests the numinous, the postmodern sublime. The cycle also breaks the grimly linear path that most apocalyptic fixations favor, and in doing so suggests deeper rhythms, however dark and ultimately mysterious, that cannot be blueprinted, preprogrammed, and obsessively followed. If visions of American history brim and bristle with apocalyptic scenarios and maps, then *Damascus Gate* at the very least points in other directions, breaking that hypnotic devotion to the apocalyptic, at the same time it skewers the apocalypse at the heart of much of contemporary American faith. Stone seems to suggest that as an American writer he can never really entirely shake off the apocalyptic burden and tradition. Whatever his impulses to the contrary, it sings in his dark blood as he tries valiantly to transcend it.

4

Joan Didion

The Fatal Glamour of Conspiracy

Joan Didion's fiction inhabits the volatile territory staged and posited by the dynamic dialectic between postmodern and conspiracy theory and the postmodern sublime. In terms of the postmodern vision, she often blurs distinctions between epistemological perspectives—How do her characters discover and understand things? Do they at all?—and ontological foundations—Exactly what has happened? Who betrayed whom? What really occurred in the backrooms of bureaucrats and the chambers of conspirators? The structure of her novels also reflects postmodern theory in its fragmented, disjointed, often contradictory montage of images, flashbacks, and context-deprived conversations and collisions.

More than Pynchon and DeLillo, Didion often relies on actual conspiracies to shape and propel her plots, whether they are part of the Iran-Contra scandal in *The Last Thing He Wanted,* capitalist machinations behind the Vietnam War in *Democracy,* or Central American "revolutionaries" in *A Book of Common Prayer.* In each instance the reader can eventually piece together an actual conspiracy and figure out who is on whose side (less so, perhaps, in the murkier *Democracy*). Thus structure and content clash. The former dismantles the well-oiled trajectory of conspiracy, thus raising doubts about its success and goals as the role that chance and coincidence play expands and resonates, while the latter underscores the narrative drive of the plot. Again epistemological and ontological perspectives shift, infiltrate one another, and remain elusive and open-ended, indications of the postmodern sublime.

Didion's use of the postmodern sublime, I believe, also lies in the tantalizing opacity of her characters. We can never be certain how much her would-be heroines—Charlotte Douglas, Inez Victor, Elena McMahon—know and understand, whether or not they experience a shock of recognition and choose to act deliberately or act impulsively in a more or less blind and oblivious manner. Do they know what's going on and how they have affected the action that surrounds them? Do they ever realize how their own actions affect that world? Or do they stumble through life in a benumbed and solipsistic manner, oblivious to circumstance and consequence? Didion keeps these issues fluid and open-ended, as if appalled by and drawn to the mysteriously murky motives of the human heart, forcing the reader to pursue those mysterious ambiguities at the center (if there is one) of these women, at once awed by their courage and dismayed by their seemingly delinquent nonchalance.

Didion territory reveals itself in her opening pages. In *Salvador* the reader is immediately plunged "directly into a state in which no ground is solid, no depth of field reliable, no perception so definite that it might not dissolve into its reverse" (1983, 13). *The White Album* insists that "we tell ourselves stories in order to live. . . . We live entirely, especially if we are writers, by the imposition of a narrative line upon disparate images, by the 'ideas' with which we have learned to freeze the shifting phantasmagoria which is our actual experience" (1979, 11). In *Slouching Towards Bethlehem,* Didion explains, "If I was to work again at all, it would be necessary for me to come to terms with disorder" (1968, xii). "She made not enough distinctions. She dreamed her life. She died, hopeful" (1978, 3), begins Grace Strasser-Mendana on the first page of *A Book of Common Prayer. Democracy* opens with a litany:

> The light at dawn during those Pacific tests was something to see.
> Something to behold.
> Something that could almost make you think you saw God, he said.
> He said to her.
> Jack Lovett said to Inez Victor.
> Inez Victor who was born Inez Christian. (1984, 11)

And later: "I have: 'Colors, moisture, heat, enough blue in the air,' Inez Victor's fullest explanation of why she stayed on in Kuala Lumpur" (16). The facts of Elena McMahon's life in *The Last Thing He Wanted* "lacked coherence. Logical connections were missing, cause and effect. I wanted the connections to materialize for you as they eventually did for me" (1996, 6).

The image catches the reader's eye, surrounded as it often is by white space on the page: "the light at dawn," "colors, moisture, heat." We are confronted with Eliot's "heap of broken images" and the cry, "I can connect / Nothing with nothing" (1996, 41). The reader experiences Didion's chaotic wasteland of mind, as if the writer had conspired to undermine all possibilities of a linear, chronological text, reducing it to a realm of isolated cells and passionate but disconnected moments. Such a text at first mirrors Rodolphe Gasche's comments on Paul de Man's literary criticism: "His is a world of unrelated singulars, each so idiosyncratic that in it everything universal becomes extinguished; it is a world of heterogeneous fragments forming a whole only insofar as, by their mutual indifference and lack of generative power, they are all the same, endlessly repeating the punctuality of their lone meaninglessness" (in Norris, 2000, *Deconstruction,* 143). The reader has entered the postmodern realm with its "radical meaning-variance, framework relativism, and paradigm incommensurability" (39). What was once considered "objective truth" becomes in Didion's texts stylized artifice and contrivance, all systems of thought reduced to basic images in search of seemingly arbitrary human connections.

Didion has clearly spelled out her methods: "I began each of my novels, with no notion of 'character' or 'plot' or even 'incident.' . . . I write entirely to find out what I'm thinking, what I'm looking at, what I see and what it means. What I want and what I fear" (Eggers n.d.). As Ihab Hassan suggests, "Didion's stylized, indeed mannered, sentences maintain our epistemological uncertainty" (1990, 34, 111). We can also clearly see the influence of Hemingway, as Didion has admitted, with his focus on exterior details and cinematic descriptions that convey or suggest an interior condition or state of mind, the images and motions that create the emotion, for Hemingway, the real thing.

In "The Waste Land" T. S. Eliot concludes with a famous line: "These fragments I have shored against my ruins" (1962, 46). If we focus on the fragments, the products and images of the poem, then we are left with disorder, a ruin of Western culture and history. But if we focus on the act of shoring, then this process takes on a more positive outlook. Eliot may have only "a heap of broken images" (30) with which to surround himself, but by shoring them "against my ruins," he is undertaking a task of personal restoration, a kind of self-redemptive act if only to hold himself together and intact. As Hassan explains in relation to Didion, "the spare, liturgical ring of the prose seems to suspend death for an instant as it exorcises the mournful frolics of the human condition" (1990, 112). Each image, each line becomes a lifeline, a detail to cling to, with the hope that some kind of connective thread or meaning will develop along the way. "You have to make it up every day as you go along," Didion acknowledges in her *Salon* interview on the Web (Eggers). "And then you have to play the cards you already have on the table. . . . Otherwise it's going to get linear, 'and then she said, and then she said. . . . ' " Her style and writing process, as she describes it, reflect the process of emergence theory, her texts built from the ground up, from local bits and pieces, not from the top down in any globalized manner, the vision emerging as she clings to "the light at dawn" and "colors, moisture, heat."

The liturgical formality of the prose emerges in Didion's repetition of images and phrases almost as precise as a chant, casting its own hypnotic spell like the workings of a mind slowly coming into focus or a consciousness waking. The spell builds and binds the various images, not providing connections early on but creating a rhythm and a cadence that sounds like, feels like it is generating connections. "Our subjectivity," Mikhail Bakhtin advises, "rather than being a place, quality, or agent, is a process of interpretation. It is a continuous intentional movement through history and language, not toward some ultimate self-realization [although Didion's female characters seem to be grappling with precisely that struggle either in trying to confront their lives and circumstances or trying to elude and avoid them], which could only be a form of death, but within the emerging discourses that make up our 'reality' and that—knotted, partial, indistinct—demand interpretation" (O'Donnell 1986, 155). The chant posits the possibility of connection if only in its rhythms and repetitions.

The compulsive ritualism of Didion's prose raises questions about the images, events, and details she describes. Do they lead to connections, as the designs of the modernist texts, in such works as Faulkner's *The Sound and The Fury*, Joyce's *Ulysses*, and Eliot's "The Waste Land," do? Are there "compulsive rituals" that lead to a greater significance? Do images and details reveal themselves as pieces of some larger puzzle, as traces of a secret web of significance? Is Didion struggling with the notion or vision of the sublime, defined by Christopher Norris as "the failure of understanding to grasp what lies beyond its utmost scope of comprehension"? When the reader confronts disturbingly powerful and violent images, does she at the same time confront "this point where understanding despairs of bringing intuitions under adequate concepts [Norris's Kantian description may parallel Didion's conception of art] that we are somehow made aware of a higher realm—a realm of 'suprasensible' ideas" (2000, *Deconstruction*, 58)?

Critics quarrel at the point where they begin to grapple with Didion's vision. Is she merely fascinated with what Barbara Grizzuti Harrison has called "the futility of human endeavor," within which "all connections are equally meaningful and equally senseless" (1980, 10)? Does she merely romanticize "privilege and terminal lassitude" (6)? Are her opinions, therefore, "disguised as instinctual, idiosyncratic reactions to ephemeral phenomena, and thereby rendered less threatening and more winsome" (11)? Is hers a mere stylistic tic or apocalypse in which doomsday becomes a lifestyle and a fashion statement?

Or is Didion's vision more sinister and postmodern? Is she wrestling, as David Casey contends, with "the inadequacy of language and the destruction of modernist American systems" (2001)? If "we are continually exposed to the mismatch between, for example, image and idea or made conscious of the verbal residue that remains after we have plumbed a passage for its significance" (O'Donnell 1986, 143), is she then presenting a relativistic vision of the horrors of the essentially human and contemporary human condition, exploring the same dark and contradictory self that so fascinated writers such as Faulkner, Hawthorne, and Joyce Carol Oates? Is hers a postmodern localized humanism that is appalled by the corpses modern politics leaves behind, by the waste and despair implicit in the contemporary American values of compulsive consumerism, public-relations parades, and the brutalities of contemporary bureaucracy and business? Can she be presenting postmodern characters who lack an even basic sense of self and who, therefore, cannot construct a meaning out of their visceral experiences? Is this cop-out or cosmic conspiracy, passing the buck or a vision darker than that of most American romantics? Is Didion a modernist or a postmodernist?

If nihilism, fashionable or otherwise, hovers close to Didion's characters and texts, how then can we account for the developing and sharpening use and exploitation of conspiracy in her fiction and nonfiction? Can we discern such development from the apparent nihilism of *Play It As It Lays* to the familial politics of musical chairs in *A Book of Common Prayer*, from a vague uneasiness with American capitalism and the fall of Saigon in *Democracy* to the very real conspiracy of the Iran-Contra scandal during the Reagan administration in *The Last Thing He Wanted*? Has an initial neurasthenic nihilism evolved into particular conspiracy theories in her later work? Is her idea of conspiracy generated by her earlier fascination with death and despair, and can it be seen as a resolution of that more evasive state of soul?

The self in postmodern theory, a victim of forces beyond individual control, becomes a contested category, a creature and function that is more socially conditioned than personally directed, so much so that it might not exist at all but appear only as a creation of language and desire. As Didion writes, so the Didion woman begins to emerge, image by image, event by iconic event. The character's self, therefore, emerges from the text Didion constructs, but each one—Maria, Charlotte, Inez, Elena—can be viewed in diametrically opposed ways. Are these passive, compulsive creatures seeking refuge from all self-reflection, or are they searching for catalysts for reflection? Are they compulsively entranced by a consciousness they choose to numb and practically abandon, or are they carefully and instinctually trying to cope and survive their often-extreme circumstances?

Didion has maintained, for instance, that in *A Book of Common Prayer,* Charlotte Douglas is very much in control, but one could easily make the case, given the images and encounters that both embody and entrap Charlotte, that her staying on in Boca Grande at the end of the novel reveals her mere surrender to events, her submitting herself to whatever fate lies in store for her, and a giving in, a giving up. Didion, in the *New York Times* of February 8, 1987, has said that her characters "are searching for some kind of salvation" (2), and we do feel the pressure of their anxieties and depression, but the method or manner of searching may be as much about surrender and self-destruction as it is about sacrifice and self-revelation.

Maria Wyeth in *Play It As It Lays* may be the quintessential Didion character, shorn of any of the political context and possible conspiracies that begin to emerge in the later novels. She exists in the superficial cinematic California of easy sex, good looks, and endless parties and deals. Hers is a numbed, embalmed landscape of emblematic encounters, monochromatic anomie, and a blurred sense of time. She functions, barely, by coasting, driving on freeways, keeping "my mind in the now," turning everything into an endless relentless present, "watching the dead still center of the world, the quintessential intersection of nothing" (1978, 6, 66).

The form of the novel reflects Maria's "blank tape" of a mind in its eighty-four chapters of fitful glimpses, its switch from first-person to third-person narrative, the amount of white space on each page that threatens to overwhelm the text, and the fragmented episodic structure, completely reflected in the world around her: "The stillness and clarity of the air seemed to rob everything of its perspective, seemed to alter all perception of depth . . . an atmosphere without gravity" (169, 75).

Maria accepts her father's view of life as a crap game to be played as it "lays," and under every rock lurks a snake, a persistent image that haunts the entire novel. She often repeats the words "none," "less," and "nothing" as if chanting to keep herself intact, but there is more than nothing here. The snake itself, of course, suggests evil with all its mythic and satanic heritage.

Maria's numbed functioning rests on her sense of punishment: "I believe my sins are unpardonable" (2). With her four-year-old retarded daughter Kate in an institution, the memory of her mother's car accident, the guilt that haunts her because of her abortion, and her divorce from Carter, she "did not particularly believe in rewards, only in punishments, swift and personal" (72). At one point she cries with abandon for her mother, for Kate, and for herself, and that instance occurs on the day her baby would have been born had she not aborted it. Her sense of "unspeakable peril, in the everyday" springs from this sense of failure and grief: "In the whole world there was not as much sedation as there was instantaneous peril" (99). However self-inflicted and self-aggrandizing this abiding sense of punishment and sin is, it lodges in her consciousness as grievously as consciousness itself.

Maria's nihilistic sensibility springs not from anywhere or just the Hollywood scene but from her own deeds and despair. To think otherwise is to misinterpret the novel and avoid the very reasons for her state of mind. She has reduced herself to a kind of entranced soul not merely for some functional desire but because of the harsh morality with which she judges her actions and her circumstances. One should recognize as well that, as Casey maintains, while postmodernism denies the possibility of meaning, "denies that human volition and resolve can do the metaphysical work of a transcendental, modernist theory, it does not deny, as nihilism certainly does, that human beings, individually and collectively, cannot believe in anything . . . more than the metaphysical claim that 'there is nothing'" (2001).

Didion suggests possible salvation, however limited and ruthlessly post-modern in her manner of not spelling out a solution or describing the force—of will? Of soul? Of compulsion?—that drives her, by Maria's awareness of questioning, doubting, and continuing to "play." Yes, she avoids issues, she reacts more than she acts, she numbs herself on the free-way and with casual sex, but her love for the damaged Kate grounds her, and she is very aware of the company she keeps: "I don't like any of you. You are all making me sick" (189).

Maria's postmodern paranoia and stunned stunted manner certainly subvert the more modernist sense of willed choices and designs, but she does make those choices, however fitfully and passively, and recognizes in the typical postmodern manner of such characters, "I never in my life had any plans, none of it makes any sense, none of it adds up." Her focusing on the lack of connections in her life becomes its own carapace of survival, buffeted by her world and circumstances "at once too deep and too eva-nescent for any words she knew[. Everything] seemed so vastly more com-plicated than the immediate fact that it was perhaps better left unraveled" (5). Unraveling in this instance suggests not so much a muted, dimwitted nihilism but Eliot's heap of broken images shored up against her ruin. Such an experience creates the hunger for apocalypse with its intimations of the postmodern sublime, for sudden revelation that hovers just beyond Maria's ability to discern or understand it, "suggested an instant in which all anxieties would be abruptly gratified. . . . The notion of general devas-tation had for Maria a certain sedative effect" (49, 103). It suggests the same impulse within the fundamentalist lust for the world's end, the con-spirator's desire to expose the ultimate elitist cabal, the postmodernist urge to recognize the ultimate lack of meaning that remains forever out of reach, unfathomable, arbitrary, and finally nonexistent.

Didion, like Maria, concentrates on "certain facts, certain things that happened." She will suggest but not "invent connections" (2), although her non-invention of them only drives the reader forward to try and dis-cover some in her own right. It is Didion's pursuit of possible connections, while recognizing that all has to be necessarily arbitrary because these con-nections are forged by her and by us and do not exist in some transcendent absolutist realm, that links her in part to the great American romantic writers from Hawthorne to Faulkner, Melville to Morrison. Her starker presentation of that pursuit in her clipped precise encounters and sharply contoured images and events reveals her more postmodern sensibilities. We continue to interpret, signify, and pursue connections, all the time recognizing that this enterprise may itself be ultimately futile if necessarily all too human. We must seek meaning and make choices—it is a basic human compulsion to do so, which Didion clearly recognizes—but the postmodernist knows (or thinks she does; how can we ever be certain?) that there are no beginnings, no endings, and no ultimate point other than the seeking itself, the path of the postmodern sublime. As Casey suggests, what terrifies us about the postmodern outlook "is the revelation that there is no longer any coherent reason behind tragedy, death and suffering and no longer any transcendental moral grounds on which to condemn it . . . " (2001).

In her later novels and essays Didion extends her vision to include both the self-conscious craft of an eyewitness recounting events that have transpired and the possibility of secret and elusive conspiracies that lie just beyond the grasp of the narrator. These two artful designs anchor her postmodern vision in particular themes and forms, the reporter trying to discover and sift through the facts and actions of a woman's life and the intimations that this life has somehow become enmeshed in a wider political and cultural milieu that creates other witnesses, other victims, and other darker networks of greed, power, and design. The woman in question, whether Charlotte Douglas, Inez Victor, or Elena McMahon, grapples with similar problems that plagued Maria—dead daughters, estranged daughters, marauding but fascinating men, deals and scenarios that vary depending on what is at stake (the control of Boca Grande, the loss of Vietnam, the war in Nicaragua), the particular Didion experience of evasion, denial, deferral, disintegration, dread, and the pervasive fear of ultimate catastrophe—but the context conjures up more extensive cultural and political consequences that involve more than individual dislocation and disconnection.

Didion also extends her range as a novelist in her first three novels. *Run River,* her first, relies on a chronological narrative form, the historical cause-and-effect of a family saga, which surrounds and encapsulates Lily Knight McClellan's numbness and morbid sensitivities. *Play It As It Lays* uses a more cinematic approach. Both reader and heroine are trapped in a seemingly merciless present, similar to John Updike's *Rabbit, Run.* By the time *A Book of Common Prayer* was written, Didion views her narrative as a kind of personal testimony, the first-person narrator who reflects on the actions of others, a structure similar to such great American novels as *The Great Gatsby* and *Absalom, Absalom!* In this later instance the reader must remain wary of the narrator's point of view and judgment at the same time she is being seduced and spellbound by the fictional process itself.

Grace Strasser-Mendana in *A Book of Common Prayer* becomes the first self-conscious narrator and witness who will eventually become "Didion" herself in *Democracy* and *The Last Thing He Wanted.* She describes herself in the first sentence of the novel as Charlotte's "witness" and at the conclusion, "I have not been the witness I wanted to be" (1978, 280). Her development underscores this transition since she first sees herself as a kind of witness for the prosecution in terms of Charlotte's passion, which she defines as delusion: "I have been for fifty of my sixty years a student of delusion" (4); "The most reliable part of what I know, derives from my training in human behavior" (53). She distrusts her anthropological methods but insists that Charlotte "made not enough distinctions. She dreamed her life." The undeluded Grace will try to explain and fathom the passionate but wrongheaded Charlotte. At the end of the novel Grace has become more the kind of witness we see in the gospels, someone who attests to the mysteries and attempts to interpret the deeds of a Christ-like figure, in the sense of self-sacrifice and scapegoat, for a thoroughly corrupt and politically avaricious society. She has not "solved" Charlotte Douglas's character, but she has borne witness to and for her, a very different kind of witness than her quasi-scientific approach initially suggests. Her awareness of her own imminent death sharpens her sense of judgment and disgust, flattens her embittered view of her environment, compelling her to view Charlotte and Boca Grande in stark, deliberate terms like "the light in Boca Grande, how flat it was, how harsh and still. How dead white at noon" (13).

As the novel develops, Grace and Charlotte seem less and less different from each other. Both are *norteamericanas,* Charlotte the outsider, Grace in Boca Grande the insider. Both have children who are lost to them, Grace's son Gerardo and Charlotte's daughter Marin. Both children involve themselves in political and potentially lethal crusades yet lack any real political commitment or program. Grace draws closer to Charlotte as if attempting to define herself more clearly. She cannot do certain things because she is a member of the politically and financially powerful Strasser family. She may, in fact, envy Charlotte's wayward sexuality and lack of concern for consequences. Grace may embody the "ego" in relation to Charlotte's "id." Grace wonders how Charlotte can possibly live such an unfathomed and unfathomable life—"She seemed aware of nothing she was doing. She was reflexively seductive" (33); "I think I have never known anyone who led quite so unexamined a life" (111)—but she also recognizes "the equivocal nature of even the most empirical evidence" (279). The dynamic dialectic between Grace and Charlotte ultimately blurs the distinct identity of each, making Grace's tale of passion and delusion ultimately suspect and full of doubt. Even Grace at the last suggests that perhaps "the delusion was mine" (280).

As *norteamericanas,* despite their very different circumstances, both Grace and Charlotte have been formed by Didion's frontier ethic, by North American culture and myth. Grace's father was a wildcatter who struck it rich in Colorado minerals. Charlotte's second husband, Leonard Douglas, runs guns. She may see herself as "immaculate of history, innocent of politics" (56), as many North Americans do from Grace's and the outside world's point of view (and it may be Charlotte's lack of political awareness that gets her killed), and she might "believe the world to be peopled with others like herself" (57), but in many ways so does Grace. Politics for her is nothing more than a series of family feuds and musical chairs. Her view of what little is at stake in the political conspiracies of Boca Grande may be the result of her viewing herself as separate and different from the Strasser legacy. Grace's sardonic testimony about Charlotte's use of euphemism may be no different from her own belief in "fear of the dark [as a] protein" (5): "Give me the molecular structure of the protein which defined Charlotte Douglas"; "As usual I favor a mechanical view" (206). This, of course, is the view that finally fails her.

Both Grace and Charlotte remain Didion women, burdened with "that sense of living one's deepest life underwater, that dark involvement with blood and birth and death" (1979, 116–17). Both suffer from dreams of "sexual surrender and infant death, commonplaces of the female obsessional life." Is it any wonder that Grace finally confesses, "I no longer know where the real points are. I am more like Charlotte than I thought I was" (1978, 53, 276)?

The conspiracies at the center of *A Book of Common Prayer,* a forerunner to those in *Democracy* and *The Last Thing He Wanted,* involve the Strasser family. Luis Strasser, Edgar's brother, Grace's brother-in-law, and the former president of Boca Grande was assassinated in April 1959. Victor, the third brother, used guerrillas against Luis to overthrow his regime and took over the government. Antonio, the fourth brother, has also been using and financing the guerrillas against Victor and eventually succeeds. Gerardo, Edgar's and Grace's son, has thrown his lot in with his uncle Antonio. The problem for Charlotte occurs when she finds herself sleeping with both Victor and Gerardo, who are on opposite sides of the latest lethal family squabble. "When I told Charlotte in March that there would come a day when it might be possible to interpret her presence in certain situations as 'political,'" Charlotte responds by describing herself as "not 'political' in the least" (201), a position, of course, that entirely misses Grace's point.

By reducing Boca Grande politics to in-house musical chairs, Didion clearly castigates the corruption of Caribbean politics in which no real changes ever occur. "Transition" provides only more of the same, confirming Grace's grim description of Boca Grande that is relentlessly changeless: "The politics of the country at first appear to offer contrast, involving as they do the 'colorful' Latin juxtaposition of *guerrilleros* and colonels, but when the tanks are put away and the airport reopens nothing has actually changed." Even Edgar and Charlotte's husband Leonard Douglas have at one time been involved with the guerrillas to pursue their own interests, a revelation that surprises Grace who thinks she knows exactly what her son Gerardo is up to. Politics, therefore, becomes the kind of public narrative and transcendent tale that Didion's vision and style consistently subvert and demolish, her postmodern "take" on such fables as cynically astute as Grace's. No wonder Grace observes a cosmos in which "there is no perceptible wheeling of the stars in their courses, no seasonal wane in the length of the days or the temperature of air or earth or water, only the amniotic stillness in which transformations are constant" (6, 157). The very attenuation of that sentence embodies Didion's political vision.

Charlotte Douglas embodies many of the circumstances and numbed consciousness of Maria Wyeth, but in *A Book of Common Prayer* we view her only at a distance through the lenses of Grace's intelligence, speculation, and mystification. Grace wishes for Charlotte to signify *something,* and her pursuit becomes the book's compelling and obsessive focus. Charlotte deifies her thoughtless daughter, Marin, who commits acts of supposedly revolutionary violence that change nothing. She runs off with Warren

Bogart, then abandons him to his own dying in New Orleans. She gives birth to a daughter who dies an hour later in a parking lot. She visits airports as if expecting Marin's imminent arrival but then continues to do so as if the ritual holds her elusive life together. She is one more Didion obsessive, self-absorbed and existing on cruise control, building her life from revisions and erasures that allow her to tell others that all is well, as if she were living underwater, wandering, and unable to come up for air.

Such weightlessness demands Grace's thirst for signification. Charlotte's apparent blankness demands Grace's need to interpret, understand, and explain. That she is unable to do so leaves the reader and Didion confined to a decidedly postmodern realm, not nihilistically created but mysteriously and ambiguously open-ended. Who can finally fathom the depths of the human heart or the contradictory motives of the human will? Mystery trumps methodology and keeps us guessing. This is not a mystery to be solved but a mystery to experience as in the mysteries that lie at the center of religious faith and eternal human doubt on the road toward the postmodern sublime.

A Book of Common Prayer introduces various images and objects—the emerald ring, the red shoes, Marin's gold bracelet—out of context and then slowly links them to the wider and more elusive environment. This has become a distinctive Didion trademark by now. Marin's gold bracelet, which Charlotte gave her, winds up on the bomb she used to try and blow up the Transamerica building in San Francisco. Edgar Strasser, who had financed the guerrillas (like everyone else has done in their quest for personal power), gave the emerald ring to Leonard who passed it on to Charlotte who eventually mails it to Grace. Children wear red shoes in the tropics. Charlotte's daughter Carlotta is buried in them. Didion forms links and connections and then leaves them suspended in her text, iconic objects that act as benchmarks for the conspiracies that surround and engulf them. We follow them like a detective pursuing clues, only to watch how they are moved from place to place, tainted by the characters who possess and deliver them. They are postmodern objects, fraught with contradictory and ambiguous meanings, afloat in the fluid inconsistencies of human lives and fates.

Charlotte's deciding to remain in Boca Grande when the "revolution" breaks out dooms her. Her death becomes a foregone conclusion. Does she know this and choose to stay, or does her own inertia paralyze and entrap her, submitting to whatever fate has in store for her? The ambiguity of her decision, if it can be called that, epitomizes the ambiguities of her unexamined life, her *norteamericana's* belief that she is somehow above and beyond mere politics, "immaculate of history." She is not, of course, and her "body was found, where it had been thrown, on the lawn of the American Embassy. Since all Embassy personnel had abandoned the building the point was lost on them. Although not on me" (277).

This is, after all, not *THE Book of Common Prayer* but only a postmodern apprehension of it. Witnesses change and doubt their own methods. Conspiracies swirl about the characters and devour them. Logic leads nowhere. Mystery tantalizes and shimmers in all things beyond human comprehension and understanding. Grace perceives moral values, however transitory: "I have noticed that it is never enough to be right. I have noticed that it is necessary to be better" (164). Words become chants. Chants both mesmerize and particularize, consoling and anesthetizing the lost soul in the music of calm repetition. And each—facts, words, personalities, mythic patterns, landscapes, conceptual and political schemes—leads only to further mystery and wonder, broken and scattered, fragments of the postmodern sublime.

Once again in *Democracy* Didion begins with images, a scene, snippets of a conversation in her decentered manner of writing fiction. As Steven Johnson suggests in terms of emergence theory, nature and the cosmos begin to organize from the bottom up, from the local to the global, revealing "the movement from low-level rules to higher-level sophistication" (2001, 18): "Local rules lead to global structure—but a structure that you wouldn't necessarily predict from the rules" (90). As if describing Didion's fictional method, he believes that things "mix, mutate, evaluate, repeat. . . . What drives each process is a hunger for patterns, equivalencies, likenesses; in each the art emerges out of perceived symmetry" (171, 128). So does Didion's tale begin to emerge out of her selected images and encounters, reflecting "the capacity of all life-forms to develop ever more baroque bodies out of impossibly simple beginnings" (14). As Johnson adds, "We have a natural gift for associative thinking, thanks to the formidable pattern-matching skills of the brain's distributed network" (200).

Tai Moses in his "Fear of Meaning" argues, "To reject the search for meaning negates the very impetus for writing, which may be why Didion shows us throughout her work glimpses of the writer grappling with her craft" (1996, 7). Didion does not reject the search for meaning at all. She rejects ever finding an ultimate meaning and solution, rejecting the rational belief that life is like a popular mystery novel within which all loose ends are pulled together in the last chapter. Instead she exposes her own postmodern doubts about meaning in general, revealing the precarious state of the writer's attempting to understand and comprehend, placing her own uneasiness with "final solutions" in the forefront of her narrative, performing the postmodern sublime as endless pursuit. As Johnson explains, "The stories that we most love are ones that surprise us in some way, that break rules in the telling" (2001, 189), and Didion breaks the rules of linear and chronological storytelling because she doesn't believe in them. In the foreground of *Democracy* lurks this uncertain, meditative, self-eviscerating, self-conscious narrator, suffering from postmodern overload, surfeit, and uncertainty.

Also in *Democracy* the growth of conspiracies lurks in the background. Politics and business mix and mutate at a time in 1975 when Saigon is falling to the North Vietnamese armies. Jack Lovett's mysterious dealings and the convoluted deals of the Christian family and their cohorts intertwine with just enough information to tie them together in terms of betrayal, entitlement, and murder. Conspiracy by its very nature remains invisible, so that this invisibility, carefully hinted at and suggested by Didion throughout the novel, like an ever-present mist or aura in a dark murky wood, like faith, establishes the elusive proof of its own existence, permeated with postmodern paranoia. Its very absence, which is present in various clues and intimations—Lovett's career, the relationship between the Christians and the Omuras—becomes the "secret" metanarrative, the subtext of *Democracy*.

The famous gaps in Didion's meticulously disconnected narratives leave room for conspiracy, paranoia, doubt, and uncertainty to infiltrate and ferment, smolder and fester. Absence establishes presence as her deconstruction of a linear plotline leaves her text open and vulnerable to provocative images, rumors, gossip, suggestion, self-scrutiny, and alien (because largely unknown) maneuvers. Images and details take on a more sinister aura because they are left unprotected, unassimilated, seemingly disconnected from a larger murkier context but uncannily luminous and resonant in the unfolding pursuit of Inez Christian Victor's and Jack Lovett's clandestine and long-standing love affair.

The self-conscious narrator, "Joan Didion," explicitly reveals her postmodern uncertainty: "I have no unequivocal way of beginning [this novel], although I do have certain things in mind," such as a poem by Wallace Stevens with "a gold-feathered bird . . . without human meaning, / Without human feeling" and "Inez Victor's fullest explanation of why she stayed on in Kuala Lumpur . . . 'Colors, moisture, heat, enough blue in the air.'" She also has a recurrent dream of tropical green, watching "the spectrum [of a rainbow] separate into pure color," and then admits, "Consider any of these things long enough and you will see that they tend to deny the relevance not only of personality but of narrative, which makes them less than ideal images with which to begin a novel, but we go with what we have." These separate images conjure up the memory of her own lack of certainty at a time when "I began thinking about Inez Victor and Jack Lovett," celebrities whose public confidence and image contrast her own lack of "that minimum level of ego which all writers recognize as essential to the writing of novels," of conviction, patience, and "faith even in my own technique" (1984, 16,17). Thus the novel's introduction of Inez and Jack coincides irrevocably with the narrator's own gaping self-doubts and anxieties. Somehow the following story must assuage that condition, suggesting a re-enacted process of healing and/or exorcism within which the postmodern narrator finds herself.

Didion's self-revelation spirals and expands. She has "no Tropical Belt Coal Company," no central image like that from Joseph Conrad's novel *Victory*. Perhaps all she has is her technique, her "self-correcting maladjustment . . . to structure," her "*ironic-but earnest tone*," her compulsion to return "*again and again to different details of the scene*," resulting in a particular atmosphere but in no "definite convictions about what happened down there in the spring of 1975, or before" (17–18). The reader is intrigued by such a confession. What must have happened must have been so terrible or so shocking that its effects may have damaged the narrator's ability to grasp them fully. After the list of abandoned stories and accounts that follows, Didion finds herself floundering but determined to press on.

"Imagine my mother dancing" is an opening line Didion has abandoned. She surrenders her "study in provincial manners, in the acute tyrannies of class and privilege by which people assert themselves against the tropics" (22), while documenting the existence of the Christian family in Hawaii, the arrival of Carol Christian there, the two daughters of Carol and Paul, the odd comment that Paul Christian "had reinvented himself as a romantic outcast" (26), and a brief discussion of fortunes made, construction contracts arranged in Vietnam, and deals arranged "to squeeze Dick Ziegler out of windward Oahu and coincidentally out of the container business," something to do with Wendell Omura. Didion rejects the novel of manners "in that prosperous and self-absorbed colony," of which the Christians seem to be the most outstanding example, and instead, like Emily Dickinson lingering over certain slants of light and imperial afflictions, finds herself mesmerized at "a certain hour between afternoon and evening when the sun strikes horizontally between the trees and that island and that situation are all I see" (27, 30). This suggests Poe's hypnagogic state, that twilight zone between waking and sleeping when images and events blur and tantalize, forever eluding human consciousness but haunting the mind and spirit like the postmodern sublime. Only at this point does Didion begin to zero in on her characters, starting with the mysterious Jack Lovett, a creature of the twilight zone and a possible key to Paul Christian's murder of his daughter Janet and her lover, Wendell Omura.

Democracy begins with snippets and shards that gradually come into focus but do not reveal their context. The images of the light at dawn as "something to behold . . . that could almost make you think you saw God" suggest the moment of biblical creation, except that the dawn Jack Lovett describes to Inez Victor occurs "during those Pacific tests" in 1952 or 1953, the expanding age of nuclear destruction and of American military might. Lovett's reaction with its soothing repetition of "sky," "flowers," and "gardenias," complete with their aroma and wetness, parallels Didion's own style, with the exception that he is reacting aesthetically to a scene of vast destruction, thus revealing his own amoral comprehension of the world around him (11). As part of the national security state in his role as CIA agent and/or secret government adviser, his very detachment suggests his remoteness and the Machiavellian mysteries that Didion suggests lie at the heart of his secret networks and spurious deals. In the fourth chapter he is the first character she pursues, describing him as "solitary, unattached to any particular institution . . . reserved, wary, only professionally affable . . . one of those men for whom information was an end in itself" (34). Part of his allure resides in his belief that "all behavior was purposeful," that other people like other nations were "wild cards, useful in the hand but dangerous in the deck" (36), viewed as part of some overall abstract design, imminently conspiratorial and forever unknown. According to his visa applications and business cards in 1975, "he was a business man . . . a consultant in international development" (39).

What the reader doesn't know, of course, as the novel begins is that Jack Lovett is speaking with Inez Christian Victor on their eleven-hour flight from Hawaii to Hong Kong on March 30–April 1, 1975, after Inez's sister Janet's death and all the public relations spinning that has been going on since she and her lover were shot to death by her father. "Oh shit, Inez," Lovett tells her. "Harry Victor's wife." The phrase finds its context on page 187, where Inez's response is to forget "the correct thing" and flee with her lover on Easter Sunday night, the flight that she describes as "an eleven-hour dawn. . . . Dawn all the way. . . . Something to behold." Thus when Didion admits that "this is a hard story to tell" (188, 915), it is because the complications have not yet fallen into place, if they ever will, and human motives remain as murky as the eleven-hour dawn is light.

Didion's setting herself up as the journalist-narrator implies, at first, that *Democracy* is a traditional modernist text, in that a real world exists beyond the narrator's consciousness of it, and the real epistemological problems occur when she tries to figure out both the actions and motives of her characters. Her first view of Lovett at *Vogue* in 1960, where Didion and Inez were both working, initially sparks her curiosity about the couple and Lovett's "temperamental secretiveness, a reticence that had not so much derived from Jack Lovett's occupation as led him to it" (41). It also launches her quest to try and fathom the chronology of events and the motives of her characters with her references to the piece of film "on March 18, 1975, one week exactly before Paul Christian fired the shots that set this series of events in motion [in which] Inez Victor can be seen dancing with Harry Victor" (42) and her growing awareness that Inez, embalmed in photo opportunities and public-relations scenarios, "had lost certain details" and describes the price she has had to pay as memory. Like Maria Wyeth and Charlotte Douglas before her, Inez's comment suggests either a strategy on her part, a conscious "way of fixing her gaze in the middle distance" or a virtual loss of memory, "as if you'd had shock treatment" (51). The ambiguities of Inez's condition remain unresolved and lend her that postmodernist aura of a public icon bereft of personal significance and reduced to a superficial film clip. To Didion both she and Lovett remain "equally evanescent, in some way emotionally invisible; unattached, wary to the point of opacity, and finally elusive. They seemed not to belong anywhere at all, except, oddly, together" (84).

In that spring of 1975 Didion happened to be teaching at Berkeley, and she insists "that the way a writer constructed a sentence reflected the way that writer thought" (1984, 71). If this is true, then the narrator Didion is as much in awe of celebrity and fashion as is Inez, although Didion continues pursuing the possible significance of the murder, political and commercial corruption, and the American imperial entitlement and colonialist mentality as revealed in Hawaii. The capitals in Southeast Asia are falling, Saigon is on the verge of collapse, and while this suggests "a graphic instance of the black hole effect," her own sense of time is collapsing as well, "falling in on itself, the way a disintegrating star contracts into a black hole" (72). Yet she persists: "When novelists speak of the unpredictability of human behavior they usually mean not unpredictability at all but a higher predictability, a more complex pattern discernible only after the fact. Examine the picture. Find the beast in the jungle, the figure in the carpet. Context clues. The reason why" (72). Meaning is not nonexistent, yet; it remains just beyond her abilities to find it. At the last she gives up the ghost, her epistemological dilemma becoming ontological as well. "We keep our attention fixed on the wire" (215), she suggests, aware of the precarious nature of her quest and pursuit, arranging and rearranging "certain objects, talismans, props" (108), distrusting "other people's versions" (124) of what has happened. She finally admits that she has produced not ultimate understanding and inevitability but a "novel of fitful glimpses. It has not been the novel I set out to write, nor am I exactly the person who set out to write it. Nor have I experienced the rush of narrative inevitability. . . . Anything could happen" (232–33).

The reader has also changed from what she set out to read. She has witnessed the process of Didion's initiation into and recognition of the postmodern perspective, stranded as Didion appears to be between the idea of Inez's doing penance for her follies and her family's at the refugee camp in Kuala Lumpur or staying on "until the last refugee was dispatched" (234) because she has nowhere else to go and ends up as suspended in time as the narrator. Didion's "fitful glimpses," as Norris contends, question "the existence of an objective, observer-independent reality" (2000, *Quantum,* 79) not just in terms of incomplete human knowledge but also in terms of its very essence. Didion's vision embodies what Norris in his discussion of Bohr's vision of the subatomic world has described as "the quasi-mystical idea that . . . 'reality' is indeed so unthinkably strange —so remote from our utmost powers of conceptual grasp—that it points beyond the limits of human reason to a realm of deep paradoxical truths which inherently elude the logic of classical (bivalent) truth and false-hood," virtually a definition of the postmodern sublime. She "inverts the realist order of priority between ontology and epistemology by transfer-ring the burden of unresolved doubts, paradoxes, uncertainties . . . from our restricted *knowledge* of whatever transpires in [reality] to the *very na-ture* of . . . 'reality'" (185, 195).

Didion provides enough facts for us to sort out family and business relationships. We can also unravel the chronology of Holy Week that un-derscores the un-Christian-like behavior of the Christians. For example, Dwight Christian, Paul's brother and a consummate operator, teams up with Wendell Omura to oppose Dick Ziegler's development project and container business. Ziegler is married to Janet Christian and is, therefore, Dwight's nephew-in-law. At the same time Wendell Omura is Janet's lover whom Paul discovers when he murders the both of them. Paul has under-gone some kind of spiritual conversion or mental breakdown in or after his visit to Tunis, lives at the YMCA, and attempts suicide after he has been institutionalized. Inez's husband, Harry Victor, is a fatuously liberal politician who spouts euphemistic hogwash almost as well as Billy Dillon, his spin-master, does, except that Dillon is the complete image-maker and public-relations scriptwriter who is appropriately cynical and savvy about every one of his orchestrated moves. The worlds of media politics, Ameri-can imperialism, and the collapse of Saigon conspire to disconnect every-one from any sense of the past, leaving them suspended in a world of drug addiction, publicity photos, and vacuous celebrity.

As in *A Book of Common Prayer,* Didion draws a bead on American colonialism and the sense of self-absorbed entitlement that comes with it, embodied and incarnated as it is in the Christians' good looks, old money, lucrative financial dealings, political clout, and aristocratic hierarchical sense of ownership. Their sense of exemption from most of life's struggles and realities parallels Inez's "local conviction that the comfortable en-trepreneurial life of an American colony in a tropic without rot repre-sented a record of individual triumphs over a hostile environment." This perspective underscores her "capacity for passive detachment as an affectation of boredom, the frivolous habit of an essentially idle mind. . . . I thought of it as the essential mechanism for living a life in which the major cost was memory. Drop fuel. Jettison cargo. Eject crew" (211, 70).

The murder and the body of her sister Janet provide Didion with the primal scene in *Democracy*, her "leper at the door, my Tropical Belt Coal Company, my lone figure on the crest of the immutable hill" (78), but the narrator's attempts to contain, resolve, and explain exactly what has led to that scene and why remain both uncertain and the focus of her own primal self-doubt and lack of conviction. Reading in London of Inez's comment that "she would be in Kuala Lumpur until the last refugee was dispatched" (234), Didion knows "how it feels to fly into that part of the world, of the dense greens and translucent blues and the shallows where islands once were, but so far I have not been back." She shares and recognizes "colors, moisture, heat, enough blue in the air" with Inez and delights in "the palm at the end of the mind . . . a foreign song" (16) but has been unable to fathom Inez's motives or state of soul. American imperialism has maimed her in some way, as have her husband's political scenarios, Billy Dillon's public arrangements, and the comfort and wealth of her Christian background. She lingers in Didion's narrative as an evanescent icon, beautiful and strange, having either consciously chosen numbness in order to survive or become an actual blank, reduced to mere icon and photo opportunity. This is perhaps what modern American democracy has wrought, but Didion the narrator experiences only a heap of broken images, which she has tried to shore up against her postmodern ruins. She remains an incurable romantic and a pessimist as far as understanding the world and the people in it who ignite her meticulous fascination. She has wandered into the postmodern vision and made it her own as carefully as she has crafted and experienced it.

Joan Didion as the reporter-narrator appears again in 1983 in *Salvador*. It is her first book-length study of an actual place and situation, the social and political landscape of the civil war(s) in El Salvador in 1982, and the reporter Didion is very much like the narrator "Didion" in *Democracy*.

In *Salvador* language becomes the first casualty, since the politically simplistic notions of right and left, right and wrong, and sides in general no longer apply. A reporter's objectivity, as in *Democracy*, proves futile when faced with the terror and bloody postmodern landscape of El Salvador. Political scenarios crumble and collapse in the wake of the horror of body dumps, the infinite spin on conspiracies within conspiracies, and the ongoing slaughter of the disappeared. Like Harry Victor's rhetoric when confronted with the strife in Indonesia, Ronald Reagan's rhetoric from Didion's point of view appears vacuous and dangerous in terms of what is actually going on. His notions of human rights and land reform, of democracy and "the initiation of a democratic political process" radically clash with the realities of perpetual murder and unending terror. Ideas such as "improvement," "pacification," and "perfection" become part of a hallucinatory litany, as the men and women like Harry Victor, who use such terms, may only be hoping that "an apparent statement of fact often expresses something only wished for, or something that might be true" (1983, 38). Grumbles Didion, "Language as it is now used in El Salvador is the language of advertising, of persuasion, the product being one or another of the *soluciones* crafted in Washington or Panama or Mexico, which is part of the place's pervasive obscenity" (65). The American program is a sham: "The American effort in El Salvador seemed based on auto-suggestion, a dreamwork devised to obscure any intelligence that might trouble the dreamer" (92).

In El Salvador Didion discovers the very landscape she has been creating in her fiction, and perhaps the urge to portray herself as "Didion" in *Democracy* stems from this shock of recognition. Now any scenario—public relations, political, governmental, celebratory—manufactures simplistic narratives in place of ultimate chaos and despair. To visit El Salvador in 1982 is "to plunge directly into a state in which no ground is solid, no depth of field reliable, no perception so definite that it might not dissolve into its reverse" (13). We're in Boca Grande once again or in a celebrity world of icons and emblematic encounters hawked to the public as "reality." El Salvador may as well be Boca Grande, since "the Salvadoran mindset . . . turns on plot [and] all the players here are densely connected" (30) through hierarchies and family networks. Conspiracy lurks everywhere, permeates the air, leaving bodies in its wake but no perpetrators, conjuring up a realm of "moral extinction" (31), within which "even the most apparently straightforward event takes on . . . elusive shadows, like a fragment of retrieved legend" (92, 67). Such a place produces "the jitters" (52), an ultimate uncertainty about all things, the postmodern terror of invisible forces and cabals stalking more victims.

Images proliferate but leave little in their wake except fear and paranoia.

Jeep Cherokee Chiefs, reinforced with steel and bulletproof Plexiglas, carry away the disappeared and the (soon-to-be) dead. Vultures eat the soft tissue of bodies first, such as the eyes or the penis. Walls topped with barbed wire and glass surround the houses in San Benito. Colonel Salvador Beltran Luna dies in a helicopter crash, but no one knows exactly where or how. The unfinished Metropolitan Cathedral, a "vast brutalist space" (79), becomes an icon of disaster. "Terror is the given of the place" (14), and "the exact mechanism of terror" (21) can co-opt any situation at any time, turning it into yet another instance of dark postmodern forces at work.

Of course Didion "knew how to interpret, the kind of inductive irony, the detail that was supposed to illuminate the story" (36), but as in Poe's visionary domain, terror trumps everything. One's obsession with body counts can just as easily be seen as one's being possessed by an evil elusive landscape. As Didion tries to track down the stories of the Mozote massacre or the whereabouts and defining roles of death squads and Major Roberto D'Aubuisson—Does he work for the government? Did he work for the government? Do the death squads work for the government? Are the death squads trying to overthrow the government?—she wanders into a twilight zone that refuses to offer any answers. She also wanders into a politically fragmented landscape in which various groups create their own conspiracies and splinter into further groups within groups, such as the FMLN-FDR, the PRTC, the FARN, the FPL, and the PCS.

Didion's El Salvador looms as a nightmarish domain of sheer terror, in which "overheard rumors, indefinite observations, fragments of information . . . might or might not fit into a pattern we did not perceive" (45). It is the landscape of *Democracy,* a postmodern place that needs the illusion of the reporter's existence and observations to make it feel more real, more present. *Democracy* like *Salvador,* fiction and nonfiction, becomes "less a 'story' than a true noche obscura" (36), where evidence, such as there is, may as well be "signals from space, unthinkable, inconceivable, dim impulses from a black hole" (102). It is a place in which "I began to see Gabriel García Márquez in a new light, as a social realist" (59), where "there are no issues [but] only ambitions" (34). The politics are here, the political parties are here, American aid and its consequences are here, and the facts about the government's responsibility for the climate of violence, the closing of the university, and the ridiculous shell of a land reform program are here as well, but it is the landscape that catches Didion's eye and reflects her own postmodern fears and speculations.

Democracy, Didion's "novel of fitful glimpses" (1984, 232), published close to the same time as *Salvador,* embroiders and expands the role of the narrator as investigative reporter, a position that will grow to include her latest novel to date, *The Last Thing He Wanted,* and her "take" on American politics in general in *Political Fictions.* It incarnates her postmodern vision of an increasingly postmodern world "out there" both in her nonfiction and in her fiction. It is no mere aesthetics of despair but a genuine visionary revelation of postmodernism at its corrosive worst.

The stories and conspiracies within conspiracies that Didion spins in *Miami* (1987) "were low, and lurid, and so radically reliant on the inductive leap that they tended to attract advocates of an ideological or a paranoid bent. . . . Stories like these had been told during the Watergate investigations in 1974" (202). She creates a dark tapestry of anti-Castro Cubans, each group intolerant of the others' agendas, each trying to become the sole voice in the struggle, "La Lucha," against Castro, full of machismo, the "absolutist" and "sacrificial" temperament of Hispanic culture, bombings, assassinations, jihads and jeremiads, "an unloosing of fratricidal furies" with no end in sight (110), like her style a series of seemingly isolated cells of misdirected frustration and fear. Passion demands action and commitment, a kind that is alien to the American politics of compromise and issues. Didion's investigations zero in on the beating of Arthur McDuffie; Eduardo Arocena, the terrorist or the freedom fighter; Bernardo Benes, who became a traitor for meeting with Castro; Emilio Milian who lost both legs to the cause; Max Lesnik who favors negotiations with the Castro regime and thus is seen as a traitor by the splintered Cuban resistance; Jose Elias de la Torriente, the traitor who was assassinated; and Orlando Bosch, who attempted to bomb a plane and was jailed in Caracas. Rumors erupt, split off from one another, and surface somewhere else, complete with Kennedy's refusal to fully support the Bay of Pigs invasion in 1961, relationships between Cuban groups and the CIA, intimations of the involvement of Lee Harvey Oswald, Oliver North, and the Voice of America.

Once more Didion portrays herself as the self-conscious reporter in a nightmare landscape of violence, murder, betrayal, and death. Once again we are engulfed by the "tropical entropy" (27), oblique surfaces that tend "to dissolve here" (36), and "fragments of the underwater narrative" (202):

"Havana vanities come to dust in Miami" (11). Boca Grande and El Salvador have come to American shores, spawning a dominant Latino American culture, in which "many people in Miami regarded such violence as an inevitable and even a necessary thread in the social fabric" (134). Washingtonians invent scenarios of "human rights" that "must be abandoned and replaced by a non-interventionist policy of political and ethical realism" (183), while arms, cash, and assassins change hands, and terrorists who have been supported by the FBI and the CIA are arrested for breaking the law. *Miami* reveals a Didion landscape run amuck.

For Didion *la lucha* "had become, during the years since the Bay of Pigs, a matter of assassinations and bombings on the streets of American cities, of plots and counterplots and covert dealings . . . " (30). Conspiracy and the search for conspiracy become the operative metaphor for what she uncovers and traces, acquiring as she does "a certain fluency in cognitive dissonance" (99). She quotes Anthony Lewis's *New York Times* article of September 1975: "The search for conspiracy only increases the elements of morbidity and paranoia and fantasy in this country. It romanticizes crimes that are terrible because of their lack of purpose" (203). Paranoia, anxiety, elliptical narratives that blur the lines, if they exist, between cause and effect, and unprovable tales increase the basic postmodernist sense of the loss of personal agency, of skepticism in regard to any definitive interpretation or solution, and of the virtual disconnection between seemingly discrete events and incidents and the invisibility of their sources, all underscored by the sense of some vast subterranean conspiracy.

Didion may have crossed an invisible line here. It is one thing to sense a world caught up in the throes of conspiracy theories and possibilities but another to seize on them as more than metaphor, as a deliberate and/or possible heart of darkness at the center of that world. There exist men in Washington, she insists, "who understood that the distinction between a crisis and no crisis was one of 'perception,' or 'setting the scene,' particularly close to the center of power. They were all, in varying degrees, ideologues, people who had seized or been seized by an idea. . . . " (185). But how, one might ask, is this significantly different from Didion's perception and setting the scene? Has the metaphor of conspiracy mesmerized her in such a way that the perception has become reality, analogies become labyrinthine truths, hearts of darkness become darkness visible? The vague but viscerally palpable conspiratorial aura and atmosphere of *A Book of Com-*

mon Prayer and *Democracy* that fed her dark and desperate vision of the human condition emerge in *Salvador* and *Miami* as actual possibilities. Conspiracy looms like the solution not the perception. Just as in Robert Frost's poem "Design," spiders and moths and flowers have become actual pawns in a universe steeped in demonic design and violent divinely ordained plots. Frost pulls the rug out from under his metaphorical escalation. Didion does not.

This may account for the imbalances of her novel *The Last Thing He Wanted* (1996). Reality intrudes so ominously and fully—Didion as reporter attempts to straddle real *and* fictional worlds—that it practically smothers the tale of Elena McMahon and Treat Morrison, doomed lovers yet again. Elena may be too emblematic of the 1980s, experiencing the same weightlessness that Didion ascribes to that era, suggesting "a sustained reactive depression, a bereavement reaction to the leaving of familiar environments" (4). In fact the novel begins with a mini-essay on the 1980s in Didion's lyrically repetitive style, introduces us fitfully to Elena McMahon and the first time Treat Morrison sees her, and moves on to include a roster of real names—Elliott Abrams, Robert Owen, Richard Secord—followed by references to an avalanche of documents, depositions, testimonies, libraries, and transcripts that literally dwarf the McMahon yarn. That yarn looks like a mere footnote to the actual facts of the Iran-Contra scandal with its ten volumes of published transcripts from the congressional hearings, all "two thousand five hundred and seven pages" (10) of it.

"Some real things have happened lately," the novel begins, and immediately they take center stage. From there Didion, remembering the process of beginning the novel in her *Salon* interview, recounts her creation of "a reconstruction. A corrective, if you will, to the Rand study" in an attempt to make logical connections in the story of Elena McMahon who "got caught in the pipeline":

> One of the first things I had started with in this book was the idea of this woman walking off a campaign. Because I'd covered some campaigns in '88 and '92, I wanted to use some of that sense of a campaign. So then, I didn't know, then she would go to Miami to see her father. Then, I couldn't figure out where she'd been. Then I decided she ought to be from Los Angeles and had been married to

someone in the oil business. That kind of gave me a fresh start. But then I was having to get her from Los Angeles to being a political reporter, right? It was a really hard thing to do. It was also a lot of fun. (Eggers n.d., 13, 12)

Elena McMahon's story seems smaller and more elusive when set within and against the overwhelming cascade of Iran-Contra facts, as if actual conspiracy has upstaged and crushed Didion's fictional vision. The vague forebodings and the atmospheric angst of back-stage doings and ominous plots in her earlier novels are too factually and too prominently fore-grounded here, laying waste to any real concern with one individual soul who ends up stranded on a runway "in a black silk shift bought off a sale rack at Bergdorf Goodman" (1996, 72). At one point Didion quotes Nietzsche: "'When man does not have firm, calm lines on the horizon of his life—mountain and forest lines, as it were—then man's most inner will becomes agitated, preoccupied and wistful'" (74). In *The Last Thing He Wanted,* the firm calm lines of the political horizon are so firmly in place and so assiduously drawn that the narrative of Elena's unlucky plight seems a minor distraction within a major disaster.

"At heart storytellers," Didion insists, are "weavers of conspiracy just to make the day come alive, and they see it in a flash, comprehend all its turns, get its possibilities" (55). Toward the end of the novel, Mark Berquist, a senior foreign policy aide in the Senate who has conspired to cre-ate an assassination plot that involves U.S. Embassy figure Alex Brokaw, and who, having played the game so well, gets himself elected to the Sen-ate later on, confronts the narrator: "I can see you've bought hook, line and sinker into one of those sick conspiracy fantasies that, let me assure you, have been thoroughly and totally discredited" (213). In the novel the "sick conspiracy" fantasy exists. Berquist knew when the false target of the as-sassination, Alex Brokaw, was changed to the real target, Treat Morrison, but in the structure and telling of the tale, Berquist is also correct. Didion herself has become a weaver of the very conspiracies she sees elsewhere as false scenarios, giddy theatrics, comfortable rationalization, and govern-mental ploys. Her presumed objectivity, her fascination with process and the "Big Picture," her insider status, and her setting up Elena as both vic-tim of and catalyst for the second assassination plot parallel Berquist's per-spective. Conspiracy has leaped from metaphor to fictional structure and scheme, linked to a real conspiracy in such clear and decisive terms that the characters pale in comparison. The brutal logic of Iran-Contra produces a very real world that threatens the existence of the disconnected dreams of Elena McMahon.

In *The Marble Faun* by Nathaniel Hawthorne, the detailed descriptions of Rome disrupt and distort the narrative to such an extent that they often stop it dead in its tracks. In fact the public made his fourth novel his most popular since they often relied on it as a guidebook to the Eternal City. In a similar manner, the more real the conspiracies and the conspirators in *The Last Thing He Wanted,* the more elusive and evanescent Didion's narrative of Elena McMahon becomes. Like Hawthorne she needs a twilight zone to thrive in, a fictional realm somewhere between fact and fiction that borders on the allegorical—Boca Grande, the Hawaii of the Christians— where the human condition can be rendered as an eerie, vaguely conspiratorial realm of betrayal, self-doubt, and anxiety. It is not her fashionable world that is at fault. That is too much like the old argument that John Cheever was merely an apologist for suburbia, which, like all such sweeping pronouncements, is only a mischievous half-truth. Rather it is her tale in this most recent novel that remains incidental to its surroundings and environment, a wisp of missteps in a very real tapestry of deceit, deception, duplicity, and death. A doomed romance—"I want those two to have been together all their lives" (227): the last line of the novel—pales in comparison to the overarching actuality of illegally selling U.S. arms to Iran in order to use some of the proceeds to help the Nicaraguan Contras from October 1984 to October 1986.

By the time Didion's exposure of "a series of fables about American experience" (7) used by professional politicians, media pundits, and campaign managers surfaces in *Political Fictions* (2001), her position looks as though she has decided that there really is a political cabal, a conspiracy of loosely interconnected men and women, "a kind of managerial elite" who "prefer the theoretical to the observable" (20, 39). They are the ones who have so rigidly staged American political campaigns that the American people have just tuned them out. Invented narratives command the airwaves and monopolize all "talking points" in the campaign. As such, "the prevailing tone, on all sides, was self-righteous, victimized, grandiose; a quite florid instance of what Richard Hofstadter has identified in 1965 as the paranoia style in American politics" (16).

We have come full circle where a description of a particular style has usurped the style of mainstream politics and culture, to the point where no other style is possible, at least in Didion's view of our contemporary postmodernist world. Such an outlook makes for superbly focused essays but weakens the threshold of her later fiction, that more elusive world between dream and reality, nightmare and social routines where her best characters cavort, freeze, stagger, and perform. Once "the political process, which had come to represent the concerns not of the country at large but of the organized pressure groups that increasingly controlled it" (238) has taken over, fiction can either imitate the scenarios and conspiracies of "the nation's permanent professional political class" (280) or abandon itself to reef dreams and other particularly personal obsessions. The dimensions of "real" conspiracies limit and kill the fictional possibilities of such a cosmic vision, and the darkness of the human heart shrinks to the dark but traceable lineaments of class warfare and paranoid scenarios.

5
Don DeLillo

Mystic Musings in a Paranoid's Paradise

"It often seems that DeLillo and Didion are crouched on the same fault line," writes John Leonard, "alert to the same tectonic tremor, full of the same nameless, blue-eyed willies" (2001, 14). Commenting in the *New Yorker* on *Libra* (1988), Don DeLillo's ninth novel, Terence Rafferty not only applauded the "quality of demented lyricism" in DeLillo's prose style but also suggested that perhaps the author "might almost have written this novel to exorcise his own tendency toward paranoid mysticism, to take a clear look at the nature of the thrill he gets from conspiracy" (1988, 108, 109). He also described DeLillo's "home turf [as] a realm of indeterminacy, unknowability, half-apprehension, a nightmarish connectedness that either is showing us the way things really are or is simply a shimmering mirage, just another deceptively suggestive metaphor" (108), a description that bristles with postmodern skepticism and the postmodern sublime. Rafferty's review illuminates the questions that DeLillo's fiction generates, how to relate the sense of mysticism and mystery, however paranoid, to "a clear look at the nature of the thrill he gets from conspiracy," how to relate "a nightmarish connectedness" to indeterminacy and unknowability, and whether or not the reader is meant to view DeLillo's world as "real" in terms of its cultural and thematic vision or "unreal" in terms of "a shimmering mirage, just another deceptively suggestive metaphor." How does the open-endedness of mystery in its wider sense as the postmodern sublime connect with the more specific lineaments of conspiracy and conspiracy theory? Does conspiracy with its suggestive connections and intricate narratives reduce and imprison a more "transcendental" or at least ambiguous sense of mystery, or does mystery in a more cosmic and vaguely mystical and religious sense manage mysteriously to outwit and outmaneuver the starker trajectories of conspiracy?

DeLillo evades as much as he tries to explain his situation as a writer. On the one hand he maintains that, as he told Anthony DeCurtis, his "work has always been informed by mystery; the final answer, if there is one at all, is outside the book. My books are open-ended" (1991, 55). He specifically links this to his own religious background: "I think there's a sense of last things in my work that probably comes from a Catholic childhood. . . . [A] Catholic [is] raised with the idea that he will die any minute now and if he doesn't live his life a certain way death is simply an introduction to an eternity of pain" (Keesey 1993, 10). In the *New York Times Magazine* of September 7, 1997, he even goes as far as declaring that "at its root level, fiction is a kind of religious fanaticism, with elements of obsession, superstition and awe. . . . We depend on disaster to consolidate our vision" (62, 63).

On the other hand, DeLillo explained, "Maybe [the assassination of John F. Kennedy] invented me. Certainly when it happened, I was not a fully formed writer . . . it is possible I wouldn't have become the kind of writer I am if it weren't for the assassination" (Keesey 1993, 12). Most Americans, he maintains in his *Rolling Stone* article of 1983, "American Blood," "entered a world of randomness and ambiguity" after Kennedy's death, that new postmodern space, which incarnates "our uncertain grip on the world" and in which "conspiracy is now the true faith" (22, 28). From the myth of Camelot, the popular vision turned to the "belief in the secret manipulation of history" (24), exacerbated as that belief was by technology's "advanced state of hardware and the general decline in such values as loyalty and patriotic commitment" (27). John A. McClure attempts to breach the gap between "religious" mystery—the unanswerable, the unknowable, the revelatory—and contemporary conspiracy—in theory unanswerable but in practice leading to possible answers—by suggesting that conspiracy "replaces religion as a means of mapping the world without disenchanting it, robbing it of its mystery" (1994, 103), thus having your cake and eating it too. That may, however, just beg the question.

Conspiracy theory supposes that events are ultimately rational. The final clue or missing piece will reveal the cabal behind the ongoing plots and networks. Yet religious mystery suggests the non-rational, the beyond-the-rational in terms of visions or ideas that can only come in the form of revelation, in dreams, in elusive mystical symbols and experiences. The two, conspiracy theory and religious mystery, remain virtually incompatible, so to suggest that the one has "replaced" the other only blurs the issue. The dilemma in DeLillo's work remains: does conspiracy become the means and the method of his pursuit of mystery, or does it take over and anchor his work in a more postmodern contemporary manner? Is conspiracy the working out in the contemporary postmodern world of a sense of ultimate mystery by embodying and incarnating it, where systems and secret networks "replace" divine design and possibility, or does it confine and narrow that sense of ultimacy? What happens to mystery when it gets channeled into a conspiracy theory or at the very least mired in the aura of conspiratorial cabals? Is it reduced and confined in the way it is in fundamentalist sects and cults, the non-rational become a literal spelling-out of apocalyptic visions and narratives of ultimate punishment and damnation?

McClure also suggests that DeLillo "has been unable to extricate himself from the spell of conspiracy" (1994, 115), thus maintaining that DeLillo's complicity in the thrill of conspiracy mars and limits his fiction. As David Remnick in the *New Yorker* declared, DeLillo has been called "the chief shaman of the paranoid school of American fiction" (1997, 43). Paul Gediman writing about *Underworld* maintains that DeLillo's is "a vision of a world governed not by mere randomness but by something—with its proliferation of patterns and subpatterns and counterpatterns—very like a holy mystery" (1997, 48). Tom LeClair joins him in this: "Establish your right to the mystery; document it; protect it," adding that the "ritual and repetition of ceremony, the fear and guilt of catechism [generates] a sense of the invisible and unknown" (1989, 15). DeLillo himself has attempted to finesse the issue by suggesting both that "the sweeping range of American landscape and experience can be a goad, a challenge, an affliction and an inspiration, pretty much in one package" (1997, "Power of History," 60), thus in effect passing the buck by commenting on the complexities of the cultural environment in which he writes, and by admitting that "The secrets within systems . . . are things that have informed my work. But they're almost secrets of consciousness, or ways in which consciousness is replicated in the natural world" (DeCurtis 1991, 61), thus suggesting an almost Emersonian notion of the mysterious relationship between the psyche or the self and, of all things, "the natural world."

One way to tackle this conundrum to try and get more clearly at what DeLillo is up to, what place conspiracy has in his fiction, is to view conspiracy and mystery not as essences but in relation to each other, as functions of each other. In this manner the empirical evidence of possible conspiracy looms as the detailed presence of a wider and more transcendent absence. The close-up focus on characters who believe in conspiracy theories suggests greater mystery in a world that remains ultimately unknowable. Stark presence breeds elusive absence: the detail when pressed suggests a broader background of uncertainty and indeterminacy, facets of the postmodern sublime.

DeLillo foregrounds the spectacle of contemporary culture as embodied in the media, sports, terrorism, language, money, sex, and consumer capitalism. The background of his fiction hints at some kind of ultimate visionary mystery, buttressed by his characters' inchoate spiritual yearnings and longings, probably nourished by DeLillo's own Catholic past and schooling. The postmodern disconnection often occurs between foreground and background, between the presentation of the poststructuralist materiality of language and culture and the aura of metaphysical uncertainty that hovers within and behind or beyond it.

DeLillo also recognizes that everything in our contemporary era comes to us as already mediated, "pre-digested," stereotyped, packaged, and marketed, thus making it next to impossible for his characters to separate foreground from background or to assume that the material foreground is all that exists. At the same time he conjures up the elusive possibilities of connection between the two, and characters often feel as if they are on the verge of linking terrorism to some ultimate mystery of the human condition or the media and its pulsating images to some transitory mystery of consciousness, but they never can fathom those possible connections. Commodities and the desires they generate and embody may lead to or inhabit the realm of some "higher" cosmic vision that cannot be grasped but like some smoldering religious longings remain ever present, troublingly persistent, and querulously frustrated.

This essential "religious" yearning distinguishes DeLillo from Pynchon's more viscerally and comically satiric approach to Western culture and fuels DeLillo's need to subvert conscious intention in pursuit of rapture and in doing so, opens up the possibility of submission to some greater unnamed and uncommodified power. Materiality, therefore, incarnates part of a *via negativa* toward an ungraspable but ghostly presence, felt only by its persistent and often cruel absence. Dread and reverence reflect each other as the "radiance in dailiness" suggests fleeting liturgies and other sacred rites that remain just out of reach.

DeLillo saturates his images and characters with menace and paranoia. "What I sense," he has said, "is suspicion and distrust and fear" (DeCurtis 1991, 66). He defines that sense more specifically: "There's a connection between the advances that are made in technology and the sense of primitive fear people develop in response to it. . . . This extraordinary wonder of things is somehow related to the extraordinary dread, to the death fear we try to keep beneath the surface of our perceptions" (Keesey 1993, 6, 9).

Postmodernism despises the metanarrative, the sweeping and transcendent design that underscores all things, and therefore embodies or at least focuses on that sense of disconnection and disruption that lies at its very core. Could that disconnection be at the core of DeLillo's fiction as well? Could the very presence or aura of conspiracy indirectly point to the invisibility, the palpable absence of mystery? Could mystery suggest the metanarrative as absence, the "ultimate" vision as unknowable possibility, as postmodern sublime?

De Tocqueville described the ideas of the democrat as "either extremely minute and clear or extremely general and vague; what lies between is a void" (1945, 82). This may help define DeLillo's strategy as a contemporary writer: he focuses on the dark details of contemporary life and then intimates at darker, ultimately unknowable forces beyond or behind those details, never spelling them out but leaving the reader and his characters with that vague sense of distrust and paranoia that hovers within the "essential" outlook of the postmodern experience of conspiracy that grasps for some kind of certainty but simultaneously recognizes a witheringly almost obsessive skepticism. De Tocqueville's vision of the void, that gap between minute, clear ideas and extremely general, vague ones that for him defines the difficulty with ideas in a democracy, throws the individual "back forever upon himself alone and threatens in the end to confine him entirely within the solitude of his own heart" (106). Expose that heart to anxious dread, paranoid suspicions about vast technological and global systems beyond the individual self's reach and comprehension, and a numbing uncertainty that every possible avenue of explanation and interpretation may be ultimately futile, and we approach the frisson and disorientation of the postmodern sublime as it appears in DeLillo's fictional vision.

For cultural critics like Walter Benjamin the aura of a painting or a work of art "is inseparable from its being imbedded in the fabric of tradition" (1935, 20). It grew out of religion, out of a tradition of the worship of art objects that "found its expression in the cult" (5), and out of the ritual associated with that cult: "Artistic production begins with ceremonial objects destined to serve in a cult" (5, 130). Once a painting, Da Vinci's *Mona Lisa,* say, gets reproduced again and again on everything from T-shirts to coasters, the original aura, itself a cultural product, dissipates and dissolves: "When the age of mechanical reproduction separated art from its basis in cult, the semblance of its autonomy disappeared forever" (123). The reproduced image floats unanchored in time and space, offering from Benjamin's perspective more distraction than contemplation, losing its original connections and significance.

DeLillo describes this as "the debasing process of frantic repetition that exhausts a contemporary event before it has rounded into coherence," and this process "tends to transform *you,* to make you a passive variation" of whatever the event is that you are watching again and again (1997, "Power of History," 62, 63). He saturates this process with a sense of dread and disruption, the postmodern anxiety that accompanies such disconnected images. They must mean something, they must signify something, but perhaps they can only suggest vague and terrifying forces that mysteriously align themselves with money, power, some visible but carefully guarded elite cabal, vast networks, and secret systems. Conspiracy, therefore, provides the contemporary aura that Benjamin described as originally surrounding the cult object.

Unlike his characters DeLillo controls and positions the dark forces he unleashes in his fiction. He is attracted to but not imprisoned by his characters' fascination with and belief in conspiracy theories. He and they hunger for "the presence and/or absence of verifiability of an explanatory, or causal point of origin," realizing that the pursuit will never end. DeLillo's scanning for signs and his characters' scanning for signs parallel what Kathleen Stewart describes as that "skeptical, paranoid, obsessive practice" of conspiracy theory, but for DeLillo, as we will see, conspiracy theory does not "become a stable center in itself" (1999, 14, 15).

"For me the crux of the whole matter is language," DeLillo insisted in Remnick's 9/15/97 *New Yorker* piece, " . . . in which a book is framed . . . sentence by sentence, page by page. . . . It's hard to talk about" (47). It is hard to talk about, but we can see DeLillo at work using it. He believes that "language can be a form of counterhistory. . . . Let language shape the world. Let it break the faith of conventional re-creation . . . the tendency of the language to work in opposition to the enormous technology of war [exists]" (1997, "Power of History," 63). All metaphor remains "deceptively suggestive," but unlike Rafferty's negative spin on that phrase, DeLillo works "himself into raptures of ambiguity" (Rafferty, 1988, 108) because that embodies his postmodern perception of our contemporary culture and world. Ambiguity inhabits de Tocqueville's American void and feeds the flames of apocalyptic desires for ultimate conflagration, that combustible and incendiary desire that fuels fundamentalist thought, conspiracy theory, and millennial visions. Bottomless ambiguity expresses the open-ended visions of DeLillo's novels. His characters may attempt to harness and confine that vision to particular conspiracies and plots, and DeLillo glories in that dark uncertain sensibility that lusts for certain origins and solutions, but he avoids those characters' pitfalls and claustrophobic perceptions in the language he employs. Paranoid mysticism is just another way of contemplating the disjunctions of postmodern existence.

The opening paragraphs of *Libra* reveal DeLillo's fictional strategy. As an adolescent Lee Harvey Oswald, as yet unnamed, rides the New York subway for the sheer thrill of riding it: "He was riding just to ride" (1988, 3). He thirsts for "the edge of no-control," revealing a giddy recklessness and an unformed or "unconscious" sense of selfhood that will propel him through all his attempts at self-definition and self-creation that will follow. Infinite desire propels his "riding just to ride," as the present participle makes way for the infinitive. Nothing for Oswald at this moment can surpass the "purer form" of the ride he finds "in these tunnels beneath the street." At the same time DeLillo as narrator steps outside of Oswald's vision and describes the subterranean world around him. People stand "bunched like refugees . . . staring nowhere." They enter the train "looking out past the nearest heads into that practiced oblivion." For Oswald "it had nothing to do with him," the indefinite pronoun embodying simultaneously the people, the subway, the ride, the workmen with their lanterns, and the noise. That "it," of course, will have everything to do with him as he tries to find a place for himself in an incomprehensible world. Conspiracy will eventually serve Oswald well in his quirky search for self-definition, as that self shifts and shivers when he constantly repositions himself, trying to fit into stereotypical roles, media-inspired scenarios, and other people's plots.

DeLillo manages, however, to suggest in this opening paragraph a wider mystery, a greater void, a space Oswald cannot even envision with its sense of "oblivion," "nowhere," and "the dark." That space suggests an ultimate mystery, de Tocqueville's void, that lies beyond the reach of conspiracy theory but which for Oswald will become embodied in it. DeLillo's "purer form" suggests the open-endedness of mystery, while Oswald will rush to confine and contain it in order to confine and contain his own uncertain sense of self. At this point he could go either way, his soul in the balance, Libra-destined, but DeLillo clearly distinguishes between the riding, the venue of conspiracy that Oswald will ultimately choose, and "to ride," that infinite realm of mystery and possibility, however haunted with visions of dread and paranoia, that DeLillo can face but that Oswald cannot.

DeLillo achieves the same effect in the opening pages of *Mao II* (1991). The reader first encounters a photograph of the famous mass wedding of Moonie disciples in Yankee Stadium with the large black title, "AT YAN-KEE STADIUM," printed across it. She then turns to the text, which offers a description of the event in an impersonal distant prose style that captures the size and the strangeness of it. All "are grouped"; they are "marching into American sunlight"; "the music draws them"; "they assemble themselves . . . crossing the vast arc of the outfield . . . the effect is one of transformation . . . one continuous wave" (3). The mass wedding becomes a "spectacle . . . so many columns set so closely . . . approaching division strength . . . an undifferentiated mass." They are not exactly a crowd since the procession is uniform: "They take a time-honored event and repeat it, repeat it, repeat it until something new enters the world" (3). The images DeLillo uses suggest the military, geometry, mass society, a movie scene, each an overview of the people involved that adds to "a strangeness down there that he never thought he'd see in a ballpark" (4). Rodge, the father of Karen, who is being married in this vast ceremony, wonders: "And here is the drama of mechanical routine played out with living figures. . . . This really scares him, a mass of people turned into a sculptured object" (7).

Clearly it is DeLillo's prose style that renders the mass as "a sculptured object." The repetition, which he also provides, contributes to the "something new [that] enters the world." That "something new" suggests something mysterious, massive, militant and menacing, within which individuals are swallowed up and reduced to mere integers in some larger equation or formula. DeLillo's machinelike precision in his style and "the drama of mechanical routine played out with living figures" mirror one another, and the spectacle that astonishes Rodge also astonishes his creator. The cool quality of the prose also distances DeLillo from Rodge's thoughts. He watches his character reacting but with none of Rodge's emotion. Instead DeLillo expresses "a sense these chanting thousands have, wincing in the sun, that the future is pressing in, collapsing toward them, that they are everywhere surrounded by signs of the fated landscape and human struggle of the Last Days . . . " (4, 7).

DeLillo's apocalyptic musings suggest a sociologist's or anthropologist's description of a particular cult's state of mind as he juxtaposes Karen's perspective with her parents'. That more omniscient point of view extends beyond their individual responses as characters and views the spectacle as a contemporary American phenomenon that both fascinates and appalls. The ceremony confines and entraps Karen and her parents from their different perspectives of it, but DeLillo confines them and the ceremony in his overall sense of dread, terror, awe, and the claustrophobic nature of conspiracy itself, an example of something larger than the Reverend Moon's religious zealotry and lust for spectacle. Rodge sees conspiracy and design. DeLillo sees that and more. Rodge sees "mechanical routine" and "a sculptured object." DeLillo sees this as well but expands his vision to include Moon's astonishing ability to answer the yearning of his disciples, "unburdens them of free will and independent thought," a deeper mystery and more disturbing sensibility, a product of postmodern times, that will resonate throughout *Mao II*: "See how happy they look" (7).

Players (1977) opens in a manner similar to *Mao II* and *Libra*, but unlike *Mao II* conspiracy forms a major part of the narrative both in terms of plot and structure. Pammy Wynant, the wife of Lyle, remarks at one point: "It's amazing, it's almost supernatural, really, the way people get an idea, a tiny human hankering for something, and it becomes a way of life, the obsession of the ages" (20). Lyle will become obsessed with an elusive conspiracy that may involve blowing up the Stock Exchange, double agents, and the CIA and begins with the murder of George Sedbauer on the floor of the Exchange. Later A. J. Kinnear, a mysterious, shape-shifting member of the conspiracy, both its ostensible theorist and possibly a mole bent on undermining it, muses about the point of it all: "It's this uncertainty over sources and ultimate goals," he explains. "Our big problem in the past, as a nation, was that we didn't give our government credit for being the totally entangling force that it was. They were even more evil than we'd imagined." He goes on making references to Watergate and Kennedy's assassination: "Why were the papers shredded. . . . Why does this autopsy report differ from that one? Was it one bullet or more? Who erased the tapes?" (104).

Kinnear also raises one of the main themes in the novel: "Behind every stark fact we encounter layers of ambiguity. This is all so alien to the liberal spirit. . . . This haze of conspiracies and multiple interpretations" (104). He might have been describing Lyle Wynant who, eager for some adventure and danger in his otherwise alienated and cocooned existence in New York City, becomes involved with a new secretary in his office, Rosemary Moore, who leads him to Marina Vilar Ramirez and Rafael Vilar, the man who shot George Sedbauer. Marina's husband Luis wants to put Lyle in George's place to get into 11 Wall Street and blow it up, but then Lyle meets the mysterious Kinnear who thinks the conspiracy has been compromised and betrayed. From there the tangled web of plot involves Frank McKechnie, two men named Burks, and Kinnear's disappearance into Canada, where Lyle follows him with $3,500, meets Rosemary again, and winds up waiting for Kinnear's telephone call in a motel.

Which returns us to the opening lines of the novel in the prologue, "The Movie": "Someone says: 'Motels. I like motels. I wish I owned a chain, worldwide. I'd like to go from one to another to another. There's something self-realizing about that'" (3). Once again DeLillo distances himself from his characters and shows them as reacting to events, to the subway ride in *Libra,* to the wedding extravaganza in *Mao II.* In the prologue unnamed characters occupy a piano bar in a plane and are about to watch a movie in which terrorists invade a golf course and kill the golfers. The nameless characters replicate the characters who will appear in the rest of the novel and, watching the film, are "steeped in gruesomely humorous ambiguity, a spectacle of ridiculous people doing awful things to total fools" (9): a preamble to the ensuing narrative.

DeLillo surrounds these characters with information about the airplane that surrounds them: "It's as though they're realizing for the first time how many systems of mechanical and electric components, what exact managements of stresses, power units, consolidated thrust and energy it has taken to reduce their sensation of flight to this rudimentary tremble." All of these things, including "one second of darkness," contribute to making "each journey something of a mystery to be worked out by the combined talents of the travelers, all gradually aware of each other's code of recognition." Watching the film parallels DeLillo watching his characters, each of whom will play a role in the novel to come, which will end in the motel with which "someone" associates "self-realization," except the character Lyle at novel's end becomes merely a "propped figure [who is] barely recognizable as male. Shedding capabilities and traits by the second. . . . We know nothing else about him" (3, 212).

Kinnear is correct when he suggests that the "layers of ambiguity" that multiply "behind every stark fact we encounter" undermine the American self-image: "This is all so alien to the liberal spirit" (104), that spirit of "can-do" and self-mastery, the myth of the autonomous spirit, which can initiate action through its will. "Americans are doomed to perform heroic deeds" (147), Marina Vilar suggests. Such an American is, indeed, a "player," a person of action, in the loop, directing decisions and deeds. Doing becomes a function of being in this myth, since consciousness precedes and creates its own circumstances.

However, as DeLillo describes the systems in play in the second paragraph and the "glamour of revolutionary violence" in the images of the film that mesmerize and numb the spectators—"The violence, after all, is expert and intense" (8, 9)—the reader views these characters as products of the system, passive reactors to both the flight and the film. "One of the things that informed my subsequent work, or all my work," DeLillo has explained, is "the notion of the medium between an event and an audience, film and television in particular" (Keesey 1993, 4). He explores this in greater detail in *Libra, Mao II,* and several of his other novels, but in *Players,* as well as in earlier novels, this vision persists. Systems and circumstances create and circumscribe these characters and their consciousness in a kind of Marxist interpretation of the media and our technological age. They appear as functions of a larger complex system, whether it is technology or conspiracy. As such these "players" sense that outside forces are controlling them, even as they attempt to seize initiatives and follow their own pursuits. The self becomes not a player but a victim, not an agent but a function, as DeLillo's postmodern vision legitimizes procedures as opposed to premises. Everything becomes operational and therefore ultimately a maze "of conspiracies and multiple interpretations" (104).

Relations, functions, transitions, and sequences replace categories, purposes, boundaries, and hierarchies in Louis Menand's (2001) description
of the intricacies of pragmatism. The player in actuality performs as the
played upon, the played with, and the played out.

In describing the external actions of his characters, DeLillo reduces
them to soulless puppets with a glimmer of sensitivity and ennui but not
much more than that. Being becomes a function of doing, and doing gets
filtered through film, television, and technological systems, so that the per-
formers perform roles that have already become stereotyped by the films
and television series, which replicate these similar roles over and over again:
"Everything that was directly lived has moved away into representation,
where images chosen and constructed by someone else have everywhere
become the individual's connection to the world formally observed for
himself" (Keesey 1993, 13). Add to this the postmodern drift and sense of
disruption, and DeLillo's characters are left with that vague sense of being
manipulated and programmed while they do their best to chart their own
courses of action, which have already been charted for them. They are not
predetermined to act in a certain way. Rather they have no other choice
but to play out their mediated existences—cocooned, alienated, anxious,
and quietly desperate—again and again in a contemporary world that
lacks reality and "essence." Theirs becomes a kind of paranoid pragmatism, an empirical tracing of someone else's footprints in dust that blows
away as soon as they think they are moving forward.

In a sense DeLillo operates from a nominalist's position. Reality appears
as just one thing after another with no or very little connection, which
prompts his characters to search for conspiracies, patterns, significance,
just as DeLillo and his readers do on a larger scale—as writer and reader
of the entire novel—apart from the characters' encounters. Since nominal-
ism acknowledges only individual beliefs and actions—general truths are
"simply conventions of language, simply names" (Menand 2001, 228)—no
communal or social dimension exists. In the postmodern era that shock of
recognition can only add to the ominous anxieties the characters and we
share in regard to vast systems, vaster networks, and global cabals. Everything that has already been mediated in some fashion or other, especially
in terms of representation, suggests something else. Each is a sign, but as
in deconstruction each sign leads on to only further signs, leaving Lyle
alone in his motel room "shedding capabilities and traits by the second . . .

barely recognizable . . . imagining that this vast system of nearly identical rooms, worldwide, has been established so that people will have somewhere to be *afraid* on a regular basis" (1977, 212, 210).

Watching television and having sex appear in *Players* as tired, monotonous rituals that are content-free. The Wynants reveal an obsessive desire for order, ritual, and control, attempting to turn the flux and contingency of their repetitive lives into meaningful patterns, as if projecting an autonomous self or personal agency on a world that rejects them. Watching television Lyle "explored content to a point," but he really enjoys "the tactile-visual delight of switching channels. . . . Watching television was for Lyle a discipline like mathematics or Zen" (16, 34). The watching provides the experience and the content. Sex between Lyle and Pammy takes place in a closed, air-conditioned room: "It is time to 'perform,' he thought. She would have to be 'satisfied.' He would have to 'service' her. They would make efforts to 'interact'" (72). They might as well be oiling machines or participating in group therapy. Intimacy suggests one more session of "compulsive information-gathering," the kind of grief management counseling that Pammy works at (70). Lyle's working with numbers and stock symbols, the very nature of his job, "return[s] to him an impression of reality disconnected from the resonance of its own senses," a pattern that affects every one of his actions. Even Pammy with her offices in the World Trade Center wonders what it actually is or stands for. What does it signify? "Was it a condition, an occurrence, a physical event, an existing circumstance, a presence, a state, a set of invariables?" (48). Reducing empirical and visceral experiences to abstractions distances both the Wynants and DeLillo, but his omniscient point of view reveals the vapidity and hollowness of theirs.

Objects seem more alive and in control than characters. Circumstance creates and shapes consciousness: "The city was unreasonably insistent on its own fibrous beauty, the woven arrangements of decay and genius that raised to one's sensibility a challenge to extend itself" (107). Pammy's having sex with Jack, object to object, results in his self-immolation and his partner's eternal grief. She returns to New York to watch television and "experienced a near obliteration of self-awareness" (205), which recalls Ethan's, Jack's partner's, earlier comment: "Fear is intense self-awareness" (139).

DeLillo develops and replays these motifs throughout the novel—the numbness, the conspiracy that leads only to further ambiguity and blurred roles and identities, the electronic system of money that Rafael wants to disrupt and destroy in order "to incapacitate it, even briefly . . . to set loose every kind of demon" (107, 183), the parallels and reflections among the characters in "The Movie" and those in the narrative, the vision of isolated souls in isolated rooms, momentarily suspended but a condition that suggests an eternal stasis. Perhaps Mark Osteen is right when he insists that "DeLillo suggests that the revelation of his own game and our complicity with it is the real subject of *Players*" (2000, 152). As readers reading a text, according to George Marcus, DeLillo forces us to seek "an order behind the visible" (1999, 17), as he seeks to explore the signs and sensibilities of our postmodern age that baffle his characters within their more limited and disconnected perspectives. Like them "we're waiting for something to happen—a drama, an endpoint, something to break the enclosure of untouchable systems and the drone of an endlessly repeating present" (6). The recognition of an actual conspiracy for them would suffice, but for DeLillo and us it will never be enough.

The luminous cul de sac of *Players* for many critics only reinforces the notion that DeLillo "has been unable to extricate himself from the spell of conspiracy" (McClure 1994, 115), and one way to look at his later novels is to view them as a means of escaping from that possible dead end. DeLillo continues to reinforce his vision in which he separates the human condition and impulse that yearn for significance and design from the actual conspiracies his characters construct and pursue. In *Libra* he wrestles with the paramount conspiracy theory of contemporary American culture, the Kennedy assassination, and brilliantly manages to offer both a possible solution from his characters' point of view and the ever-present mystery and ongoing quest that offer no solution but maintain the pursuit as if it were essential to the human spirit. From a typical postmodern perspective DeLillo remains skeptical about the finality of any particular system of belief or unmasking of any conspiratorial cabal but keeps the process of inquiry and the scanning for signs of further significance wide open.

James Wood insists that "the problem is that DeLillo veers toward complicity with the very culture he wants to defend the novel against" (1999, 186). That "veering toward" allows him to create "the paranoid vision [that] incorporates a certain restless despair that makes the creation of rounded individual characters impossible," and therefore his fiction "comes to seem complicit with the paranoia he describes" (191, 185). In *Libra* De-Lillo does create a possible conspiracy in terms of Kennedy's assassination, complete with a dizzying labyrinth of anti-Castro, pro-Castro, imagined anti-Castro, imagined pro-Castro, anti-Castro masquerading as pro-Castro, pro-Castro masquerading as anti-Castro, mercenary, paranoid and randomly violent factions and folks, but the narrative suggests contingency and chance more than successful conspiracy.

Oswald's plotless, rootless, aimless life and his ideological inconsistencies and blathering just happen to coincide with Win Everett's plan to set up a shooter to miss Kennedy but to link the would-be assassin to pro-Castro forces in order to discredit them. In fact Everett hopes to create a fake Oswald and a false trail to promote his cause, but circumstances surprise him and force him to change his plans: "It was no longer possible to hide from the fact that Lee Oswald existed independent of the plot. . . . It produced a sensation of the eeriest panic, gave him a glimpse of the fiction he's been devising, a fiction living prematurely in the world" (1988, 178, 179). Chance contributes to this particular conspiracy, drawing on the likes of a gay pilot, a participant in the Guatemala coup of 1954, a cowboy involved in the Bay of Pigs fiasco, a mob kingpin, and a former FBI agent. The crossed paths of this motley crew suggest Didion's description of the political mazes and conspiratorial backwaters of Miami. The conspirators' readjusting their plot to find a person to activate it come upon Oswald, the very person in search of someone's plot that he can become part of and, thereby, perform some notable historical deed. Coincidence and conspiracy coincide and produce a kind of appalling balance, for which the astrological sign is, of course, Libra.

DeLillo freely admits his attraction to the dark romance of conspiracy, a state of mind he has discovered and scrutinizes in postmodern contemporary American culture. It exists, and it seduces:

If we are on the outside, we assume a conspiracy is the perfect working of a scheme. Silent nameless men with unadorned hearts. A conspiracy is everything that ordinary life is not. It's the inside game, cold, sure, undistracted, forever closed off to us. We are the flawed ones, the innocents, trying to make some rough sense of the daily jostle. Conspirators have a logic and a daring beyond our reach. All conspiracies are the same taut story of men who find coherence in some criminal act. (440)

DeLillo explores conspiracy as a theory and, as Osteen suggests, "a separate world, a form of social magic [where] alienated members can discover the sense of belonging, meaning, and order that postmodern American life so rarely provides" (2000, 158). But he remains the outsider, one of the "flawed ones . . . trying to make some rough sense of the daily jostle." With Nicholas Branch he determines "that the conspiracy against the President was a rambling affair that succeeded in the short term due mainly to chance" (441). DeLillo's fictional strategy reveals both the pull and the lure of "the same taut story of men," but ultimately its limitations and spurious claims fail to explain exactly what has happened.

DeLillo recognizes and re-enacts the "natural law that men with secrets tend to be drawn to each other, not because they want to share what they know but because they need the company of the like-minded, the fellow afflicted" (1988, 16). Such a "law" may underscore the American fascination with fundamentalism, apocalyptic judgment, and elite cabals. It is the basic impulse DeLillo registers and explores, not the finite intricacies of a genuine conspiracy. His character, General Edward Walker, testifies against "The Apparatus [that] we can't see or name. . . . It is the mystery we can't get hold of, the plot we can't uncover . . . men who know each other by secret signs, who work in the shadows to control our lives" (283).

DeLillo agrees with that sense of elusive mystery but, clearly, not with Walker's notions of an ultimate "Apparatus." He delights in David Ferrie's idea of inevitable connections that "[come] out of dreams, visions, intuitions, prayers, out of the deepest levels of the self" (339), but he rejects Ferrie's conspiratorial concoctions. This may "veer toward" conspiracy or "seem complicit" with Ferrie's mystical vision of destiny and paranoia—these are the "stuff" of contemporary vision and cultural mythologies to DeLillo's eye—but it does not support and extol them. DeLillo recognizes that "rapture of the fear of believing" (352) that we have recognized within apocalyptic cults and fundamentalist faiths—"rapture" is after all one of the basic experiences the fundamentalist believer wishes to experience as a result of his or her belief and the Second Coming of Christ—and he shares with Ferrie a distinctive Catholic background—"I made the circuit. Kneeling in the dark and whispering my sins to a man in skirts" (321)—but he does not accept the consequent paranoid plans of his characters. Their "theology of secrets" (442) fascinates the writer, but he rejects the theology. Secrets mesmerize, for they "are an exalted state, almost a dream state. They're a way of arresting motion, stopping the world so we can see ourselves in it" (26). Win Everett waxes eloquently in describing his daughter's delight in telling him a secret, but DeLillo explores that "dream state" and its compulsive, instinctive, peculiarly American qualities that underlie but do not condone specific conspiracy theories.

DeLillo employs several techniques to separate his narrative overview from the particular conspiracies that thrive like bacteria in the toxic underworld of *Libra*. The very multiplicity of characters undermines all specific designs. Oswald emerges as more of a patsy, a cipher within the conspiratorial connivings of others than his own man. DeLillo's hypnotic and often lyric prose celebrates the allure of the conspiracy but not its content. The narrative form remains unstable, an amalgam of fact and fiction, part documentary, part speculation, part dead end.

LeClair's analysis of what he calls the "systems novel" points to the dynamic processes of DeLillo's fiction, the reciprocal looping of its episodes and characters as opposed to a more static, cause-and-effect structure. Joseph Tabbi suggests that DeLillo reworks the technological forms and political narratives constructed by our culture from the inside in order "to represent or restructure the field of power and information" (1995, 179) that drives our culture. As Osteen concludes, "*Libra* is ultimately less about the conspiracy, or about Oswald, than it is about the darker secrets and deeper divisions of American culture" (2000, 161). In fact Nicholas Branch in the novel, sounding remarkably close to his creator's own point of view, pondering the labyrinthine and relentlessly unending details and information of the Kennedy assassination, wonders, "Can't a man die without the ensuing ritual of a search for patterns and links?" (1988, 379). The pursuit of patterns pulsates in DeLillo's fiction, but no one pattern dominates and explains.

DeLillo's Oswald casts no giant shadow as the brilliant mastermind and perpetrator of Kennedy's assassination. Instead "he feels he is living at the center of an emptiness. He wants to sense a structure that includes him, a definition clear enough to specify where he belongs. . . . He is a zero in the system." Conspiratorial plots and counterplots use and "invent" him in the

novel. He pulls the trigger that kills the president but only through a tortuous series of dead-ends, coincidences, accidental connections, and cross-
purposes. The only sense of self he achieves, and that only momentarily,
occurs at the very beginning of *Libra* where, riding the subway beneath
the streets of Manhattan, he feels the power of the noise, the dark, and the
view, all of which remain outside of and beyond him: "He was riding just
to ride." Only in the rush of the ride does he sense "this inner power, rising
to a shriek, this secret force of the soul," which will occur "never again in
his short life" (357, 13). He reacts, he prevaricates, he attempts suicide, he
gets himself court-martialed, he tries to defect to Cuba, but never does he
create himself as an ideologically consistent or self-directed individual.
Conspiratorial forces use and create him, not the other way around, and
this is precisely what DeLillo is up to as "his" creator. The contemporary
zeitgeist uses him. He is spawned by forces beyond his control, a product
of contemporary American culture.

When Oswald tries to write about his purpose or destiny, he remains
"stateless, word-blind, still a little desperate. . . . He could not clearly see
the picture that is called a word. . . . He saw spaces. . . . Things slipped
through his perceptions. He could not get a grip on the runaway world"
(210, 211). He yearns "to be swept along . . . in the stream of no-choice,
the single direction" (101), an isolated soul waiting for destiny to mark
his path rather than his choice to mark it for himself. Like so many of
DeLillo's misguided characters, "other people . . . fixed it so he would seem
the lone gunman . . . watching him, using him. . . . Made him a dupe
of history" (418). Grasping at the stereotype of "the powerful world of
Oswald-hero," he hungers for "the reverie of control, perfection of rage,
perfection of desire" (46), the kind of desire that DeLillo describes as fueling the contemporary lust for decisive action and a conspiratorial retalia-
tion against the status quo, but he ends up still yearning to experience
"perfection of rage, perfection of control, the fantasy of night. . . . Lee felt
he was in the middle of his own movie" (370). DeLillo does not conspire
along with him; he portrays him as becoming the dupe of other conspirators, other agents and agencies and in doing so purposefully undermines
the idea of conspiracy altogether. He remains "the negative Libran who is
. . . unsteady and impulsive. Easily, easily, easily influenced" (315), as
David Ferrie recognizes, but for that very reason he exists as a mere pawn
in the convoluted conspiracies of others.

Oswald remains confined within his own dim powers and elusive imaginings, "locked in the miniature room, creating a design, a network of connections. It was a second existence, the private world floating out to three dimensions" (277). Like DeLillo the writer "he no longer saw confinement as a lifetime curse. He'd found the truth about the room. He could easily live in a cell half this size" (435). After all "a cell is the basic state. . . . Men in small rooms, in isolation" (196) such as DeLillo's own, Oswald's own, and consciousness itself. Unlike Oswald, however, DeLillo's house of fiction contains many mansions, and he recognizes, along with Nicholas Branch, "that his subject is not politics or violent crime but men in small rooms" (181).

Wood worries that DeLillo's lyricism gets in the way of his paranoid characters as if siding too much with their cockamamie schemes and visions, but it seems to me that DeLillo celebrates more the compulsions, the impulses, and the contemporary mania for conspiracy, not particular conspirators and conspiracies. He evokes the dark forces and currents that erupt and can be diverted into the blind alleyways of dark designs, not the designs themselves. Win Everett, for instance, who has run his own agency within the CIA and wishes to create a false Oswald to discredit pro-Castro forces, in bed with his wife listens to the night:

The night was full of water moving, faint wet sounds, rainwater dripping through the trees, water falling from eaves . . . wet sounds of tires on asphalt, tires on a wet street. . . . Hollow thunder in the distance. Water silent in grassy pools, running down leaf stems, collecting in the webbed centers of leaves, trembling dreams . . . (*Libra* 1999, 75–76)

The repetition in this excerpt hypnotizes and suggests a certain ominous atmosphere, reinforced by the assonance in such words as "collected" and "webbed centers" along with the metaphor of "webbed centers" that conjures up conspiratorial plots, but the description reflects more of Oswald's sense of the elusive "nature of things" (211) rather than any particular plot. DeLillo creates that dream world, rife with nightmare imaginings, paranoiac visions, and conspiratorial auras, an underworld of American consciousness, not palpable designs.

A conversation in *Libra* also suggests the often impersonal and vague nature of DeLillo's style. Beryl Parmenter tells her husband Larry that "People think we're the strangest marriage." He responds, "What's strange about us?" and adds, "People think we're interesting." But Beryl will have none of it: "They think we're strange." To which Parmenter replies, "I don't think we're strange. I think we're interesting" (128). Their responses remain short and abrupt in their repetition of "strange" and "interesting," as well as "practical," which appears four times in four sentences. The abruptness suggests a certain obliqueness, as if they are merely responding to the other's words, not to any particular idea or content, creating a code as they continue. In such a way they appear emotionless and distant, as if they are hiding some more urgent agenda and need to dodge and dissemble as best they can. They sound like diplomats involved in an almost Jamesian thrusting and parrying, determined to keep cool at all times, as unspontaneous and self-controlled as possible. Such is the language of conspirators, vaguely ominous, consciously evasive, and compulsively guarded.

In *The Names* language itself also resonates with conspiratorial possibilities. Rife with ambiguities and uncertainties, it participates in ritual murder, personal transformation, and shifting perspectives. Deception lingers in its use, for, as Jacqueline Rose suggests, "When we speak, we take up a position of identity and certainty" (1992, 16), a position that presents its own problems and creates its own fictions. The postmodern self remains as unstable, elusive, and slippery as the language it purports to use and is as much a product of that shifting code as is the "I" characters use to identify themselves. No event reveals a single meaning, and language only complicates the process of attempting to find one. Postmodernism like deconstruction exposes the arbitrariness of words in terms of the relationship between signifier and signified as much as it reveals, in DeLillo's novels, "the intricate fabric woven by a now global economic order, in the mysterious zones produced by the system itself" (McClure 1994, 119).

The fascination with language saturates and permeates *The Names*. DeLillo serves up oblique conversations, descriptions and dialogues that are often turgid, crabbed, enigmatic, and aphoristic, clotted epiphanies and sudden shocks of recognition. The written and spoken word isolates, separates, subdues, and codifies. Tap Axton has invented Ob, his own coded language, which Osteen associates in the novel with the many ways in which language can be used: as obligation, obsession, objectification, obliteration, and oblation. Owen Brademas, the amateur linguistic archaeologist in search of the root meanings of words, mentions "a Dorian dialect . . . a style called *boustrophedon*. One line is inscribed left to right, the next line right to left" (1982, 22–23). He studies epigraphy, the revelation and translation of inscriptions, and travels to Lahore to learn Kharoshthi script. In India he pursues Brahmin script, "inscriptions cut into the stone. Sanskrit." James Axton, a risk analyst involved in insuring multinational corporations against the hazards of political disruptions, sees himself immersed in the "hard-edged and aggressive language of business . . . drawing some of its technical cant from the weapons pools of the south and southwest, a rural nurturing in a way, a blooding of the gray-suited, the pale, the corporate man" (278, 47). "The Prairie," an excerpt from Tap's novel at the end of *The Names,* celebrates the delight and terror of glossolalia, the Pentecostal ecstatic ceremony of speaking in tongues, a fierce rite that leaves his character, Orville Benton (Owen Brademas), tongue-tied and forces him to flee, stricken by incomprehension and yet compelled in future years to seek out the meanings of ancient inscriptions carved on rock.

Language names and codifies: "You will want to hurt your enemy, it is in history to destroy his name" (150). It also kills: "Every utterance of his name brings him closer to death" (294). It creates: "If you will know the correct order of letters, you make a world, you make creation. . . . If you know the combinations, you make all life and death" (152). Language connects and disconnects, exposes its own self-reflexiveness and communal possibilities, imprisons, dictates, undermines, and buries. It may reveal and conceal ancient patterns and pure possibilities, but it can also obliterate these patterns, remain as untranslatable as the stone tablets of Muenjadaro in Pakistan, and speak to the disconnections, the disruptions, and the failed decodings of history. One must wrestle with the conspiracies inherent in the riddles and revelations of language to recognize the ambiguous deconstructions of a postmodern perspective on death, dissolution, and despair.

The cult that Brademas discovers in *The Names,* "Ta Onomata," which in Greek means "The Names," when painted on a rock epitomizes the cult's desire to worship language as a physical sign, as its own dead letter. For the cultists words exist as stark graphic images, the sacred inscriptions of death, epigraphs cast in stone. They remain objects and "are what we aren't, what we can't extend ourselves to be. . . . Objects are the limits we desperately need. They show us where we end" (133), which for the cult culminates in ritual sacrifice and murder. When the initials of characters' names coincide with the initials of the name of a place—Michaeli Kalliambestsos in Mikro Kamini, Hamir Mazmudar in Hawa Mandir, James Axton in Jebel Amman—members of the cult murder or attempt to murder them. The mystery of language's power, reduced to the medium of a mark and a series of coincidental initials, produces mayhem, a murder to stop time, to uphold the sacredness of language. The cult's "means to contend with death has become death" (308), reducing language to the perverse purity of dead letters, naming to kill, killing to preserve, submitting the living spirit of language to dead letter, reducing spirit to inscription.

The presence of inscriptions on ancient stones suggests the absence of dead cultures as much as it suggests the presence of other writers, other perspectives and perceptions. The cult defies absence by creating its own, administering death in order to master and control it: "They mock our need to structure and classify, to build a system against the terror in our souls." They literally deconstruct the living spirit for the dead letter, so that each will seem to coincide with the other, but in doing so "they intended nothing, they meant nothing. They only matched the letters" (308).

DeLillo seems to be mocking postmodern linguistic theory at the same time that he is fascinated by it, while recognizing that the power to name can be more than the rite to kill. The self, if in fact it exists only as a function of language, must die, whereas the self if it can be seen as the cause and creator of language, can learn to live, however ambiguously, however warily. Naming can liberate as much as it can kill. This is the vision, the pursuit that Axton undergoes and experiences. As several critics have pointed out, at first he "stayed away from the Acropolis . . . that somber rock," viewing it only as "what we've rescued from the madness. Beauty, dignity, order, proportion" (4). He shrouds it in abstraction, freezes it as a sign of abstract qualities, in effect killing whatever life it may contain. Such a perspective parallels his own isolation as an expatriate, a businessman separated from his wife and son, cocooned and cushioned as are "business people in transit, growing old in planes and airports . . . versed in percentages. . . . We take no sense impressions with us, no voices. . . . It is dead time" (6, 7). He inhabits the terminal of postmodern skepticism, immersed in policy updates, the analysis of possible coups, collapse, and political catastrophe. He remains detached, rootless, introspectively unstable, the perpetual tourist, drifting "across continents and languages, suspending the operation of sound thought" (43), as much a creature of the new globalized system as a vaguely dissatisfied critic of it. Like DeLillo he remains enchanted and at first just a bit disgruntled with the "technocratic amaze" (McClure 1994, 135) of the new economic order of multinational capitalism.

At the end of the novel, however, he approaches the Parthenon as "not a thing to study but to feel." It no longer seems mere dead stone, the dead letter of a dead and vanished culture; it becomes "part of the living city below. . . . I'd thought it was a separate thing, the sacred height. . . . I hadn't expected a human feeling to *emerge* from the stones but this is what I found" (italics mine, 330). In that shock of recognition lie the possibilities of the dialogical discoveries of language, as communication and conversation not as catacomb and monological mausoleum: "This is what we bring to the temple, not prayer or chant or slaughtered rams. Our offering is language" (331). DeLillo does not shun or avoid the complexities and ambiguities that reside in that final sentence. Rather he celebrates language as a living ceremony in its own right, a human offering to distant or nonexistent gods in the spirit of possible communication and connection, not phonetic alphabet or dead letter but as living breath, as voice not disembodied but reincarnated in the offering he is making.

Owen Brademas flees from the incomprehensible, as Orville Benton flees from the Pentecostal madness in Tap's novel, because he seeks comprehensible origins, specifically and precisely translated cultic epigraphs, as Axton admits as well—"It eludes me. It defeats me. . . . Nothing adds up. The cult is the only thing I seem to connect with" (300)—that will purify his troubled quest and encapsulate his need to know. Axton has shared Brademas's obsession to build theories surrounding the bare act with desperate speculations, mainly to comfort ourselves" and has discovered that "nothing signified, nothing meant" (216), but at the end of the novel he also discovers flow, fluidity, and ambiguity. He seeks not to decipher inscriptions but to celebrate offerings, and language is what human beings can offer to the ever elusive, the forever mysterious, and the vast enigmas of consciousness, vanished cultures, contemporary terrors, and the cosmos. He will never see the transcendent pattern, if there is one, nor discover the ultimate sign, but he will participate in offering the means by which human beings suggest such possibilities in the intricacies and hieroglyphics of their languages, in their instinctive voicing of their open cries.

McClure joins those critics who describe DeLillo as part of the very system he criticizes. DeLillo, he maintains, celebrates "the postmodern pleasures pursued by Axton as if they were forms of liberation or resistance, when in fact they are not only consistent with, but in many cases actually byproducts of, a regime of global manipulation and control" (1994, 137). Axton discovers that the firm he works for works with the CIA: "If America is the world's living myth, then the CIA is America's myth. All the themes are there, in tiers of silence, whole bureaucracies of silence, in conspiracies and doublings and brilliant betrayals" (317). The CIA supports and underscores Axton's very existence, both his aimless drifting and his professional career. As an American businessman he can roam the globe more or less freely, encouraged by his boss, George Rowser, whose life was "full of the ornaments of paranoia and deception" (44). DeLillo's postmodern irony locates Axton right on the front lines of American imperialism: "Technicians are the infiltrators of ancient societies. . . . Whatever people need, we provide" (114).

But does American imperialism's placing him at the scene of the Acropolis undercut his new perception of language and the possibility of meaning? Do American conspiracies undermine his possible faith in the ability of language to transcend the codified and manipulative conspiracies of dead letters? McClure, insisting on DeLillo's reduction of American enemies to fanatical terrorists from the East, thinks they do: "It seems that a novelist's negotiations with enchantment influence his political vision and produce texts that are complicit with the very imperial discourses and interests they also attack" (1994, 123). I would suggest that McClure's idea that "the price of re-enchantment [in] the world of spiritual romance . . . is a repudiation of the political" (145) performs the same reduction of the spirit of language to the dead letter of specific political policies and simplistic Cold War dichotomies. He confuses and blurs epistemological and ontological categories. Spiritual journeys like Axton's, whatever their decided links to political realities, cannot be reduced to them. Axton's sense of offering, however ironic, complex, and ambiguous, is nonetheless a personal and quasi-religious act, which may be "something closer to a multilingual version of the old Latin Mass" (140), as McClure explains it, than a real celebration of diversity and difference in both East and West, but for Axton and the reader it is an act fraught with meaning. It is more personal than the communal Pentecostal ceremony that immediately follows it in "The Prairie," and it does disclose the change in perspective that Axton has come to personify.

Terror in *The Names* rests not only in "Eastern" terrorists, the fanatical cult members, but also in language itself in how it is used and how it operates. In the postmodern world the personal is the political, and the political like language infects, pervades, and saturates the personal, but like language it can also be personally liberating, however ultimately circumscribed and foretold. McClure's argument would reduce language to its incarnation as a politically and conspiratorially complicit agent in the status quo, but DeLillo's novel suggests that it can also be more. Perhaps Axton's explicit rejection of his political entanglements, however momentary, suggests the possibility, the glimpse of a wider cosmos that language can conjure up, as DeLillo has.

The Names reflects Axton's spiritual trajectory, as well as the reader's, as he journeys from the expatriate isolation and his focus on terror's cost effectiveness of "The Island" to the stone silences and the "pure rite of seeing" (182) in "The Mountain," from "the waking awareness . . . to burn away one's self" (294) in "The Desert" to the Pentecostal ravings of "The Prairie." We last encounter Axton recognizing what kind of offering he would like to make on the Acropolis, while Brademas in Tap's novel flees tongue-tied and terrified. Axton's final act may be as arbitrary and as artificial as the cult's obsession with matching letters, but the change in him and his perspective suggests a more human feeling and openness than the cult represents. Axton may still be fascinated with mysterious alphabets and their connection with death and the self, but his offering transforms sign into the intimation of significance, dead letter into spiritual action.

Osteen describes "DeLillo's vision of the author's vocation: to object to patriarchal authorities; to place verbal magic in the way of paralyzing dread" (2000, 140). Whether or not Tap's "Prairie" exhorts us "to resist consumption and force readers to rename the world" (141), DeLillo's "verbal magic," in all its complicated ambiguities and doublings, does oppose the "closed-in" qualities of cults and conspiracies. For them "inwardness is very much the point. One mind, one madness. To be part of some unified vision. Clustered, dense. Safe from chaos and life" (116). DeLillo's language is safe from neither, and it does acknowledge the attraction of the cult and the conspiracy as much as it exposes language's complicity with them, but it finally undermines and repudiates them, separating compulsion from enactment, fascination of our contemporary culture's fascination with them from supporting and reinforcing them. The politics may be slippery, as is language, but that very slipperiness in all its darker and more demonic implications and complicities upends the rigidity of the cause and the cult and offers lacerating but liberating ambiguities in place of "one mind. One madness."

"Forget relationships," exclaims film director Frank Volterra to Axton. "I want faces, land, weather. People speaking whatever languages" (199). For him the film image reigns in contemporary culture, not the word. Volterra believes that "figures in open space have always been what film is all about. American film. . . . People in a wilderness, a wild and barren space" (198). "Film is more than the twentieth-century art," he insists. "It's another part of the twentieth-century mind. It's the world seen from inside . . . we're constantly on film, constantly watching ourselves. The whole world is on film, all the time" (200). In *Mao II* DeLillo pursues more explicitly Volterra's obsession.

The image, particularly on television, threatens to subdue and overwhelm the world of *Mao II*. When linked with the litanies of disaster on the news, it mesmerizes and numbs whoever watches. DeLillo scrutinizes television news as "a kind of instrument of apocalypse. . . . We consume these acts of violence" (Remnick 1997, 48). Eugene Goodheart would agree: "The apocalypse may be the dominant media trope of our time" (1991, 122). Trope becomes vision, as apocalypse in contemporary culture, once confined to cults and cabals, invades the media, offering American spectators a steady diet of millennium-haunted violence and an end-of-the-world frisson that increases their sense of anxiety, dread, and knee-jerk terror. The apocalyptic image pervades contemporary consciousness in *Mao II* and drives spiritual consumers into the arms of fundamentalist leaders, eager to benefit from their doubt and dismay and lead their new disciples into their own regimented realms.

"We never look at just one thing," explains John Berger. "We are always looking at the relation between things and ourselves. [At the same time] every image embodies a way of seeing. . . . The photographer's way of seeing is reflected in his choice of subject" (1972, 10). The social construction of the act of seeing and images as a way of seeing fascinate DeLillo in *Mao*

II. The photographs throughout the novel show crowds, with the exception of the final one, which reveals three boys in a trench, the middle boy giving the peace sign, and yet the boys are as much functions of Rashid's terrorist plans as the members of the various crowds are functions of the events that overwhelm them. DeLillo has also superimposed titles on each photo, which are as black and visible as the photos are gray and blurred, thus privileging the word over the image. The book opens with a two-page spread of the crowds in Tiananmen Square with the title, "MAO II." Long files of couples approach the Rev. Moon: "AT YANKEE STADIUM." "PART ONE" is superimposed over the crush of suffocating spectators pressed against a soccer field fence. "PART TWO" marches across the huge poster-face of Ayatollah Khomeini at his funeral with crowds gathered beneath it, and "IN BEIRUT" hovers above the three boys in the trench.

The images share many things in common. The first, second, and fourth reveal ceremonial acts: a protest march, a mass wedding, and a funeral. Two and four show two powerful clerics, Moon and Khomeini, leaders of their own particular cults and revolutions. Three and five suggest death and violence: the mashed faces, open mouths, and twisted arms against the fence and the war zone that the boys inhabit.

DeLillo comments on the effect of these images both on his characters within the novel and in the descriptions he creates for the reader. Karen Janney (who is an avid spectator and television viewer and a cult groupie, who is later deprogrammed and becomes a disciple of the novelist, Bill Gray), one of 13,000 people married by the Rev. Moon, later watches the Tiananmen Square massacre on Brita's TV in her Manhattan apartment (Brita is the cool-eyed photographer who likes to photograph writers and believes in the power of the image). Karen watches as if mesmerized by but with no visceral response to "soldiers jogging in the streets . . . a smoldering corpse in the street. There are dead bodies attached to fallen bicycles. . . . The crowd dispersed. . . . One crowd replaced by another" (1991, 177). When she tries to interpret what she has seen, she can only grapple with vague incomplete thoughts: "But it is funny how a picture. It is funny how a picture what?" Outside she comes across a couple in the park who are preparing for the Second Coming: "We are protected by the total power of our true father. We are the total children. All doubt will vanish in the arms of total control" (178, 179). Karen's fascination with the portrait of Mao Zedong on television merges in her mind with the couple's mantra on "our true father" and "total children," thus underscoring DeLillo's exploration of the roots of fundamentalist yearnings for regimentation and the need for a forceful leader, a theme that *Mao II* will examine in great detail.

DeLillo's description of the mass Moonie wedding clearly reveals the military regimentation of the ceremony, within which each individual becomes merely one more marcher into marriage. Although DeLillo connects the scene to the perspective of Karen's parents, who are sitting in the grandstand, he obviously wants the reader to react similarly to the sheer strangeness and alienation that the scene displays with its "drama of mechanical routine played out with living figures . . . a mass of people turned into a sculptured object . . . immunized against the language of self" (7). This first scene in the novel that directly follows the photograph of the stadium's columned masses viscerally displays one of DeLillo's major themes: "The thousands stand and chant. . . . The future belongs to crowds" (8, 16).

Karen again becomes a spectator and consumer, this time of the soccer-stadium massacre and Khomeini's funeral as they are presented on television. The first she witnesses at Bill Gray's house, the second in Brita's apartment. DeLillo describes her as seeing the soccer catastrophe and the television as showing it. "Sees" and "shows" enact a litany of spectatorship with Karen reduced to an eye, a witness, a creature of almost pure reception: "She sees men and boys at first. . . . They show bodies at odd angles. They show men standing off. . . . She sees a great straining knot of people pressed to a fence. . . . They show the metal fence and bodies crushed against it. . . . " DeLillo describes exactly the photograph that begins "PART ONE." The style re-enacts the gruesomely mesmerizing acts of seeing and showing, as if language has been reduced to and "freeze dried" as some neutrally objective mode of observation and description. Agony and death pervade the scene but are described in terms of limbs, faces, bodies, hands: "It is like a fresco in an old dark church, a crowded twisted vision of a rush to death as only a master of the age could paint it" (34). Karen's emotions remain frozen, buried by and within the meticulous and objective detail, a laundry list of disaster. DeLillo's matter-of-fact prose diminishes her selfhood and reduces her individual identity to that of onlooker, in this instance reproducing the power of images on so passive a spectator.

Part Two begins with the huge fierce face of Ayatollah Khomeini, followed immediately by Chapter 8, our first glimpse of the poet-prisoner as hostage in Beirut, thus linking the Iranian revolution with the terrorists of Beirut. Karen again becomes the spectator-consumer, this time of Khomeini's funeral on television. Unlike watching the soccer debacle, however, she reacts with both horror and understanding with her hands over her mouth. She feasts on the frenzied mob scene, the "weeping chanting mourners," and feels that "she was among them," identifying with the loss of the great father, the idolized leader, the Reverend Moon to his disciples. Mourning becomes her: "We will all be a single family soon. . . . Because the total vision is being seen. . . . For there is a single vision now." Karen succumbs again to the crowd as slave to master, apostle to a god: "She had Master's total voice ready in her head" (193, 194). The self's submission to the image performs its disappearance into the crowd, whether it be protestors, brides and grooms, football fans, or Iranian fanatics. The image of the master embodies the Master's total voice. The self becomes silent devotee.

The last photograph, "IN BEIRUT" with the boys in the trench, incarnates the contemporary world as one of war, confrontation, and conspiracy. Brita's visit to the city confirms the pervasive devastation of our era: "It is the lunar part of us that dreams of wasted terrain. She hears their voices calling across the leveled city. Our language is Beirut" (239).

America's passion for images, as Jean Baudrillard describes it, creates a thirst for more images, for images *as* images, themselves embodying virtual reality, flattening all before them. In New York Bill Gray, the hermit novelist, resurfaces, appalled at "the way it simply rushed at him" (94). As a writer he associates images with his own death: "The deeper I pass into death, the more powerful my picture becomes. Isn't this why picture-taking is so ceremonial? It's like a wake" (42). The tent city that Karen stumbles upon "was a world apart but powerfully here, a set of milling images." In Beirut "the streets run with images. . . . Brita thinks this place is a millennial image mill" (149). Warhol's silk-screened images of Mao, reproduced again and again to become their own crowd, "reprocessed through painted chains of being" (229), overwhelm the viewer. The glut of Maos and the mass weddings generate an infinite procession, the brides and grooms compressed "into one accelerated mass," suggesting a "millennial hysteria" (135, 80) to Bill become a catastrophe. The totalitarianism and tyranny of images override everything in their wake, spectators become passive consumers anxiously eager to be led, yearning for leaders to discipline and define them, the individual self become the crowd enflamed by mass hypnotism and hysteria, drunk on their addiction to apocalypse.

Bill Gray, the solitary writer, fears the image and the crowd, both of which proclaim that "the only salvation lies in the dissolution of personalities into the single-headed throng" (177). Karen welcomes the crowd. It speaks to "our urgent need for certainty," as "one crowd replaced another. . . . We are protected by the total power of our true father. . . . All doubt will vanish in the arms of total control" (179). Scott, Bill's disciple, glories in the community that crowds suggest and represent; they summon our common future. George Haddad praises the "call to unity. . . . Something enormous and commanding . . . total politics, total authority, total being" (158). Crowd control: the wave of the future.

The psychological process DeLillo presents follows its predictable course. Feeling lost, alienated, and assaulted in a fragmented and crowded postmodern world, afflicted by images of disaster and catastrophe on the news and in the media, battered souls rush to join a group, a cult, a fundamentalist faith: Tell us what to do, what to believe, what to feel! Images enhance the process, beckoning icons that mesmerize would-be disciples. A fearless leader rises to control the crowd, shape and transform it, wed it, bury it, kill it, organize it into a cause, and the only creature capable of creating and employing that power in contemporary culture becomes the terrorist, the cult object, the religious guru, driven by a destiny, a vision, and a self-justified faith. As Abu Rashid, the terrorist in Beirut, tells Brita about why his boys wear T-shirts with his picture on them, "It gives them a vision they will accept and obey. These children need an identity. . . . We teach them identity, sense of purpose. . . . All men one man. . . . The image of Rashid is their identity" (233).

Mao II enacts the tale of burnt-out and reclusive novelist, Bill Gray, allowing himself to be photographed by Brita Nilsson, an act that leads to the possibility of his being exchanged for a poet held hostage in Beirut. His is also an act of despair, the novelist succumbing to the image. Forgoing his craft for his eventual death, he stages the process of his own demise, photographed, fled, dead. He has believed that "stories have no point if they don't absorb our terror" (140), but images and the images of terrorists and disaster are absorbing the culture, rendering him irrelevant and barren. Now "news of disaster is the only narrative people need. The darker the news, the grander the narrative" (42). Apocalypse has become the rhetorical and image-driven norm. George Haddad, the political scientist and go-between for terrorist groups, recognizes the problem, that "in societies reduced to blur and glut, terror is the only meaningful act" (157). It is an act of outrage, desperation, and demented postmodern rage, created by "lethal believer[s], the person who kills and dies for faith" (48), a prophecy all too chillingly confirmed on September 11, 2001.

Is this what DeLillo has managed to accomplish in *Mao II*? Yes, and no. The theme shimmers like a neon sign: the novelist, the individual self who relishes the word, vanishes beneath the onrush of the crowd and the terrorist, the pathological leader who celebrates the image, the fanatics who swoop down upon the World Trade Center towers in planes to produce the astonishing and cinematically spectacular images of catastrophe and apocalyptic collapse. Such men "don't need their own features or voices. They are surrendering these things to something powerful and great" (234). We have seen the images. They haunt our own visions and dreams, replayed across the television screen again and again as if they were just happening, still happening, repeated so often they become disembodied horrors, consumed goods, eruptions of cultural nightmares, postmodern funeral pyres: "I liked the angle of that shot better. Did you see how he caught the second plane as it banked and dove? That was awesome!"

In writing about the way we see things, the way seeing is a socially constructed act, John Berger adds, "The world-as-it-is is more than pure objective fact, it includes consciousness" (1972, 11). The consciousness within *Mao II* includes the inroads and images of terror and contemporary horrors. DeLillo's language in this novel has also succumbed to those images, absorbed the flattened impersonal response of the passive spectator. When my students confront the style in this particular fiction, they describe it as "plain, abrupt, opaque, unemotional, elliptical, cold, dead, obsessively monotonous, colorless, juiceless." Characters talk past one another or only to themselves, as if trapped in their own numbed consciousness. The style describes the act of observation, as if every action and thought were one or two steps removed from "actual" events. The style diminishes the individual, replicating the process that DeLillo accuses images of perpetrating. The "feel" of the novel incorporates a sense of drift, disconnection, an entranced torpor, the very condition and state that watching too much television supposedly induces.

Mao II strikes me as the stylistically bleakest of DeLillo's novels, not as obscure and numbing as the brilliant but ice-cold *Ratner's Star,* for instance, but as bleak as the conspiracies of image, media, and terrorism he describes. I agree with McClure that it "offers a powerfully plausible description of fundamentalism" (1994, 146), the postmodern anxiety and ennui that hungers for the sanctuary of a cult or creed, but its characters all sound alike, lecturers in a void. Osteen maintains that "DeLillo imitates the discourses he aims to deconstruct and thereby generates a dialogue with those cultural forms that both criticizes their consequences and appropriates their advantages" (2000, 210), a subversive complicity in effect, but in *Mao II* dialogue and design are too meticulously and airlessly constructed, however fascinating and seductive the tale. The death of the novelist, Bill Gray, feels too much like DeLillo's own. He hasn't so much written terror out as let it in to trample and stiffen the prose. In *Mao II* consciousness has shrunk, beaten back by images, disaster, and apocalyptic musings, a victim of its own startling discoveries, revealing a nightmarish underworld of the postmodern condition that seems to have reached its bitter end.

Despite the astute political nuances and vision of *The Names* and *Mao II,* the fact that, as Jeffrey MacIntyre (2002) suggests in his *Salon* interview on the Web, "DeLillo's version of terrorism implicates both agents of terrorism and the West in a larger web of mutually antagonistic ideologies," as Wood has concluded, "*Mao II* was a desperately unreal book, a collection of conceptual episodes. . . . That novel was dominated by the very images it sought to overpower" (1999, 189).

Wood, however, confuses DeLillo with his subject matter. Viewing paranoia as the enemy of fiction, because paranoia explicitly spells out its causes and effects whereas fiction should reflect "a free scatter through time, unpressed, incontinent, unhostaged" (1999, 190), he explains that paranoia will always reduce and oversimplify the ways of fiction, creating a more rigidly monochromatic world than the "real" world of fiction would suggest. Thus "DeLillo veers toward a complicity with the very culture he wants to defend the novel against" (186), and in Wood's discussion of *Underworld,* the novel "comes to seem complicit with the paranoia it describes" (185). The problem rests in the verbs, "veers toward" and "comes to seem."

Once having established this fact for himself, Wood goes on to point out that paranoia flattens characters. It allows no room for the more rounded characters that fiction should create, since they remain skewered by their own fantasies, yammering away like pompous, one-dimensional lecturers or cardboard evangelicals. "Political paranoia . . . makes characters unreal," Wood insists. Too many paranoids occupy DeLillo's fictional texts, shackled by DeLillo's overt preaching about them, and even if Nick Shay in *Underworld* is not one of them, he "is not a full or interesting enough character to carry much weight." Besides the very "form of the novel is against him" (1999, 183, 185), itself a kind of paranoid tract and one-dimensional vision, not to mention DeLillo's often lyrical style, which seems to support the very paranoia it is supposed to be criticizing. In short DeLillo doesn't write about paranoia. He creates it like an author hung up on one particular theme and perspective.

Of all the possible novels to use to support this argument—one thinks of *Ratner's Star* and *Great Jones Street,* for instance—*Underworld* provides the worst example. As I have maintained, DeLillo darkly delights in exploring the paranoiac impulse and American culture, not the specific paranoid projects or conspiracies of his characters. In some cases his characters do appear to be "flatter," particularly in *Mao II,* but the charge doesn't stick to *Underworld.*

Underworld strikes me as a departure from and the fulfillment of DeLillo's body of work. This grand magnificent novel enacts the process of discovering the possibility of vision implicit in its form and in his fictional techniques. Of course in the postmodern world everything is provisional. No metanarrative rushes to the rescue. No final vision transcends its place in both time and space within the novel. The reader moves from fragment to fragment, from episode to episode, eagerly searching for the connections and motifs that DeLillo has planted throughout the book. The very absence of a distinct metanarrative encourages us to seek out presence, to find a "key." As DeLillo suggested in the *Times* on September 7, 1997, "I think I was trying to be objective in the face of something revealed, an unexpected connection, a symmetry that seemed to be waiting for someone to discover it" (60). That connection, that symmetry, that "something revealed" hovers everywhere in the text, rife with intimations, glimpses, and epiphanies, a vast canvas that suggests the postmodern sublime.

Of course paranoia and conspiracy loom large, and the suggestion of anything different from them may be "all nuance and wishful silhouette," but DeLillo also clearly raises the larger issue of possibility in *Underworld:* "Or does the power of transcendence linger, the sense of an event that violates natural forces, something holy that throbs on the hot horizon, the vision you crave because you need a sign to stand against your doubt?" (1997, 824). That sign may stem only from the craving and the need, and it may be self-projected, but on the very first page of *Underworld,* DeLillo states, "Longing on a large scale is what makes history . . . [people] bring with them . . . their own small reveries and desperations, the unseen something that haunts the day" (11). Paranoia kills and entraps, but longings still remain, the kind that propel and compel DeLillo's characters, however ultimately distorted, to pursue meaning and significance, as they propel both writer and reader. As Matt Shay wonders, seduced by paranoia as so many of the other characters are but still open to doubt about the literalness of such massive conspiracies, "There may have been an underworld of images known only to tribal priests, mediums between visible reality and the spirit world" (466). Those mediums can point in more than one direction, more than to the path of least resistance, which would direct him to paranoid plots, and *Underworld* makes the most of the rampant ambiguities and contradictions that may, however fitfully, suggest a wider, more transcendent significance. Many are the tribal priests in this sumptuous novel, and many are the spirit worlds that lie beyond the oversimplified paranoid faiths.

DeLillo urges the reader to make connections, which parallels the compulsion of many of his characters, and he rigs his text to call attention to coincidences, similarities, and repetitions, but the process for the reader surpasses the more insular pursuits of the characters. His is not E. M. Forster's optimistic faith in the imperative, "Only connect." The phrase, "Everything is connected in the end" (826), near the very end of the novel, suggests more ominous possibilities. But as connections accumulate in *Underworld,* these fragments shored against certain ruins, hope does emerge.

Connections abound, and we can play the game the text conjures up for us. Take the number thirteen, for example. How many letters are there in the name Jimmy Costanza, Nick's father? Add up the digits in the name Moonman 157. Manx Martin sells the famous baseball to Charles Wainwright for $32.35. Branca, the famous pitcher of that mythic October 3, 1951, game, wears number thirteen. Add up 10/3. During the San Francisco earthquake, clocks stopped at 5:17 a.m. Kennedy's assassination, caught in the Zapruder home movie, begins at frame 313. As one character comments, "Wouldn't you know . . . there had to be a thirteen somewhere in the case" (489). The upshot: Coincidence? Conspiracy? Chance? In a postmodern world, bereft of meaning and without direction, such superstitions loom large if not in any recognizable, understandable way.

Once the game's afoot, it's hard to stop, whether counting oranges or baseballs. Agent Orange and Minute Maid Orange Juice: Charles Wainwright administers the Minute Maid account. Klara Sax wears an orange T-shirt. Prokofiev's overture to his opera, *Love for Three Oranges*, accompanies the showing of Eisenstein's *Unterwelt*. Sister Alma Edgar and J. Edgar Hoover share Cold War paranoias. Bill Waterson tells the young Cotter Manx that "the thing about baseball" as a game is that "you do what they did before you. That's the connection you make. There's a whole long line" (31), just as there is with "the long arching journey of the baseball itself" (318). Cotter Manx retrieves the ball on October 3, 1951; his father Manx sells it to Charles Wainwright; Charles gives it to his son Charlie who loses it; Marvin Lundy supposedly finds it and includes it in his baseball memorabilia in his New Jersey basement, after a search that involves Genevieve Rauch, who may have been killed by the Texas Highway Killer; Nick pays Lundy $34,500 for it, as if trying to grasp that lost momentous and innocent day of his youth, October 3, 1951, the day before Shay accidentally kills George, the heroin addict in the Bronx. Nick has to have that baseball, an icon emanating nostalgia and triumph, in his attempt to overcome "the mystery of bad luck, the mystery of loss . . . it's the only thing in my life that I absolutely had to own" (97). The ball also suggests Branca's failed pitch: "Bad luck, Branca luck. From him to me. The moment that makes the life" (132). In a wasteland of significance, drowning men grasp at such straws.

"Baseball's oh so simple. You tag a man, he's out. How different from being *it*" (678), but children can see through the game "to something old and dank, some medieval awe . . . that crawls beneath the midnight skin" (60). So can J. Edgar Hoover on October 3, 1951, at the game when he discovers that the Soviets have exploded their second atomic bomb, thus escalating the lethal competition of the Cold War. This midcentury moment defines an era, rife with contradictions spawned by baseball and the bomb, initiating an era of nihilistic connections, polarities of life and death, conceived in the Manichean machinations of the Cold War. That script shapes midcentury American history and culture. Such is the paranoid heart of darkness in DeLillo's *Underworld,* and it creates a world of nuclear waste, a contemporary world of spiritual and metaphysical waste, and a postmodern dark night of the soul that feels, in Matt Shay's words, like "a dream someone's dreaming that has me in it" (459).

DeLillo descends into midcentury's hell, into its underworld within which the consciousness of the bomb intercepts and infiltrates all things like some horrifying pagan mystery. Whatever happens, "all technology refers to the bomb" (467), and that knowledge feeds the paranoia of characters, such as Matt Shay, Eric Deming, J. Edgar Hoover, and Sister Alma Edgar among others. Deming, the bombhead, "not subject to moral ambivalence," loves "the edge. The bite. The existential burn" (405, 406). J. Edgar knows that the KGB lurks behind everything. He hugs his massive dossiers "in the endless estuarial mingling of paranoia and control. . . . The dossier was a deeper form of truth, transcending facts and actuality . . . and therefore incontestable" (241). Sister Edgar in her latex gloves feels "sinfully complicit with some process she only half understood, the force in the world, the array of systems that displaces religious faith with paranoia. . . . The faith of suspicion and unreality. The faith that replaces God with radioactivity" (251). Simeon Biggs believes the U.S. Census has been rigged to hide ten million blacks. Marvin Lundy wonders if Greenland has "some secret function and a secret meaning. But then you think everything has a secret function and a secret meaning" (316). Such are the characters who subscribe to *dietrologia,* the Italian word, which, for Nick Shay, means "the science of what is behind something. A suspicious event . . . the science of dark forces" (280). This is not the whole of *Underworld,* but the Cold War consciousness creates and supports the dietrologia of the novel.

Fallout from the Cold War seeps into, infiltrates, and threatens to overwhelm contemporary American culture. Nuclear waste remains and must be disposed of, managed, dealt with. It produces its own religious rites: "We entomb contaminated waste with a sense of reverence and dread" (88). Waste becomes "the mystical twin" of weapons, "because waste is the secret history, the underhistory. . . . We destroy contaminated nuclear waste by means of nuclear explosions" (791, 102). Nick Shay sees himself, however sardonically, as one of "the Church Fathers of waste in all its transmutations . . . a member of an esoteric order . . . adepts and seers" (185).

Nick Shay surveys the devastation of his Bronx neighborhood, a blighted wasteland, as much a product of the Cold War's billions for bombs as it is a metaphysical postmodern wasteland of a terrified new world with no script to follow. Welcome to "the age of construction debris and vandalized car bodies, the age of moldering mobster parts . . . of vermin, craters choked with plumbing fixtures and sheetrock. . . . Gunfire sang at sunset off the low walls of demolished buildings" (238, 239). The intense focus on communist conspiracies has given way to its true legacy, derelict tenements and murderous children. No wonder Eisenstein's lost masterpiece, *Unterwelt,* with its images of degradation and deformity, is a hit at Radio City Music Hall. It reminds Klara Sax of "the other *Underworld,* a 1927 gangster film and box office smash" (431), a dark realm in which you may be forced to question language "and follow the word through the tunneled underworld of its ancestral roots" (826).

DeLillo thematically pursues two other creatures of this blighted postmodern, post–Cold War world, Nick Shay and the media. In his life and career Nick has made the most of waste. As a self-proclaimed waste manager, he has organized his life to try to contain and overcome that fatal day, October 4, 1951, when he shot and killed George Manza, the heroin addict and gangster friend who had befriended the sixteen-year-old punk from the South Bronx. Rescued by Jesuits, Shay creates an isolated and desperately protected persona based on control and functional efficiency: "I've always been a country of one. There's a certain distance in my makeup, a measured separation like my old man's . . . *lontananza,* distance or remoteness . . . the perfected distance of the gangster . . . the made man" (275). In trying to imagine his father's disappearance as part of some secret mob conspiracy, he tries desperately to lend a "narrative purity" (454) to the fact that Jimmy Costanza one day just upped and took off, abandoning his family, Nick's mother, and his brother Matt. Marian, his wife, "had a demon husband if demon means a force of some kind, an attendant spirit of discipline and self-command . . . hard and apart" (261).

Nick inhabits a postmodern self, an identity built on opposition to waste, loss, and confusion. His fragile sense of self rests on what he excludes from it, a polarized position that remains barely sustainable, forever threatening to collapse and shatter if only into glittering shards of longing and loss. His presence protects a void, an absence that began with his father's disappearance and continues with his career in waste management.

DeLillo at times forces this connection, and the metaphor threatens to collapse under its own weight, but, as we shall see, Nick's "whisper of mystical contemplation" (282) suggests other routes and visions than longing and loss, a wider territory that *Underworld* creates within, above, and beyond his paranoid, self-controlled, well-guarded world. He remains selfish even in relation to "the past, selfish and protective. I didn't know how to bring Marian into those years" (345), but he can clutch a mythical baseball, even if it may not be that ball from the 1951 game, solitary in the privacy of his home at 4:00 a.m.: "There is something somber about the things we've collected and own . . . that breathes a kind of sadness . . . the grasp of objects that bind us to some betokening. . . . I long for the days of disorder . . . rippling in the quick of my skin . . . angry and ready all the time, a danger to others and a distant mystery to myself" (808, 810).

In *Underworld* Kennedy's assassination still lingers in the notorious Zapruder film, screened in the private studio and home of a video artist for drug-addled spectators who are still able to know "a kind of floating fear, a mercury reading of the sixties, with a distinctly trippy edge" (488). Unlike the ball game in October 1951, when Kennedy was shot, "people went inside. We watched TV in dark rooms. . . . We were all separate and alone" (94).

The main media spectacle, however, in *Underworld,* occurs when a twelve-year-old girl catches on videotape the murder of a passing driver by the perpetrator who comes to be known as the Texas Highway Killer. The tape stuns. It mesmerizes with that mix of torpor and violence DeLillo associates with contemporary consumerism and culture, the one feeding the other. The tape plays over and over on television, and the effects are predictable in DeLillo's world: "The more you watch the tape, the deader and colder and more relentless it becomes. The tape sucks the air right out of your chest but you watch it every time" (118). Jeff Shay, Nick's son, "became absorbed in these images. . . . He enhanced and super-slowed" them (530). Like TV commercials and stories, "whoever controls your eyeballs runs the world." As Charles Wainwright, the ad agency executive, brags, "Once we get the consumer by the eyeballs, we have complete mastery of the marketing process" (531).

The horror deepens when, without warning, DeLillo shows us the Texas Highway Killer at home. Richard Henry Gilkey, like the spectators of the infamous video, seeks escape, and he can only accomplish this by talking with a TV anchorwoman because "she made him feel real . . . he was never really who he was until he talked to her." For him the media creates a self, the persona of the Texas Highway Killer, and like DeLillo's Oswald allows him to become part of history. As with all media events, however, the fascination dissipates: "No one talks about the Texas Highway Killer anymore . . . the shootings have evidently ended and the name is gone now" (807). Gilkey's fifteen minutes of fame, of random violence, erupts and vanishes, one more postmodern sign of the times with its mix of paranoia, spectacle, and final banishment. The shelf life of a still unidentified murderer lasts as long as any media-driven fad.

So many of the characters in *Underworld* would agree with Matt Shay: "Paranoid. Now he knew what it meant, this word that was bandied and bruited so easily" (421). J. Edgar and Sister Edgar come to mind immediately, twin paranoids in the Manichean mysteries of the Cold War, but there are others at work here, artists such as Klara Sax, Ismael Munoz as Moonman 157, Sabato Rodia, Lenny Bruce, and Albert Bronzini. Sax paints abandoned B-52s in the desert left over from the Cold War. Moonman 157 paints subway trains, at once vandal and visionary. Sabato Rodia created that weird architectural collage of junk and joy. Lenny Bruce's manically comic monologues, or rather DeLillo's brilliant re-creation of Bruce's monologues, erupt and explode with "a kind of abridged syntax, a thing without connectives, he was cooking free-form, closer to music than speech, doing a spoken jazz in which a slang term generates a matching argot" (586), riffs akin to DeLillo's own talents as a novelist. Even Albert Bronzini, Sax's former husband and Matt Shay's natural sciences teacher who believes that the only art he knows is the art of walking, still speaks of "the laws of nature in their splendid harmony. . . . This is the real power. How the mind operates. How the mind identifies, analyzes and represents. What beauty and power" (734, 735). These artists and others from Truman Capote's vulgarly sumptuous Black and White Ball to Eisenstein's use of montage act as a counterpoint to the plethora of paranoids in DeLillo's text.

Nick may have spent his life controlling and managing waste, both his own and his culture's, but the Jesuits in rescuing him from a life of petty crime and the possibility of another murder strike a chord within him that he never really abandons or forgets: "The Jesuits taught me to examine things for second meaning and deeper connections" (88). He walks a precarious wire between the possibility of a paralyzing paranoia that has mesmerized his brother and an eruption of uncalled-for rapture, between self-containment and sudden epiphany. The balloon ride he gives his wife Marian as a birthday present stuns him: "Everything we saw was ominous and shining, tense with the beauty of things that are normally unseen" (126).

Others share such revelations. Klara Sax, who marries Carlo Strasser, beholds a Central Park "when there's a distilled sense of perception. . . . It was one of those days of light and scale when everything you see has the full breadth of intention" (497). Marvin Lundy comes upon a dock in San Francisco that DeLillo describes in the negligent lists of an enraptured Whitman with its "sense of enormous tonnage and skyhook machinery, tractor-trailers crooking into marked slots and containered goods stacked on the decks of tremendous ships, you almost couldn't believe how big, and the-what-do-you-call, the booms of dockside cranes swinging cargo through the mist" (305). Klara Sax in New York City discovers "a brick façade flushed with coral light, more or less on fire with light, and the brick seemed revealed the way only light reveals a thing . . . of some intenser beauty" (387). Matt Shay cannot stop looking at Landsat photos shot from outer space: "The photo mosaics seemed to reveal a secondary beauty in the world, ordinarily unseen, some hallucinatory fuse of exactitude and rapture. Every thermal burst of color was a complex emotion he could not locate or name" (415). Bronzini realizes "how language is webbed in the senses" (683).

Dark forces certainly prowl amid the rubble and postmodern drift of *Underworld,* but they provide only half the story. There are encounters and events that even paranoia cannot shape or contain and that suggest the sudden quantum leap into possibility an Emerson would have appreciated. The web DeLillo designs allows for both paranoia and possible redemption. Yes, as Leonard argues, DeLillo is "the poster boy for postmodernism [with its] randomness and incongruity"; he is "the conspiracy theorist of corporate power, government secrecy [and] malign systems"; he is "the Bombhead . . . for whom not just consumer culture but also politics and history drift deathward"; but he is also "the secret sadhu, a holy man in search of God. . . . His is a hounding after something sacred, so ecumenical it's almost promiscuous" (2001, 14, 15).

These contradictions, the polarized oppositions in *Underworld* of paranoia and possibility, death and life, define a basic relationship of DeLillo's cosmos because they do not exist to reveal the mere fact of opposition. These contradictions suggest the positive and negative poles of an electrical circuit. Yes, they oppose each other, they appear in opposition to each other, but the electrical circuit cannot be completed until both are in place. "Without Contraries is no progression," the poet William Blake declared in "The Marriage of Heaven and Hell," and the same goes for *Underworld*. The dark forces of paranoia run rampant in this world, but they are only the darkest piece of the puzzle.

DeLillo also conjures up an Emersonian vision: "We live in a system of approximations. Every end is prospective of some other end, which is also temporary; a round and final success nowhere" (Hodder 1989, 40). Unlike Emerson he stumbles on no ultimate and harmonious unity at the heart of things. DeLillo's postmodern world is a world of fragmentation, discontinuity, and disruption, but there are glimmerings of other things, sudden eruptions of the spirit, sensual epiphanies. As Steven Best and Douglas Kellner describe the "postmodern turn," "Values that modern thought takes as opposites polarized in rigid binary distinctions, such as between fact and value, determinism and chaos, and subjectivity and objectivity, implode in postmodern thought" (1997, 221), but they also expand. Stark dualisms shimmer and become dialectically dynamic. For Emerson the powers of the mind and in nature lay in transitions. Permanence and the stationary appalled him. What we would call a quantum leap was what delighted him, the reaching for an idea or a vision, seeming to grasp it, and then as quickly moving on, forever in transit, open in DeLillo's case to catastrophe as much as celebration but open, not permanently shut down by the paranoid fantasies of particular characters.

The form of *Underworld* speaks directly to this Emersonian delight in transition and juxtaposition. It enacts the process of discovering the possibility of vision, a series of possible transformations and encounters that can lead as easily to disaster as to delight. The novel leads the reader from the triumphant nostalgia of baseball on October 3, 1951, accompanied as it is by the Soviets' exploding a second atomic bomb, to October 4, 1951, when Nick Shay accidentally kills George Manza. We once again witness the fall from a scene rife with Edenic possibilities, including the serpent in the guise of the Soviet bomb and Bruegel's *The Triumph of Death,* to Cain's crime, the murder of a brother. The elaborate montage of the novel, however, undercuts the rigid Manichean script of the Cold War, the good Americans versus the Evil Empire. It subverts the absurd scenario based on the premise of total annihilation as political policy, the fallout of 1950s bomb shelters and the Demings' suburban denial of such a fate, cocooned in their world of Jell-O, chicken mousse, breezeways, and crispers. In such an unreal realm, the Demings' son Eric inevitably becomes the eager "bombhead" of the nuclear era, lusting for his "existential burn." Yet the novel moves on to Lenny Bruce's oracular comic perorations and jeremiads, the civil rights movement, the New York blackout in 1965, and Father Paulus at the Jesuit retreat. Positive follows negative; negative follows positive in their backward trajectory from 1992 to 1951 after the opening ballgame.

Underworld opens and closes in a positive manner: "He speaks in your voice, American, and there's a shine in his eye that's halfway hopeful" (1997, 11). DeLillo addresses the reader in the second voice, including her automatically, complete with the "shine in his eye," and that shine, like *Underworld* itself, is "halfway hopeful." "Das Kapital," the epilogue, leaves us with the horrors of Kazakhstan, complete with the use of a nuclear explosion to destroy nuclear waste. Weapons and waste: checkmate. The Museum of Misshapens reveals the victims of Soviet nuclear policies, and Nick, finally admitting that his father years ago just walked out on his family, remains to face the emptiness and mystery of his own existence. Someone in the wasteland of the South Bronx called the Wall rapes the young girl Esmeralda, whom Sister Edgar and Moonman 157 have been seeking to try and save, and throws her off a roof. Esmeralda's face turns up on a billboard, however, in the light of an oncoming train, no doubt a hallucination, a trick of light, but people starved for a vision gather to look for it. Sister Edgar's appearance in the crowd becomes "a verifying force— a figure from a universal church with sacraments and secret bank accounts and a fabulous art collection" (822). Irony in this postmodern world stalks all halfway hopeful visions, and Sister Edgar, complete, dies.

In cyberspace—where Sister Edgar sees the thermal explosion of the mushroom cloud, "feels the power of false faith, the faith of paranoia," and joins that old Cold War warrior, J. Edgar, "all conflict programmed out"—DeLillo lights on "a single seraphic word":

And you look at the things in the room, offscreen, unwebbed . . . the thick lived tenor of things . . . the apple core going sepia in the lunch tray . . . and the chipped rim of the mug that holds your yellow pencils, skewed all crazy . . . and you try to imagine the word on the screen becoming a thing in the world . . . its whisper of reconciliation, a word extending itself ever outward . . . but it's only a sequence of pulses on a dullish screen and all it can do is make you pensive—a word that spreads a longing through the raw sprawl of the city and out across the dreaming bourns and orchards to the solitary hills.

Peace. (825, 826)

"Longing on a large scale is what makes history" (11).

The lyrical assonance of DeLillo's prose—"chipped rim," "whisper of reconciliation," "raw sprawl"—embodies that longing while recognizing "only a sequence of pulses on a dullish screen." It mirrors Nick's longing, among others, with its hunger for "the grasp of objects that bind us to some betokening" and the loss that accompanies it in "the hour after sunset in a stillness that feels unceasing" (808). Nick also longs for his younger violent days of disarray, and DeLillo's "raw sprawl" encapsulates it in all its ambiguous and contradictory musings. But "the tissued grain of the deskwood alive in light" (827) rides in the same vision as do the yellow pencils "and the yellow of the yellow of the pencils." Emerson "preferred to balance himself at the brink of the apocalypse, before the fixing of nature, in a vision of all possibilities" (Hodder 1989, 92), and DeLillo, too, recognizes that power "resides in the moment of transition from a past to a new state" (1997, 84). That contemporary state appalls and kills, but it can also, if only momentarily, delight and transform. The perilous equilibrium of *Underworld,* as fragile as a spider's web shimmering in sunlight or shattered by a nuclear blast, resonates in DeLillo's aphoristic style and in the form of his masterpiece. Apocalypse can breed frissons of wonder as much as dread. DeLillo's novel, like Emerson's vision, "frustrates a habitually discursive reading" (Hodder 1989, 131), and if his ultimate vision remains provisional, terrifying, momentary, and hallucinatory, his practicing of that vision, his pursuit that takes him "out across the dreaming bourns and orchards to the solitary hills," does not.

Adam Begley has described *The Body Artist* as "a metaphysical ghost story" (2001, 12), but critics have also attacked it as vaporous, elusive, elliptical, opaque, enigmatic, listless, sterile, and tedious. The apparent ghostliness reflects DeLillo's extending and probing the kinds of epiphanies he explored in *Underworld,* and this pursuit suggests his developing, undermining, and subverting his "take" on the paranoid strictures of conspiracy theory and the conspiratorial state of mind. Conspiracy demands linearity, a plot that develops over time, a cause-and-effect specificity that has emerged from the religious and political overreaction to postmodern randomness and relativity. In undermining that linearity, which rests in part on the sense of time's passing in a systematic and goal-oriented manner, DeLillo upends the conspiracy mentality and eviscerates it, reaching for glimpses of the postmodern sublime.

"Time *seems* to pass," *The Body Artist* begins, and in that process "the world happens, unrolling into moments" (italics mine, 7). It is the moment that DeLillo zeroes in on here, fraught with its fragile existence in its sense of fading as soon as it appears, perhaps a particle when, once glimpsed, all too quickly turns into a wave and drifts away. With his use of second-person address, DeLillo connects the reader to a specific moment—"You stop to glance"—which he immediately describes as "a spider too pressed to its web." Such a moment resonates with Emersonian unity, the self and nature momentarily ensnared and entwined in "a quickness of light and a sense of things outlined precisely." In that instant consanguinity comes self-knowledge, not an intellectual apprehension but an instinctual intuitive one: "You know more surely who you are on a strong bright day after a storm when the smallest falling leaf is stabbed with self-awareness." As in Emerson's incarnation of such epiphanies, nature seems self-aware; that state is not merely relegated to human consciousness in isolation. Connections bristle here; the leaf and consciousness, caught instantaneously in precise language, in the length and rhythm of the line and paragraph, reflect each other. Both are stabbed with self-awareness. At that very moment, in this interpenetration of human consciousness and the natural environment, "the world comes into being, irreversibly, and the spider rides the wind-swayed web" (7).

Lauren Hartke, isolated, savoring death and her consciousness of it in the performance piece she creates later in the novel, recognizes what DeLillo is up to: "Maybe the idea is to think of time differently. . . . Stop time, or stretch it out, or open it up." It is not easy and is fraught with intimations of annihilation and loss, as Emerson and other romantic writers understood: "When time stops, so do we. We don't stop, we become stripped down, less self-assured" (107). Thus does DeLillo record the way the world registers on Lauren's consciousness, and thereby creates what Emerson hungered for in his "Divinity School Address," an "original relation" to the universe, original, perhaps, in the sense of origins, of the "fit" between the spider's web and human consciousness. Thus does DeLillo ultimately undermine conspiracy theorists and states of mind, focusing on time as a series of such moments, of such instants in the process of unfolding and revealing, for time only "*seems* to pass." As Osteen suggests, epiphany trumps irony here. This is DeLillo's antidote to paranoia and our conspiracy-addled culture.

Several such moments appear in *The Body Artist*, often in the presence of birds, like them often "elusive and mutely beautiful" (13). Gulls in flight "become . . . the slant carriers of all this rockbound time, taking it out of geology, out of science and mind, and giving it soar and loft and body" (113). In such moments birds can be "so sunstruck they were consumed by light" (21), prompting Lauren to consider "she'd somehow only now learned how to look. She'd never seen a thing so clearly . . . alert to the clarity of the moment but knew it was ending already . . . [as] if you've been near blind all your life" (22).

DeLillo's style struggles to break such moments down and open:

> She thought she saw a bird. Out of the corner of her eye she saw something rise past the window, eerie and birdlike but maybe not a bird. She looked and it was a bird, its flight line perfectly vertical, its streaked brown body horizontal, wings calmly stroking, a sparrow, not wind-hovering but generating lift and then instantly gone. (91)

Lauren decides that she has seen this only in retrospect, that she has to write it down and "re-create the ghostly moment . . . and how would she ever know for sure unless it happened again, and even then, she thought, and even then again" (91). Within such ghostly moments appears "Mr. Tuttle."

DeLillo's prose breaks down or opens up a half-conscious moment in time into its apparent images, its constituent parts—a brown body, wings generating lift. Seeing, thinking, concluding, at all times uncertain, participate in this processing of the moment, a meticulous deconstruction of it reconstructed into separate glimpses, separate senses, the only way perhaps language can really grapple with such experience. Where perception shimmers and shatters, there language falters and leaves a residue of strangeness, eeriness, ghostlier demarcations. The style slows the reader's reading down with its use of assonance, and DeLillo's meticulous cataloging of Lauren's consciousness. He suggests that "there has to be an imaginary point, a nonplace where language intersects with our perceptions of time and space" (99), and from that elusive vantage point, "there is no sequential order except for what we engender to make us safe in the world." Conspiracy, like most linear narratives, relies on sequential order and cause and effect, and we cannot live totally without these if only "to distinguish one part from another, this from that, now from then . . . by making arbitrary divisions" (83, 91). When their power is reduced, however, when their hold on the American mind is meticulously deconstructed, conspiracy necessarily loses the force and charisma of its spell.

DeLillo performs a similar operation in his description of a fallen paper clip, including the reader again in his use of the second person. The dropped clip becomes "a formless distortion of the teeming space around your body," its sound making "its way through an immense web of distances." The belated sound suggests the knowledge of what has fallen as the memory of the incident emerges to support it. The paper clip's "slipping off the edge of the page" slips into past time and memory, for then "it slipped off the edge of the page." Memory like consciousness half remembers, half sees as the paper clip makes "a sound for which there is no imitative word, the sound of a paperclip falling, but when you bend to pick it up, it isn't there" (89–90).

Mr. Tuttle—ghost, self-projection, the embodied disembodiment of grief and loss, or "a floating signifier" in the deconstructive and linguistic jargon that David Kipen (2001) uses, a postmodern self existing only in its relational impact on another, on Lauren—slips in between perception and memory, consciousness and the world, that "nonplace where language intersects with our perceptions of time and space" (99), a physically visible and visceral presence occupying the isolated moments of Lauren's being. Of course he talks like Lauren and Rey: how could he not? Of course he would pronounce such oracular truisms such as, "I am the moment. Being here has come to me" (74). Not for nothing is he unable to offer any "reassuring sequence" (77), confusing future and present. He threatens Lauren's sense of self as all such incarnations would, "unoccurring" as he is.

Lauren remains stunned and baffled by her husband Rey Roble's suicide, a much-married man who directed a film, *My Life for Yours*, and was drawn to "people in landscapes of estrangement . . . the poetry of alien places, where extreme situations become inevitable. . . . " (29). Rereading that opening scene, Lauren's and Rey's last morning together, we come upon his strange line: "I'm the one to moan. The terror of another ordinary day. You don't know yet" (15). This is underscored by the "noises in the wall" (17) of the haunted house, a situation Lauren realizes that Rey is about to discuss. Through the ordinary but conspicuously experienced separate moments within the "hyper-preparedness" of Lauren's conscious, complete with her sensations of smell and texture and sightings, we begin to sense Rey's own terror "or fear of believing, some displacement of self" (75). For Lauren it becomes "the wedge into ecstasy," into an experience beyond and outside the self; for Rey it becomes suicide.

Lauren can pursue the "lurid ruin" (116) that Rey's death confronts her with and descends into a solitary disconnection from that "soul extension, dumb guttural wonder" (37) that has always seemed to connect her to the natural world, but as a body artist she uses her body to perform various poses. Her belief and trust lie in the physicality of the body, perhaps another antidote to conspiratorial yearnings and speculations. She performs, exercises, scouts herself "to feel time go by, viscerally, even painfully" (104) to make it pass, unfold, surpass the single incantatory moments of "dumb guttural wonder" but also death. We must have narrative to move on, to survive, while at the same time recognizing the depth and exquisite densities of single elusive moments. Time also must be rooted in, experienced by the body, and from it, with it we build our myths of time.

Perhaps this underscores the postmodern myth or vision that celebrates discrete cubist fragments, each glittering and, at the same time, uneasily aligned to a wider narrative, contradictory, forever elusive, forever riding the webbed consciousness of paradox. Thus begins a mystic journey toward a different kind of Enlightenment, toward a full recognition of the postmodern sublime, as Leonard suggests, "embracing mystery . . . in this geography of the invisible [in] voices and visions, detachments and amazements . . . dark nights and rivers of light, awe and apparition, abandonment and madness, ecstasy and trance" (2001, 17). DeLillo's language wrestles with the same issues, intuitions, and intimations of Lauren's body: they both work to inscribe and describe, probing time, the self, space in minute detail, fleeing from or rejecting the metanarrative of the world in order to open it up as writer and performance artist. Use answering machines and a videotape of deserted roads in Finland in your art, as DeLillo uses language in all of its cool oracular often painfully conceptualized incarnation.

The calculated elusiveness of *The Body Artist* celebrates precisely what paranoid fantasies, fanatical fundamentalisms, and constructed conspiracies cannot. This slim novel, its postmodern performance built on moments separated from but connected to other separate moments, constructs a re-enactment of human consciousness and perception, both of themselves and the world they inhabit, not in some absolutist simplistic manner but as riddled with ambiguities and paradox as consciousness itself. Lauren and DeLillo earn their crisp bright vision, the antidote to conspiracy's relentless draining of the human spirit, at novel's end: "She threw the window open. She didn't know why she did this. Then she knew. She wanted to feel the sea tang on her face and the flow of time in her body, to tell her who she was" (124).

6

Thomas Pynchon

*The Functions of Conspiracy and
the Performance of Paranoia*

If Mark Twain casts a long shadow as the patriarch of modern American prose, according to Sherwood Anderson, Ernest Hemingway, and William Faulkner, then Thomas Pynchon certainly casts his as the godfather of the contemporary conspiracy novel, beginning with *V.* in 1963 and *The Crying of Lot 49* in 1966 and culminating in the sumptuously gargantuan *Gravity's Rainbow* (1973) and *Mason & Dixon* (1997). Not only does Pynchon focus on conspiracy and paranoia as distinct American obsessions and anxieties, but he also employs all the postmodern techniques in doing so from an assault on linear metanarratives to a delight in everything from parody to pastiche, fantastically indeterminate yarns to wildly inventive and satirical song lyrics. To read Pynchon is to immerse oneself in fiction that gyrates and spins from tragedy to comedy, loss to lunacy, religion to ribald revelries. He has so thoroughly cornered the literary market on conspiracy and all its attributes that *The Crying of Lot 49* remains his most taught novel at the university level, and his vision of conspiracies and paranoia approaches the open-ended mysteries of the postmodern sublime.

Pynchon's novels have lured literary theorists and critics to such an extent that they have spawned an industry. Not since T. S. Eliot or Faulkner has there been such an amount of critical material. The list overwhelms and stuns the avid reader, rife with Derridian deconstruction, Lacanian loss, Foucauldian power plays, Baudrillardian simulacra, Gnostic prophecies, Eastern epiphanies, and the like. The anti-linear structures of the novels almost insure that no reader will read the same text in a similar fashion, each in pursuit of his or her own point of view, focusing on some elegant fragment that purports to reveal the secret of the entire fiction, the key that unlocks the code. While I have tried to pull back and first look at the fiction from the wider perspective that I associate with the postmodern sublime's ideal of open-ended fluidity and the spirited pursuit of elusive meaning and significance, I cannot say that I am completely immune to the whispers of purported allegorical significance and elusive symbolic imaginings that haunt Pynchon's texts, but let us try to start at a "bottom line" and work our way upward or outward.

One of the key techniques of Pynchon's prose involves the density of his sentences and paragraphs. The amount of information he crams into a single sentence often boggles the mind, rife as they are with arcane information, sensuous images, imaginative riffs, and turbulent exposition. Turn a page in a Pynchon novel and you come across the look of stylistic density that suggests in appearance the fat swollen paragraphs of the later Henry James. Any opening sentence or paragraph will do:

> One summer afternoon Mrs. Oedipa Maas came home from a Tupperware party whose hostess had put perhaps too much kirsch in the fondue to find that she, Oedipa, had been named executor, or she supposed executrix, of the estate of one Pierce Inverarity, a California real estate mogul who had once lost two million dollars in his spare time but still had assets numerous and tangled enough to make the job of sorting it all out more than honorary. (1999, 1)

In one sentence we come upon the season and the time of day, the strange name of some woman who must be a suburbanite—Tupperware, hostess, kirsch, fondue—another strange character with a name that is practically unpronounceable, and a capsule history of his losing two million dollars "in his spare time," which doesn't seem to have dented his assets any, which remain "numerous and tangled." One Oedipa Mass has thus been presented with a very real task out of the blue. She then remembers a hotel room in Mazatlán, two hundred birds in the lobby, a sunrise at Cornell University, a tune from the fourth movement of the Bartók Concerto for Orchestra, a bust of Jay Gould that Inverarity "kept over the bed on a shelf so narrow for it she'd always had the hovering fear it would someday topple on them." Had he died that way, "crushed by the only ikon in the house"? How does she know so much about his bedroom? Had they gone to Cornell together? Where is Mazatlán? Why Bartók? Jay Gould was a notorious robber baron and gambler. Does that make Inverarity his disciple? How do fondue and numerous funds go together? Are the names silly because they are meant to be cartoonish and comic, the stick figures of some allegory or satiric vision? Why, when wondering about Inverarity, does Oedipa think of herself as "so sick?" Too much kirsch perhaps? And what are we to make of someone who harbors "the hovering fear" of a bust falling on someone else in bed? Is there more here than meets the eye? Or less?

Pynchon's paragraph reads like exposition, at first. It suggests a historical time period—that summer when everyone was eating fondue—upon which he lavishes his details, piling them on, at once seemingly realistic, at once silly and outrageous. The paragraph looks like expository prose. There are no quotations, no asides. The block of language on the page suggests authority and background, a Jamesian density, a Faulknerian depth, and yet we do not find out until the beginning of the second paragraph that Oedipa discovers her being named executrix in a letter. We know only that she discovers her naming, a kind of first step in a possible quest to untangle numerous assets that leaves her speaking the name of God while being "stared at by the greenish dead eye of the TV tube."

From such exposition Pynchon will suddenly leap into the fantastic or absurd without warning. He grounds his tale, anchors it in a plethora of details that may or may not connect—Bartók? God? TV? Jay Gould?—and then suddenly shifts to a long-distance call at three in the morning a year ago that reveals a "voice beginning in heavy Slavic tones as second secretary at the Transylvanian Consulate, looking for an escaped bat; modulated to comic-Negro, then on into hostile Pachuco dialect" and turns out to be Inverarity, though he calls Oedipa Margo, and then impersonates Lamont Cranston, the Shadow from an old radio crime series. The structure of Pynchon's paragraphs suggests a hefty "metaparagraph," filled with necessary exposition and information at the beginning of a novel, but the information undermines such linearity and collapses inward upon itself. Is "The Shadow" a clue? Does Margo work with or for him? Why is the Muzak at the market Vivaldi's Kazoo Concerto with Boyd Beaver as soloist? How can these odd separate bits add up to anything?

Pynchon presents at first the illusion of ordinary exposition, but then he rips the fabric into colorful tatters. He destroys "common-sensical" and conventional reality very quickly, immediately unmooring the reader. Where are we? Who are these creatures? In doing so Pynchon grounds his flights of fancy, his more fantastic and surreal riffs and tangents in the length and weight of the sentence and paragraph. The effects render the "realistic" strange and fantastic, at the same time they allow for more fantastic details and episodes to follow. Confronted with such an abundance of arcane facts and strange lore, the reader readies herself to look for the key to it all. Like coming upon the strange argot in Anthony Burgess's *A Clockwork Orange,* we become alert to a strange world, a different place, and must keep our eyes open to look for clues as to where we are or what is going on.

Conspiracies loom in the wings: who is behind this? Inverarity? Maas in her kirsch-addled state? Pynchon? What started out as historical, social, and cultural "reality" has shifted to somewhere else, seamlessly. The distance between the daily world and a more imaginative, psychological, or "fantastic" one—Oedipa's troubled mind? Pynchon's crazed leaps?—blurs and crumbles. We are either released from the world we know and expect or the linearity of that world that suddenly proves to be loonier and odder than we ever imagined. God resides there somewhere, the television eyes Oedipa strangely, and a "hovering fear" smolders within her, but these radical disruptions or disconnections reveal nothing about where they will lead. *If* they will lead.

In his review of *Mason & Dixon,* W. M. Hagen "speaks of a 'wall' of ignorance around the reader: the business of the 'wall' or the limits of one's knowing, creates a space for Pynchon's special brand of strangeness, of connections suggested or speculated that cannot absolutely be discounted" (Clerc 1983, 23). This is an extremely helpful comment, for there can be so many historical references, jargon-laced conversations, textual allusions, inside jokes between characters, and bizarre asides in Pynchon's writing that the reader automatically feels left out, condemned to the uncomfortable role of outsider and bystander, someone kept out of the secret or the context of the moment as if permanently exiled from significance and meaning. Pynchon's is not a "user-friendly" text. We intrude on another world that resembles our own slightly, but we are left without a compass, desperate to find our way in or out, eager to latch onto something recognizable—A summary? A revelatory description? An expository thread that will link one episode to another?—whether it be a trace of plot, a revelation of character, or something similar.

Faulkner often presents a scene in medias res, an action that occurs directly in front of the reader but without explanation or context. He later provides that context, fills in the blanks, and reveals the bottom line, psychological or otherwise, that most modernist fiction finally discloses. A figure in a Jamesian carpet eventually emerges. In Pynchon's work this is not the case. There is a carpet, but what figures there are strut and shimmer, disperse and dissolve, without acknowledging the reader's presence and questions. Thus we are left on our own, afoot in some surrealistically Whitmanic rush of information, characters, incidents, and objects hurled at us by the author, apparently disconnected from any overall structure or framework, from any scenic certainties. We intrude on a strange realm, filled with gothic fears and intimations of death, bubbling with paranoia and the whiff of secret cabals. Aware of such differences and remoteness, the reader yearns for the figure in the carpet, for "something beyond" or within, a thread, a crumb, a knot of coherence that will tie such separate and seemingly isolated episodes together in some recognizable fashion, fearing that much may remain untranslatable, merely overheard and beyond our range and capabilities to figure it out.

The text that Pynchon creates, ruptures, breaks open, and scatters like the most postmodern of magicians practically forces the reader to latch on to a "typical" encounter, a primal scene, or a momentary epiphany in search of the smoking gun, the missing piece, the key to the code in order to try and understand and comprehend the whole. We look for the visionary framework that would make sense of these disparate incidents and anomalies, but Pynchon only continues to set us and the text adrift, plunging into his own labyrinthine vision and withholding the thread to lead us to what we imagine may be the center or the core.

Allegory like metaphor describes one thing and suggests another in a meaning that may be oblique but that remains essential, not contingent. Christian allegory in our culture forces the text into a pattern of discovery and redemption from the dark night of the soul to a resurrection of the spirit. If we can decode the allegorical scrim, we can grasp the framework and significance of the text. However, allegory can prove to be ironic when the meaning it asserts contrasts with the words and images the writer has used. At the same time writers, such as Hawthorne, have recognized that allegorical meanings remain impermanent; they are locked into particular historical and cultural contexts and are linked to specific times and places. If they are so locked in, then we should be able to translate them by reestablishing the cultural context as carefully as we can by, in the example above, relying on the Bible or in a novel such as *Uncle Tom's Cabin,* unearthing the belief in the Christian-saturated, sentimental domesticity of the mid-nineteenth century.

From a modernist and postmodernist point of view, allegory tyrannizes a text. It can reduce it to a simplistic code that may be easily translatable. What Pynchon and his characters do, akin to Hawthorne's shifting use of allegory—one character interprets things in his rigid monistic manner, another in her more ambiguous open-ended manner—is insist on the tyranny of their own particular interpretation in their own particular ways. Such allegorizing can become a fetish, since Pynchon appears to be indulging in it as much as his most rigid characters. The text, disrupted and disconnected as it is, underscores the tyranny of such allegorizing by leaping from one allegory to another, from one interpreted incident or interpreting character to another. The reader, desperate for a framework and a scaffold within and upon which to place and stage the text, may easily side with one character or side with Pynchon when he pauses to make his allegorizing comments relatively clear and precise, only to lose her way yet again when the text moves on and shifts to something entirely different. Pynchon both exercises and undercuts the urge to allegorize, as if bobbing up out of a stormy sea to catch a sudden glimpse of land before sinking again into the fearsome turbulence that surrounds him. His texts, which force the reader to try and interpret and allegorize as she goes along, also continuously undermine that process. We are again riding a magic carpet in an often-nightmarish sky with no other figure or guide in sight.

Despite or because of the deadly seriousness of his vision—conspiracy, technology, private hallucination and/or public despair and dismay, the particular instances of which we will explore here in a selection of his novels—Pynchon consistently undercuts it by creating characters with satirically silly names; orchestrating the farce and slapstick humor of cartoons; tossing in song lyrics, doggerel, verses, and poetic pranks; interrupting as a consciously conversational narrator to comment on his own contrivances or disagree with something he's just set up, nudging the reader with a knowing phrase or aside; breaking into his own text to rearrange a sentence, add a thought about a certain character's absurd behavior, wit, or demise; delighting in the drunken and drugged revelries of sex and violence that suggest college fraternity parties run amuck as well as the hallucinatory episodes of the 1960s; and radically shifting the tone, register, syntax, and atmosphere of such stunts, incidents, occurrences, and tangents. This can become off-putting and self-indulgent as Pynchon spoofs his own spoofing, fiddling while Rome burns, as if he has taken to heart the notion that it is almost impossible to hit a moving target.

If there lurks a heart within this gothic darkness and these spotlighted pyrotechnics, it throbs with a pervasive fear of, interest in, and evasion of death, which at any time underlies and undercuts all things. A pervasive paranoia, corruptly puritanical in its insistence that something pernicious and insidious lies beyond appearances in terms of some intuitively realized forces or some ultimate elite cabal, penetrates the soul and the world. As in Poe's fictions, many of Pynchon's characters, including at times Pynchon himself, focus so intensely on their own obsessions that they seem almost demonically possessed by the nightmarish world that they often create beyond them. Western consumerism and technology conspire to evade this vision, reducing it to recognizable conspiracies and plots, but in doing so they only add to it. Since the consumer culture and technology in Pynchon's world do not ultimately satisfy some deep human yearning, they only extend that yearning and desire that can only be quenched or completed in death.

Cosmic tensions, the shards of the Judeo-Christian world, intimations of possible immortality, and strange epiphanies haunt Pynchon's landscape. The experience of absence and shattered worldviews contribute to that aura of possible presence and transcendence that lurks just beyond or within the text. Pynchon's thoroughly postmodern vision, a classic of its kind, often suggests mystical musings, a hunger for the invisible, the impossible and the irredeemable. The gothic contours of such an outlook reduce the world to power plays, insiders versus outsiders, the self versus the state, master against slave, but also open it up to glimpses of unfathomable mystery, weird epiphanies of language and light that dissolve as readily as they appear. Pynchon's characters often feel, as the reader does, that they are buried alive in someone else's conspiracy, puppet-creatures cut loose from their strings in someone else's scenario and vision, footloose but still entangled, lost but still imprisoned in a strange landscape or labyrinth beyond their abilities to comprehend it. Demons hover here and haunt the reader as well. A "hovering fear" is never very far away, and fathoming it remains just out of reach.

Mired in too much information, flooded with details and characters and incidents, webbed in dense prose, dangled somewhere between inner nightmares and an outer nightmare world that may be no more than a reflection of those inner dreams, perched outside of what may be some lethally recognizable plot and scenario, desperate for signposts that prove as impermanent as the characters and author who provide them, initiated into sudden delirious romps of sex and violence, erupting into fits of farce and hysteria, the Pynchon character and the reader embark on a quest that reveals all the yearning and longing of such a narrative path and yet erases that very path, if indeed one exists, that we attempt to follow.

Pierce Inverarity's will launches Oedipa Maas in *The Crying of Lot 49* out into the world in search of his estate and legacy. Feeling trapped, "a captive maiden" in her own suburban tower of Kinneret-Among-the-Pines with a husband who once believed in used cars and now cannot believe in his new job as a disk jockey for station KCUF, she lights out for the territory of San Narciso in Southern California "with no idea that she was moving toward anything new" (1999, 13).

Most critics have discussed the open-endedness of Pynchon's shortest and most widely read novel as if it somehow avoids the dilemma that Oedipa finds herself in: is there an underground mail system named Tristero, or is she merely experiencing the generalized paranoia that permeates all of Pynchon's texts? The novel's irresolution precisely mirrors the postmodern sense of conspiracy and often the postmodern sublime, in that no particular plot is found and resolved, but the pursuit of the possibility of its existence remains intact. That pursuit of a yet unrecognized, unidentified, or nonexistent conspiracy becomes its own self-justifying reason for being.

The Crying of Lot 49 does not undermine conspiracy thinking or theory (even though it offers no solutions to the specific conspiracy that might be the Tristero) but perpetuates it in Pynchon's craftily designed irresolution. Most conspiracy theorists thrive on their desire to locate the missing piece, the elusive detail, but were they to do so the quest would be complete and the case closed. Better to persist in an ongoing investigation—it keeps conspiracy theories and theorists alive—than to find it concluded and finished. Pynchon creates and manipulates this insistent and compulsive trajectory.

In many ways like pragmatism Pynchon's novel opposes what Louis Menand has described as "the idolatry of concepts" (2001, 425): "The so-

lution has been to shift the totem of legitimacy from premises to procedures" (432). This pragmatic pattern, shorn of the Enlightenment optimistic faith in progress and ultimate solution, underscores a postmodern perspective in which paranoia and victimhood have usurped that faith and
substituted their own anxiety and dread. Such a functional approach to
things "makes the value of an idea [in this case the Tristero] not its corre-
spondence to a preexisting reality or a metaphysical truth, but simply the
difference it makes in the life of the group" (431), or in Oedipa's case, in
the life and propulsion of her quest.

Pynchon's view of Oedipa's world conjures up a cosmos in which everything is defined functionally, relationally, rather than "essentially." It opposes absolutes, divine revelation, the idea of truth as an independent
source, a transcendent invisible order, and a cosmic plan, exactly as the
pragmatists did without the Enlightenment values that sustained their vision. From such a pragmatic and paranoid-postmodern perspective, as
Menand acknowledges, "relations will be more important than categories;
functions, which are variable, will be more important than purposes,
which are fixed in advance; transitions will be more important that boundaries; sequences will be more important than hierarchies" (2001, 124). This
vision underscores Pynchon's novel, within which Oedipa is searching for
a final revelation and answer that will never come. Her quest reverberates
in the crying.

Oedipa's quest, therefore, from the novel's point of view and structure
enlists pragmatic procedures, disconnected from enlightened reason and
cause and effect, which may exist only in her mind, in a strange and more
terrifying contemporary world of powerlessness, paranoia, and victimhood
that is abetted by and saturated with the orgy of information produced by
technological leaps in communications from television to computers. Even
if Oedipa perceives her ego as "her tower," she feels "that what really keeps
her where she is is magic, anonymous and malignant, visited on her from
outside and for no reason at all" (1999, 11–12), the black magic of a postmodern world.

In his book on the foundations and founding fathers of pragmatism,
Menand suggests that these pragmatic procedures "[belong] to a disestab-
lishmentarian impulse in American culture . . . the protestantization, so to
speak, of Protestantism" (2001, 89), that same impulse that breeds various
religious sects and splinter groups that continue to fragment and "purify"

themselves in their compulsive need to retreat from the mainstream in order to preserve more basic fundamentalist values. Such sects oppose the mainstream since that is where such values become diluted and compromised. Thus the Davidians branch off from other branches, and thus various exiled groups in *The Crying of Lot 49* become Peter Pinguid disciples, textual scholars, Inamorati Anonymous advocates, anarchists, members of the Societies for the Propagation of Christian Knowledge, and grimly predetermined Scurvhamites.

We can apply the same pragmatic procedures to the text of the novel that Oedipa seems to be applying to the world around her. The first level of the text presents an incredibly fragmented landscape, battered by disruptions and distortions from rock bands to cartoon encounters, crazily named characters to sudden eruptions of angst and anxiety, at once comic, satiric, sardonic, and tragic, an atomized world of flotsam and jetsam, the postmodern experience, that seems to flaunt its own incoherence and disunity. Siding with Oedipa, however, the reader begins to perceive a possible second level in the text in which a mystery or puzzle seems to be lurking, a deep structure that is connected to historical fact and incident, to the Holy Roman Empire, phony Pony Express riders, secret messages, the omnipresent muted posthorn image and to contemporary corporations, secret societies, and Pierce Inverarity's will. A third level, however, suggests that such connections may be circumstantial and coincidental, that they are overdetermined and ultimately ambiguous, and that an "ultimate" postmodern world of total disruption, a poststructuralist's delight in no deep structure whatsoever, exists and undermines any possibility of answers.

Another possibility suggests that what Oedipa really discovers is America in all its apocalyptic fragmentation, a place of frustrated exiles, loners, outsiders, victims, and other disinherited and disenfranchised souls who may or may not be using an underground postal system in an effort to commiserate or stay in touch with one another: "For here were God knew how many citizens, deliberately choosing not to communicate by U.S. Mail . . . it was a calculated withdrawal, from the life of the Republic, from its machinery . . . this withdrawal was their own, unpublicized, private" (1999, 101).

Like Oedipus before her, Oedipa Maas may, in fact, discover her own complicity in a lost underground world of disaffected and alienated souls.

Beneath or within the mass (Maas) popular culture lurks another world of the disconnected, Oedipa's connections revealing this vision to her. As a character she remains relatively passive, open, reflexive and reactive, a kind of barometer for the very communications-saturated nation that surrounds and inhabits her. She experiences the postmodern predicament, what John Johnston has called the "radical uncertainty about how to process the information that she had acquired. . . . Oedipa is less the site of an experience than the site where multiple connections become uncertain" (1998, 39, 47). She also is the only female among males, directed by Inverarity, as much a victim of his will, possible conspiracy and popular culture as the reader is to Pynchon.

The reader's experience reading the book reflects Oedipa's own. Her collection of information parallels ours, as more information overloads the text, which itself leads only to more information, further chaos, and possible further evidence of the Tristero's existence. Mesmerized by her growing concern with Tristero's existence or nonexistence—for her it becomes a bipolar vision: either it exists, or it does not—Oedipa becomes part of what she sees but is unable to see that that is what may be happening. Wandering into a centerless maze, stumbling on "an eternal chasm between dogma and aimlessness" (McHoul and Wills 1990, 94), she maintains her quest, as does Pynchon, and arrives at the novel's end awaiting yet more information which, true to the novel's trajectory and structure, can only lead to further "crying," to other possibilities that will remain possibilities. Pynchon keeps Oedipa, the reader, and the novel perched on the lip of this carefully controlled and crafted abyss, this "either/or" that remains precariously balanced and a perilous equilibrium, a structural strategy that keeps the conspiratorial theorist still searching and hoping, if only for the next circumstantial clue.

Pynchon meticulously plots Oedipa's progress in terms of the connections she makes and how she makes them. It is a process most of his characters will pursue in later novels. At first her mind leaps from one random association to another, from the Cornell campus to a bust of Jay Gould, each of which is connected in some way to her past relationship to Inverarity. She literally describes as a "vast sprawl of houses" the city of San Narciso that she first looks down on but then sees them "like a well-tended crop." From that simile she rapidly moves on to a more metaphorical description, describing the place as the "first printed circuit" she had ever seen inside a transistor radio "with the same unexpected, astonishing clarity as the circuit card had." She then ups the ante of the analogy, for "there were to both outward patterns a hieroglyphic sense of concealed meaning, of an intent to communicate." Now the scene has become something to decode, something to translate. Something has been concealed within it that is intended to communicate. To her. From sprawl to circuit, from "ordered swirl" to "hieroglyphic sense": Oedipa, like Hawthorne discovering the scarlet letter on the second floor of the Customs House in Salem, moves briskly from literal to allegorical to symbolic description, changing physical objects to icons that carry more metaphysical meanings. But she doesn't stop there. She hovers on the edge of "an odd, religious instant," of revelation that strikes her "on some other frequency, or out of the eye of some whirlwind rotating too slow for her heated skin even to feel the centrifugal coolness of . . . words . . . being spoken." Such a revelation carries with it an apocalyptic aura that the image of the whirlwind suggests. Pynchon has slipped through discrete boundaries, ushered Oedipa and the reader into some other realm, some other world, such that, as David Porush contends, "the ground of the literal threatens to dissolve in favor of the system of interlocking meaning implied in those metaphors" (1994, 43)—printed circuit, hieroglyphic sense, an intent to communicate, the eye of some whirlwind. At such a moment Porush concludes, "epistemology and ontology . . . dissolve into each other [and create] a transcendental realm" (43) or at least the possibility of one, a liminal space with its frisson of postmodern paranoia and the postmodern sublime.

Oedipa can never hear or translate what "words were being spoken," and the "religious instant" passes away as quickly as it had occurred "as if a cloud had approached the sun or the smog thickened" (1999, 14–15). The incident becomes a memory, lodged just beyond her comprehension as she remains, "remembering her idea about a slow whirlwind, words she couldn't hear" (16). The fragility of her perception and the likelihood that nothing happened at all haunt her and set up the pattern or parameters of her eventual search for the Tristero.

At the beginning of Chapter Three, in a paragraph that contains three "ifs," three "logicallys," and one "perhaps"—one thinks of Hawthorne's multiple choices craftily held in place by his characters' devotion to either/or solutions, while he as the author transcends them—Pynchon exposes Oedipa's developing perspective. Perhaps she is drawn to her quest because it may "bring to an end her encapsulation in her tower." Perhaps she comes to label "something . . . the Tristero System or often only the Tristero" because Tristero "might be something's secret title." Her quest probably started with "that night's infidelity with Metzger"; that "would logically be the starting point for it; logically." The second "logically," of course, undercuts the very idea that logic could in any way have been part of what seems to be happening. In any case all of this "would come to haunt her most, perhaps: the way it fitted, logically together." A logical fit becomes a haunting "as if (as she'd guessed that first minute in San Narciso) there were revelation in progress around her" (31). Pynchon provides more than enough qualifiers for the reader to be wary of Oedipa's progress, and yet he has saturated the novel with so many possible connections that we all too easily can fall in lockstep behind her. That "revelation in progress," so tenuous to begin with, alerts us to Oedipa's own innocence and possible ignorance with its attendant paranoia that suggests something may be up somewhere, most likely "all around her" (31).

The tale of the American soldiers' bones in Lago di Pietà in Italy and Miles's (a member of the rock band The Paranoids) remembering a similar incident in a play he has just seen, "The Courier's Tragedy," leads Oedipa to interrogate the play's director, Randolph Driblette, which leads to her realization that Driblette's smile "was exactly the same look he'd coached his cast to give each other whenever the subject of the Trystero assassins came up. The knowing look you get in your dreams from a certain unpleasant figure" (61). Oedipa is off and running. And so are we.

At one point in her conversation with inventor John Nefastis about Maxwell's Demon and the concept of entropy, Oedipa wonders "if the Demon exists only because the two equations [between thermodynamics and information theory] look alike? Because of the metaphor?" (85). She later recognizes that "the act of metaphor then was a thrust at truth and a lie, depending where you were: inside, safe, or outside, lost" (105). Pynchon here relies on two of the basic assumptions of the postmodern perspective that the act of observation affects observation itself and that language may be nothing more than a self-referential and self-reflexive code that generates metaphors, which feed on themselves—like Robert Frost's "Design"—but lead only back into the linguistic morass out of which they have come.

Thus Oedipa's impasse: "Behind the hieroglyphic streets there would either be a transcendent meaning, or only the earth. . . . Another mode of meaning behind the obvious. Either Oedipa in the orbiting ecstasy of a true paranoia, or a real Tristero. For there either was some Tristero beyond the appearance of the legacy America, or there was just America . . . " (150–51). The possibilities that the Tristero exists, that it is a hoax staged by Inverarity, that Oedipa is hallucinating and paranoid, or that she is a victim of her own cause-and-effect logic and/or her sense of victim-hood gather and proliferate. In every case all, as Brian McHale asserts, possibilities "are logically exclusive of one another." They are "probability functions . . . each of the four possibilities represents a virtual state of the same underlying semiotic structure" (Johnston 1998, 43). The novel circles back on itself, its last line the same as the title, a kind of whirlpool from which no "ultimate" meaning can escape except the paranoid pragmatic procedures at large in a postmodern space.

As William James explained, "Thinking just is a circular process, in which some end, some imagined outcome, is already present at the start of any train of thought" (Menand 2001, 353). Pynchon's outcome exists in his sustained open-endedness within which specific conspiracies may be derailed and unproved, but the conspiratorial impulse continues to thrive and expand, feeding on its own compulsive paranoia. As Hanjo Berressem suggests, "The apocalypse is not a final cataclysm, it is *inherent* in every sign. It is not their destruction that is apocalyptic, but their growth and continuation" (1993, 114). It is the immanence of that conspiratorial impulse that remains intact, free-floating, ever present, pervasive, not the existence of some transcendent cabal. Such apocalyptic yearnings have always fueled American culture and fiction, but Pynchon incarnates them in full cry in our contemporary times.

Generally speaking, Pynchon applies the second law of thermodynamics, the existence of entropy in every system, to his fiction. Each act produces a loss of energy in some fashion, as every closed system harbors within itself its own eventual breakdown, even though there are variables that cannot be accounted for, since energy can be dispersed in a million different ways. Pynchon's application of this law to communications suggests that more and/or too much information can only increase entropy, can only lead not to further knowledge but to further chaos and dissolution, as if emergence theory, pressed beyond comprehensible limits, like all metaphor must break down. Robert Frost once described metaphor as riding on its own melting, that is, it can take us to some newer level of insight and possibly "revelation," but like all human wisdom or glimpses of "the truth," it finally dissolves and makes way for yet another metaphor, another revelation that helps us, as Emerson would suggest, climb "the stairway of surprise." For Pynchon entropy appears to be the only metaphor that does not break down, that remains intact in his fictional cosmos, his framework for his vision of our contemporary world.

In fact Oedipa's initial suburban world reveals a kind of entropy in its disconnected, glib, and superficial manner. Her swiftly plunging into ideas of conspiracy, revelation, and hidden meaning, while generated by Inverarity's will, nevertheless could also suggest her overreaction to her prior pedestrian entropic experience of her environment. It's as if entropy breeds conspiracy as much as conspiracy, once rigidly formed, immediately begins to breed entropy. The tower of Oedipa's ego suggests a closed system within which entropy will automatically occur, unless she manages to escape from it, and yet in doing so, in moving briskly from a passive and reactive mode of thinking to a more active and conspiracy-tinged one, she only assures that entropy will again occur.

Entropy, like postmodernism and deconstruction, is both an antidote to and a force that helps initiate conspiracy theory. This unrelieved polarization operates at the dark heart of Pynchon's second novel, deconstructed only perhaps by the even bleaker view of an America populated by loners, exiles, alienated individuals, and isolated drifters. And that view, of course, is played off against the Yoyodyne culture of corporate efficiency, functionality, and group response. In either case Pynchon seems convinced that we seek models of explanation at the same time recognizing that all models of this kind necessarily break down and collapse under their own weight.

In *The Crying of Lot 49* entropy in terms of information overload remains intact, although one could also argue that Oedipa becomes the novel's Maxwell's Demon, separating the fast from the slow molecules of incident and episode, as she sees them, in an attempt to keep the novel in perpetual motion. The novel's open-endedness does achieve a kind of state of perpetual motion, since nothing is or can be resolved. Is that what conspiracy theorists try to achieve, a perpetual motion that Pynchon knows must eventually decay and can never be permanent but that provides the illusion of an ongoing investigation, a continuing pursuit of the unpursuable? Is this the secret that underlies metaphor and language? It is the crying that persists despite the recognition that what it cries for can never be found. That is our lot in life, saturated as it is in contemporary times by paranoia and postmodern disruptions. So Pynchon keeps us perilously perched, seeking the conspiracy that will connect all the dots, recognizing that there can be no such thing, certain only that death and decay are inevitable and that most of us continue to look to some "priesthood of some remote culture; perhaps to a descending angel" (152).

Gravity's Rainbow looms like Olympus or a Himalayan peak surrounded by mountains of criticism, lesser peaks but towering in their own right. One approaches the ascent carefully, the air thinning as you struggle from precipice to crag, at all times dwarfed by Pynchon's achievement and the sheer turbulent bulk of an American *Ulysses*, akin to such other literary wonders as *Absalom, Absalom!* and *Moby-Dick*.

From the first "screaming across the sky" to Captain Geoffrey "Pirate" Prentice's famous Banana Breakfasts, from page three to page five, the reader already experiences vertigo. The nightmare of flight and collapse shifts to the vapor trail of a V-2 rocket, Prentice's sprawled hung-over mates, the odor of breakfast described as a defense against death, a Romanian's paranoid fantasy about Transylvanian Magyars, Prentice's strange talent for slipping into others' fantasies, three songs, W. C. Fields, H. A. Loaf, and the attack of a giant Adenoid. Are we dreaming or awake? Where, at the very least, is an Oedipa Maas to cling to?

Beginning any new novel we like to be seduced, to submit to the spell of the text, giving it the benefit of the doubt and surrendering our critical faculties, more or less, while the words tantalize and dance before us. With *Gravity's Rainbow* we let ourselves be sucked into a maelstrom of language and then become desperate to make connections, look for clues, make sense of what's happening on the page. Mired in details we long for context, eager to figure out a framework or blueprint and yet ride with the strange and often alien images and incidents Pynchon presents.

We become conspiracy theorists in search of the overall plan, as the novel, a conspiracy in its own right with its assault on modernist conventions and linear metanarratives, lures us onward. We begin to perform the role of several of Pynchon's characters, of Tyrone Slothrop or Pointsman, determined to put the pieces together and not only endure but prevail over the wildly disconnected text. We begin to suspect as Pynchon sets up the various episodes, the burgeoning web of characters, and the harrowing truth about the V-2 rocket, that our own paranoia—This *is Gravity's Rainbow*! It *is* an important book! It will be *impossible* to understand!—"is nothing less than the onset, the leading edge, of the discovery *that everything is connected,* everything in the Creation . . . " (1973, 703).

Gravity's Rainbow functions as a conspiracy. We feel forced to seek an order behind the visible text and tales. We begin early on to speculate whether or not there is some cabal present or nothing. Even the absence of visible connections suggests that these lie just beyond our reach. We scan for signs, look for evidence, as Kathleen Stewart emphasizes, "waiting for something to happen—a drama, an endpoint, something to break the enclosure of untouchable systems and the drone of an endlessly repeating present" (1999, 16). As de Tocqueville takes to task the American mind in a democracy, we experience "an ardent and sometimes an undiscerning passion . . . craving to discover general laws in everything, to include a great number of objects under the same formula, and to explain a mass of facts by a single cause" (1945, 16). *Gravity's Rainbow* assaults and forever disrupts that yearning, threatens whatever logic of metaphor, allegorical scaffolding, or chain reaction we think we see emerging within the text in Pynchon's burgeoning language, at once "fantastic, incorrect, overburdened, and loose, almost always vehement and bold" (62).

The novel, structured like a conspiracy, undermines all those specific conspiracies it pays homage to. History and, by analogy, all linear meta-narratives reveal a terrible truth: "What passes is a truth so terrible that history—at best a conspiracy, not always among gentlemen, to defraud—will never admit it" (1973, 164). The text never really connects the dots but creates trails, crumbs for the reader to follow in order to try and make sense of what is going on. It is the postmodern compact, the paranoid covenant to suggest all kinds and degrees of secret conspiracies and leave them unresolved, hovering on the brink of extinction, if in fact they ever really existed at all. Pynchon and the novel conspire to initiate and undermine links that seem to lead to deeper truths. Like Slothrop we can stalk the Firm, try to figure out exactly how "Pirate" Prentice connects with Teddy Bloat who connects with Roger Mexico who connects with Edward W. A. Pointsman who connects with Brigadier Pudding who connects, somehow, with L. Jamf, who has invented Imipolex G, which is connected to Slothrop's erections and the V-2 rocket. The Firm swallows the book—

"No one has ever left the Firm alive, no one in history—and no one ever will" (543)—but if history remains a conspiracy to defraud, then what seems at first intimately connected may only exist in a conspiracy theorist's mind.

The reader can play the conspiracy game as most critics have. We begin to cross-reference names and objects, search for hidden networks and labyrinthine webs of intrigue, precisely what Pynchon has in mind, having created this paranoid epic out of just such impulses and intuitions, the heart of a postmodern darkness. Like a web the structure lures and entraps, but when Slothrop and others finally make it into the Zone, ambiguities rule, overdetermination thrives, and everything blurs and dissolves. At one point Seaman Bodine offers, while laughing, "*Everything* is some kind of a plot, man," while various plots point in various directions, and Slothrop continues to hope that "this network of all plots may yet carry him [and the reader] to freedom" (603).

John Storey views *Gravity's Rainbow* as a series of perpetual presents, a spatial sequencing of radically different incidents that create emotional involvement at one minute and ironic detachment at the next (1998, 187, 195). Epiphanies flourish and flame out. Revelations resonate and retreat. Are we to dance to Enzian's tune that "our real Destiny [as] the scholar-magicians of the Zone" is to locate "a Text, to be picked to pieces, annotated, explicated, and masturbated till it's all squeezed limp of its last drop" (1973, 520)? Can we assume "that this holy Text had to be the Rocket," or seduced by the rocket's trajectory and death-dealing powers; do we miss what may really be going on, "while the real Text persisted, somewhere else, in its darkness, our darkness . . . " (520)? Since so much of *Gravity's Rainbow* focuses on the rocket, its crews, its construction, and its disciples, and its "screaming across the sky" reflects both the gravity and the rainbow arc, the trajectory of the text, then "the Rocket has to be many things, it must answer to a number of different shapes in the dreams of those who touch it" (727). At the very least this provides an organizing principle within the text, the image that breeds interpretations like so many schools of criticism, industry and science, from the letter-by-letter analysis of the Torah to the Gnostic sense of an ultimate secret, from Manichean mysteries of good and evil to kabalistic musings, each its own form of conspiracy, cosmic or otherwise. And yet because of the micro-political localism of most postmodern theory, the idea of particular matters as opposed to some overarching metanarrative, "Each will have his personal Rocket" (727), while any "ultimate" text or interpretations will continue to multiply "by a conspiracy between human beings and techniques" (521) and remain unavailable, since they probably do not exist at all.

Pynchon weaves elaborate carpets only to pull them out from under us. He conjures up the conspiratorial spasms of our contemporary times, acknowledging their power and compulsive force, but leaves us twitching and irritated, the very arc of conspiracy intact pulled by gravity toward some apocalypse or reckoning but left screaming across the sky: "Now everybody—" (760). The western urge, the American need, the Enlightenment thirst for rational resolution and "problem-solving"—"Holy-Center Approaching is soon to be the number one Zonal pastime" (508)—remains convulsively intact, recognized as an often lethal force, but at the same time "separations are preceding. Each alternative Zone speeds away from all the others, in fated acceleration, red-shifting, fleeing the Center" (519). The desire for comprehension cannot outrun the postmodern experience of uncertainty, incompletion, and doubt, as Pynchon's characters and by analogy his readers seek "the comfort of a closed place, where everyone is in complete agreement about Death" (299). Desire and death provide the process and the product of *Gravity's Rainbow,* the bookends of a gothic nightmare and a technological landscape that, at first, promises the fulfillment of the former and relentlessly creates the reality of the latter.

Gravity's Rainbow does furnish us with a historical "bottom line" despite the gaps and fissures, the cartoon escapades and the rampant sexuality, the bizarre characters and warped psyches. In 1944 German V-2 rockets caused death and destruction in London. That fact colors the entire novel, permeates and saturates all incidents and characters. Explanations wander off into various dreamscapes—ACHTUNG and Operation Black Wing and The White Visitation and PISCES—and there very well may be a connection between the rockets and Slothrop's erections, which leads him to pursue the Schwarzgerat and Imipolex G—even though Mickey Wuxtry-Wuxtry tells us, "Jamf was only a fiction, to help [Slothrop] explain what he felt so terribly, so immediately in his genitals for those rockets each time exploding in the sky . . . that he might be in love, in sexual love, with his, and his race's death" (738)—but the text resolves none of this. Of course, Pynchon's vision of history remains extremely selective, focused solely on death as the goal of technological innovation with tangential scurryings into wartime love affairs, individual obsessions, and endless, drug-addled revelries.

Gravity's Rainbow, a triumph of postmodern paranoia and conspiratorial imaginings, both in form and content, spawns multiple interpretations, the text a site of rampant ambiguity, overdetermined meanings, and endless connections. Storey has described it succinctly as "the structured articulation of a number of contradictions and determinations" (1998, 115), as episodes shift from one to the other horizontally. One episode does not lead to the next, although they do connect in many ways in terms of characters, motifs, visions, and certain objects, particularly when one re-reads the text. The initial reading experience emphasizes the flatness and depthlessness of each yarn with its foregrounded focus on immediate details and conversations that defy connection and remain open-ended and unstable. The characters and the reader are locked into an ongoing process that reflects Derrida's persistent deferral of meaning, a seemingly infinite series that moves forward in the linear fashion of print but not toward some ultimate explanation or solution. Words imprison and screen as much as they promise to liberate and define.

Characters with their silly and satirical names proliferate like subatomic particles run amuck. As one of them suggests, "Names by themselves may be empty, but the *act of naming* . . . " (366). It is the act, the performance that counts, as if we were moving rapidly from one stand-up comic's routine to another in breathless pursuit of still more. The structure performs its acts of conspiracy and paranoia, dizzy with Pynchon's riot of detail and naming. The process of signification remains endless and always threatens to self-destruct. We are meant to participate in Eliot's shoring up of fragments even though they remain fragments, forever shattered and scattered.

Such fragments include the labyrinthine recurrence of characters in a dazzling maze and network of spies, lovers, agents, bureaucrats, bunglers, and control freaks. Follow one and you stumble into nests and cabals of others. We can certainly see Pynchon's obsessions with technology, industrial monopolies, the compulsion of the West to command and kill, and the ever-present shadow of death and destruction. For example, in a completely circular episode, which begins and ends with the same language and phrases, we come upon Katje Borgesius, Blicero (the SS code name for Weiszmann) and young Gottfried involved in perverse sex games that involve Pynchon's persistent psychological vision of master and slave, domination and submission. Borgesius turns out to be a British spy whom Slothrop has been set up to rescue from the clutches of an enormous octopus on the Riviera, so that she can seduce him, someone can steal all his clothes and identity papers, and then he can pursue the mysterious Schwarzgerat rocket in the Zone under various assumed names and costumes. The evil Blicero, described as "malignant . . . the Zone's worst specter" (on page 666: Aha, the mark of the devil!), akin in his overall thirst for power to the omnipotent and omnipresent Jamf, he of Imipolex G, and involved in the German genocide in South Africa against the Hereros, seduced the boy Ndjambi Karunga while in South Africa and nicknamed him Enzian. Enzian turns out to be the half-brother of one Vaslav Tchitcherine, a Soviet agent roaming the Zone in search of the rocket, who sees himself as Slothrop's main opponent and is in love with the good witch, Geli Tripping, who has also slept with Slothrop. Enzian becomes devoted to the rocket, helps to lead the Schwarzkommando in Germany that is looking for it, and is involved in Operation Black Wing, at first a fake operation filmed by Gerhardt van Goll to mislead the enemy.

Once addicted, it is hard to stop. Margherita Erdmann, a film actress who once worked for von Goll and thoroughly enjoyed the sadomasochism of his films, meets Slothrop in the Zone. Her husband, Miklos Thanatz, turns out to have witnessed the launching of the huge rocket, 00000, within which Blicero has imprisoned his boy-lover Gottfried who will die when the rocket descends to earth. Her daughter Bianca, a thoroughly corrupted young wench among the sex-crazed passengers aboard the ship Anubis, becomes Slothrop's lover and is later murdered. Who can forget Byron Bulb who holds out against the system and the electricity cartel by not expiring as bulbs should; or Franz Van der Groov who exterminated dodoes; or Gerhardt von Goll who is also known as "Der Springer," a black-market entrepreneur who seems to know everything that's going on; or Francisco Squalidozzi, the Argentinean anarchist who is seeking asylum in the defeated Germany; and Ludwig who is searching for Ursula, his lost lemming?

While the text seems to be tracking these characters and their obsessive plots and plans, Pynchon abruptly short-circuits them, plunging into Bakhtinian revelries and grotesque carnivalesque carryings-on. The drugs, the alcohol, the sex, and the singing contribute to sudden ribald and raunchy eruptions of sheer exuberance and decadent farce that stop the novel in its tracks: party-time on the lip of the abyss. Slothrop performs as Plechazunga, the pig hero, in a pig costume, which ends up on Major Marvy, who is then castrated by mistake; Marvy has been after Slothrop for months, chasing him out of the Germans' rocket assembly plant, attacking from a plane the hot-air balloon, which Slothrop escapes in, and ends up being bombarded by pies from said balloon. In a drugged dream Slothrop falls down a toilet in Roseland, looking for his lost harmonica, which he discovers at the end of the novel before he disappears. Pointsman, with a toilet bowl stuck on his foot, chases after a dog to use in his Pavlovian experiments. Slothrop as Rocketman comes upon Mickey Rooney at the conference in Potsdam where friends have buried some hashish that Rocketman is sent out to retrieve. At one point Slothrop feels as though he is lodged within his own cock, perhaps the safest place to be. At another, Roger Mexico hurls an alliterative menu of disgusting culinary possibilities at an august dinner party, this after having urinated on one earlier. All these wild revels seem determined, in true 1960s fashion, to undermine official occasions and policies, to bombard the bureaucrats and technocrats as often as possible.

Each of Pynchon's bizarre characters has moments of insight and revelation, and each can be seen as a representation of some larger theme or concept. For instance, Slothrop's quest for the rocket and the relationship between his erections and the rocket's targets provide the novel with one of its major plotlines, and yet Slothrop, his quest, and the question of erectile response dissolve and scatter in the Zone: "It's doubtful if he can ever be 'found' again, in the conventional sense of 'positively identified and detained'" (712). The storyline evaporates, eviscerated by the Zone's incongruities and inconsistencies.

Gravity's Rainbow reveals several nodes of thematic intent, motifs that recur, self-contained clusters and epiphanies that, however disconnected and abandoned, tend to resurface in other guises and incidents. One can pinpoint the pervasive influences of death and desire, of the human hunger to control and in some way synthesize them, shackled to "human consciousness, that poor cripple, that deformed and doomed thing" (720). Journeys northward lead to "death's region. There may be no gods, but there is a pattern" (322). The State and its conglomerates "need our terror for Their survival. . . . They are only pretending Death is Their Servant"

(539, 540). Fathers and mothers, both actual and surrogate, inflict death and terror on their children, whether they be Jamf and Slothrop, Slothrop and his own father, the Germans and the Hereros, Frank Pokler and his daughter Ilse, Gerta Erdmann and Bianca, or Pointsman and the children he wants to abuse for his Pavlovian experiments, "dreaming up ever more ingenious plots against their children—not just their own, *but other people's children too!*" (441).

Paranoia pervades all thought and action, the expressed functionality of Pynchon's vision of the human condition, whether "operational," "creative," puritanically derived or otherwise. Slothrop thrives on it, as do Prentice, Roger Mexico, Tchicherine, and others. In fact Slothrop/Pynchon produce five proverbs for paranoids, everything from "If they can get you asking the wrong questions, they don't have to worry about answers" (251) to "*You* hide, they seek" (262). "Paranoids are not paranoids [Proverb 5] because they're paranoid, but because they keep putting themselves, fucking idiots, deliberately into paranoid situations" (292). Once again we are incarcerated in the nightmarish landscape of *The Crying of Lot 49:* "If there is something comforting—religious, if you want—about paranoia, there is still also anti-paranoia, where nothing is connected to anything, a condition not many of us can bear for long" (434). It sounds like the postmodern *cri de coeur* and can be underscored by the proliferation of possible conspiracies in the text, from the ever available Masons and the Illuminati—"Lovers of global conspiracy . . . can count on the Masons for a few good shivers and voids when all else fails" (587)—to perpetual quests themselves, a compulsion wired into the human psyche: "The rest of us . . . at the mercy of a Gravity we have only begun to learn how to detect and measure, must go on blundering inside our front-brain faith in Kute Korrespondences . . . finding in each Deeper Significance and trying to string them together like terms of a power series hoping to zero in on the tremendous and secret Function whose name, like the permuted names of God, cannot be spoken" (590). Alas, I, too, am guilty.

If there is broad philosophical combat undertaken in *Gravity's Rainbow,* it involves Roger Mexico and Edward Pointsman, the believer in chance, randomness, and statistical possibilities and the disciple of Pavlovian cause and effect. In Pynchon's functional metaphysics, Mexico affirms that between the 0 and the 1 a certain randomness persists. On the other hand Pointsman, a typical Pynchon villain who is "running" Slothrop, insists that all is predetermined; it is either 0 or 1, never both one and the other; cause and effect must operate in and underscore all things. Of course the very structure of the novel undermines such pedantry while recognizing the power of its conceptual certainty and belief that the human psyche will eventually turn out to be purely physiological. Pynchon's tales of séances, spirits, and voices from beyond suggest that bureaucracy extends beyond the grave and that our own earthbound version of it remains deadly and terrible: "In each case, the change from point to n-point carries a luminosity and enigma at which something in us must leap and sing, or withdraw in fright" (396).

Critics have belabored, and rightly so, Pynchon's cultural and historical vision that saturates the novel: America as the European extension of death and analysis, the cartelized state of the contemporary world, war as both a theatrical excuse for technological experimentation and monopoly and a complex technological machine in its own right, the rocket as the male symbol of power and control, and religion as not only the opiate of the people to be manipulated by the elite but also suggestive of enigmatic cosmic possibilities, "data behind which always, nearer or farther, was the numinous certainty of God" (242). The enigma, however, remains: "There was no difference between the behavior of a god and the operations of pure chance" (323). Fragments of this vision occur in different characters' perceptions and, therefore, remain scattered, the explanatory bursts that may or may not add up to some overall perspective, but Pynchon circles them again and again, indicating at the very least his fascination with such interpretations: Enzian's reading the rocket as the ultimate text, Tchitcherine viewing the State as one more representation of the rocket cartel and alphabets as agents of oppression, Pokler's expounding on male submission and subservience to the creation of the corporate city-state, William Slothrop praising the preterit Judases of the world in place of the Jesus that the Elect chose to worship and manipulate for their own sakes.

In every instance, when it comes to sex, death, visions, or conspiracies, Pynchon's characters are always at the mercy of gravity. However far-reaching the arc of technology or obsessive faith, everything eventually falls, at least on Earth. The rocket and humanity's skewed aspirations may momentarily ascend, but the inevitable descent remains: "The Rocket . . . promises escape. The victim, in bondage to falling, rises on a promise, a prophecy, of Escape . . . " (758). Leland Bland, achieving astral projections of himself, evades gravity's pull, but we cannot, trapped by that force which is "Messianic, extrasensory in Earth's mindbody" (590). Nora Dodson-Truck, a spiritual medium, recognizes "the Force of Gravity. *I am Gravity, I am That against which the Rocket must struggle*" (639): the conscious choice of gender roles is obvious. The rocket's rainbow, its parabolic arc, cannot last. Perhaps it is only the doomed Slothrop who can recognize the life-giving, metaphorical potential of that rainbow: "A stout rainbow cock driven down out of pubic clouds into Earth, green wet valleyed Earth. And his chest fills and he stands crying, not a thing in his head, just feeling natural . . . " (626). Of course Slothrop's vision like Slothrop is scattered and lost in a gothic world that recognizes only domination and death.

When it comes to an overall evaluation of *Gravity's Rainbow,* standing back and attempting to view it in its entirety, critics fume and fight, and the debate rages on. During the past thirty years since its publication, however, certain things clearly relate it to its cultural era. Pynchon pits the rambunctious skepticism of the 1960s against the idea of "the System," a reified totality that takes on a life of its own, "which sooner or later must crash to its death . . . dragging with it innocent souls all along the chain of life. Living inside the System is like riding across the country in a bus driven by a maniac bent on suicide" (412), an apt description in many ways of the experience of the novel. Victor Strandberg would agree: "In sum, we find at the base of all Pynchon's work the temperament of a hippie rebel against tradition, convention, and all forms of social hierarchy" (2000, 103). The System, however, permeates all things, including the individual self, "because submission and dominance are resources it needs for its very survival. . . . It needs our submission so that it may remain in power" (1973, 737). Perhaps this is why Pynchon's psychological vision and the wild parties he creates seem dated. The gaudy antics strike me as overdrawn and obsessively insistent.

Jane Kramer in *Lone Patriot* describes the leader of the now extinct Washington State Militia John Pitner's cranky querulous vision as a fear of the New World Order that "had sent warships *and* the Germans, and that it was only a matter of time before Germany had access to all the secret technology America was keeping from its own citizens. The two-hundred-year light bulb [Byron?]. The toaster that lasted a lifetime. . . . David Rockefeller and his friends had paid off the man who invented it"

(2002, 167). Thomas H. Schaub describes *Mason & Dixon* as "surely a novel for the people, as antigovernment as any Idaho militiaman" (195). Such a position reflects Pynchon's own.

Pynchon's "all-round assholery . . . less a fighting team than nest full of snits, blues, crotchets and grudges" (1973, 676) often leads to characters' acknowledging that "they are both so blitzed that neither one knows what he's talking about . . . and the rest are not exactly sure what's going on" (442, 597). He also recognizes that no two observers see or experience anything in the same way, part of the persistent postmodern siege against modernist and absolutist "bottom lines." The structure of *Gravity's Rainbow* capitalizes on this. Episodes appear to be "Parallel, not series. Metaphor. Signs and symptoms. Mapping on to different coordinate systems" (159). Those signs reveal that "we are obsessed with building labyrinths" (264), as the Argentinean anarchist Francisco Squalidozzi suggests, "where before there was open plain and sky. . . . We cannot abide that *openness:* it is terror to us" (264). What truths there may be can only come in psychic flashes or be revealed by strange omens, intuitive leaps that coincide with the 1960s psychic vision. And yet "in each of these streets, some vestige of humanity, of Earth, has to remain" (693).

Critical analyses of the novel stand divided between a blessed rage for order that lies within the text for critics to ferret out and identify, and a ribald rage for disorder, an ultimate chaos that totally undermines and deconstructs Western logic and rationalism. Such a bipolar battle often fails to recognize a third category, which I favor, that envisions disorder and disruption as themselves an immanent order.

Various commentators have described *Gravity's Rainbow* as the pursuit of a lost coherence, whether that vanished vision of unity exists in actuality or not. The goal may be a kind of eco-spiritualism, an Edenic view of Earth as a living creature that humanity continues to defile, the Gaia perspective that Pynchon sets against the labyrinthine conspiracies the rational Western mind delights in. The novel, thus, becomes a legitimate mapping of this search or quest, at the same time it recognizes that there may be none. The dread of finding no design propels characters and Pynchon to continue to pursue the hope of finding it. This may parallel Lacan's idea of "an endless quest in search of an imagined moment of plenitude . . . for a non-existent object, signifying an imaginary moment in time" (Storey 1998, 93), a psychological compulsion that drives all humanity, another incarnation of the postmodern sublime. Language exists to construct the very subjectivity and selfhood that defines itself in terms of this quest, but it also makes that fictional self aware of the feeling of lack and loss that propel it. Language, therefore, dooms humanity to being both expressive and repressive, fueling desire and thwarting it at every turn, a necessarily fragmented and tortured perspective that ceases only in death. And that Pynchon suggests may even continue forever after death in a spiritualist world.

As Stephen Whittier has suggested in a letter to the author, the pursuit of a lost coherence carries with it a decided nostalgic edge. That nostalgic imperative "must always be repressed by the dominant cultural logic" of late capitalism. An elite will always control institutionalized truths in a manner that attempts to suppress capitalism's paradoxical and contradictory nature: the self or individual vs. the system, the self as a product of the system, the self vs. the consumer economy, the self as the ultimate consumer. This suppression, part of the scenario to satisfy desires and at the same time keep them forever open-ended, relegates such nostalgic pursuits to narratives, which allow us to domesticate, regularize, organize, and enjoy "our anxieties, paranoias, and unconscious desires through alternate (but complicit) structures . . . like 'conspiracies.'" The multiple conspiracies of the novel, therefore, share this nostalgic narrative whether in prophesying an apocalyptic future, a nostalgic past, or a coherent present. In this sense conspiracies reflect the actual quest and are part and parcel of it, mapping certain cultural and political alignments, perceiving order and unity and our role in them, if only as the victims with vengeance and frustration in our hearts.

Critics who confront *Gravity's Rainbow* negatively complain of its ultimate chaos, of its essentially fragmented coherence that may deconstruct Western rationalism but that also deconstructs everything else in its path, leaving the reader bombarded by separate, disparate incidents that are so skeptically and satirically conceived, they remain comic, ironic, obscene performances of a work of fiction that barely functions. These critics complain of confusion, of a monotonous vision of collapse that leads only to a polyglot mess of entropic disintegration that is ultimately static and self-defeating. As readers we can search for an order that isn't there, try to connect the dots that only exist to thwart and victimize us, Pynchon's having the last laugh as scholars and critics produce reams of argument and analysis, all of which he has meticulously deflected and dissolved. For Thomas LeClair the novel remains a cacophony of voices, "an ensemble of voices—oral routines gathered together by a garrulous narrator" (1989, 53). For Richard Poirier "the rage to order . . . is merely a symptom of accelerating disorder [with] the capacity to dislocate us" (1987, 111). These "infinity of moments" (Cooper 1983, 213) linked by "the motif of autodeconstruction" (Berressem 1993, 244) create only an infinite instability, a thoroughly gothic world of terror and destruction that undercuts every attempt at interpretation and destabilizes every sign in a gender-bending, racial-deconstructing, postcolonial-dismantling mélange. Hostile to and subversive of every possible theory or concept, *Gravity's Rainbow* produces only a series of polarized pieces without end, revealing no hope of any origin whatsoever nor any ultimate hopelessness for that absent, nonexistent origin. Every teleological system is reduced to a mere shape, the shadow of some unscrupulous invisible system that kills and crushes (McHoul and Wills 1990, 167).

But what if the novel's very structure of disorder produces its own sense of order in which fragmentation can be viewed not as mere chaos and collapse but as a strategy of liberation, as Deborah L. Madsen (1991) suggests, seeming to create a space beyond or outside of all systems, beyond and within the boundaries of Western logic and analysis? Since practically everything in *Gravity's Rainbow* can be seen as serious and comic, riding on puns, dirty jokes, and parodic allusions, what if the novel embodies the kind of incestuous infinite play that Derrida locates within the heart of language itself? If language both resists and incorporates, why cannot the novel in its aesthetically spasmodic form and function?

Susan Strehle maintains that Pynchon's fiction derives its energy from quantum physics. One of Pynchon's teachers at Cornell marveled at "his apparently voracious appetite for the complexities of elementary particle theory" (Levine and Leverenz 1976, 9). At one point Enzian feels as if "the details . . . swirl like fog, each particle with its own array of forces and directions . . . he can't handle them all at the same time, if he stays too much with any he's in danger of losing others" (1973, 326–27). At another "the deeper and true Self is the flow between cathode and plate. . . . We live lives that are waveforms constantly changing with time, now positive, now negative" (404). Particles and waves in league with chaos or emergence theory: each episode acts up, performs, plays out, and then is superseded by the next one without segue or set-up. These initially separate particles exist in one continuous wave that becomes the novel itself, and once the wave crests and ebbs, the reader can begin to perceive particles within particles, which reveal a kind of spasmodic coherence, nodes of themes and vision.

Strehle believes that Pynchon would side more with Roger Mexico's statistical view of the world than with Pointsman's Pavlovian patterns. In that case a statistical "wave" or overview discovers or generates a cosmos that continues to be as discontinuous, energetic, relativistic, subjective, and uncertain as subatomic reality appears to be, wherein energy trumps matter, and existing "particles" can be viewed no longer as discrete entities but as part of an overarching field, a curved gravitational force (1992, 10). *Gravity's Rainbow,* therefore, creates a "network of relational independence . . . the way energy transforms matter and shapes an interconnected field" (23). I don't wish to reduce the novel to a quantum grid that exists to reveal the subatomic cosmos as the "ultimate truth" at the base of the postmodern vision but only want to point out that it does offer a way of describing and coping with the functionality and performance of the novel as a novel. Thematic nodes—particles in the wave of the entire structure—appear and disappear, keeping the entire text open-ended, multiply suggestive, and extremely fluid. Much like emergence theory, the novel emerges from the ground up, from episode to episode as it skitters and twists from one to the other, keeping in its direct sightlines the gaps, fissures, and disruptions that the postmodern vision warrants.

Gravity's Rainbow neither produces nor endorses total annihilation or total transcendence. Instead it walks a perilous tightrope across the yawning chasm between them. In its outlook it is decidedly apocalyptic, thus participating in that American cultural phenomenon that underscores many points of view in the last half century. As Molly Hite (1983) wisely suggests, the novel only propels its characters and its readers toward revelation, but there is none in sight. Apocalypse has become a function of the postmodern vision, not reduced to some fundamentalist truth or conspiratorial explanation but as open-ended as it can be. The postmodern sublime virtually bristles with apocalyptic possibilities. Meaning becomes displaced, dislocated, and deferred, but the trajectory of the novel participates in the apocalyptic thirst for some ultimate epiphany that will never come. All myths of origins and endings provide fodder for the epic sweep of Pynchon's vision. As Stewart asserts, "conspiracy theory is a skeptical, paranoid, obsessive practice of scanning for signs and sifting through bits of evidence for the missing link . . . seeking an order behind the visible" (1999, 14, 17), but like its apocalyptic cousins it "can become a stable center in itself" (15), as we continue to wait for something to happen that will never happen but that we feel compelled to pursue. *Gravity's Rainbow* gives us that conspiratorial apocalyptic vision as a function of our contemporary postmodern way of perceiving the world around us. There is no God, no demon, no master manipulator to unveil and accuse, but there is our apocalyptic craving for the deluge, revelation, catastrophe, "truth." We persist in searching for what can never exist, and Pynchon's novel embodies this quest as certainly as it dismantles it.

One of Pynchon's many strengths as a writer is his ability to hint at dark conspiracies that underlie all things without ever clearly identifying them or reducing them to visible cabals. The atmosphere of elaborate but elusive conspiracies permeates his novels, keeping the reader off base and forever alert to more evidence, more clues, more trails. As he confirms in *Vineland,* Pynchon's true zone remains "that phase of twilight, full of anxiety, when mercy in this world and the others is apt to be least available. Energies were on the loose, masses could materialize . . . " (1990, 275).

Critics have lambasted the linear groundedness of *Vineland,* complaining about its overt polemics in terms of the Nixon Repression and the Reagan era undermining and eviscerating "the Mellow Sixties, a slower-moving time, predigital, not yet so cut into pieces, not even by television" (38). The dream "of a mysterious people's oneness, drawing together toward the best chances of light . . . the people in a single presence . . . being seen to transcend" (117) has ended, destroyed by government agents, government snitches, and co-opted flower children who betray their own kind. Drugs, the "Sacrament of the Sixties," have become the "Evil of the Eighties" (342). Aging hippies have flocked to their various retreats in disarray and despair, to the Sisterhood of Kunoichi Attentives, into New Age Zen, to Katmology Clinics, and to the spirit-haunted realm of Vineland itself, ever mindful of "the call to attend to territories of the spirit" (317).

The political "purity" of the Sixties in general, however, and of the People's Republic of Rock and Roll in particular has long since been compromised and betrayed by insiders as well as outsiders. Even Frenesi Gates, perhaps the most dedicated character to the "Sacrament of the Sixties" of the period and Pynchon's most complex character here, really enjoys being "privileged to live outside of Time," an almost archetypal Pynchonian desire, "to enter and leave at will, looting and manipulating, weightless, invisible" (287). When she sleeps with, goes to work for, and is ultimately subsidized by the government that underwrites Brock Vond, she continues in her passive manner "to go along in a government-defined history without consequences, never imagining it could end" (354), whether betraying, setting up, and filming the murder of Weed Atman or marrying Zoyd Wheeler and Flash. Committed to the 24fps revolutionary film group, she all too easily sheds that role for others, as if Vond's take on the Sixties is not that far off the mark, acknowledging "not threats to order but unacknowledged desires for it. . . . [They] needed only to stay children forever, safe inside some extended national Family" (269). However romantic Pynchon makes the Sixties in terms of the proverbial "Lost Cause" or in contrast to the television-mesmerized, imminently compromised 1970s and 1980s, he still can imagine the shifting, often selfish motives that may have contributed to the "revolution" and its failure.

The politicized landscape of *Vineland*, however, is not the cause of the novel's flatness and more linearly structured plot, despite the wacky and bizarre characters and episodes, the flashbacks from 1984 to the 1960s and the 1970s, and what Joseph Tabbi has described as the novel's "debased literary realism" (1995, 91), within which Pynchon has constructed a world infiltrated by pop culture and computer graphics. Instead the more clearly defined lines of conspiracy and deals ground the text all too solidly. We can easily trace the network of informers and snitches, of double agents and double-crossers from Frenesi and Vond to Hector Zuniga and DL's failed assassination of Vond, from the failed union activities of the 1930s and 1950s to the new Reagan realm where "background shopping music" penetrates the landscape, "originally rock and roll but here reformatted into unthreatening wimped-out effluent, tranquilizing onlookers . . ." (328). In a world where male motorcycle clubs transform themselves into the Harleyite Order of nuns for tax purposes or ancient Ninja orders have been "made cruel and more worldly, bred of spirit . . . not the brave hard-won grace of any warrior, but the cheaper brutality of an assassin, [a world of] incrementalists, who cannot act boldly and feel only contempt for those who can" (127), "the merciless spores of paranoia" (239) may breed everywhere, but the connections between various groups and individuals stand out starkly. Gone or at least muted is Pynchon's conspiratorial aura, here replaced by specific deals and particular betrayals.

Pynchon still creates his paranoid landscape. Chipco, that "shadowy world conglomerate" (142), may be a part of "some planetwide struggle . . . still governed by the rules of gang war and blood feud" (146), but coming after *Gravity's Rainbow*, *Vineland*'s enervated domain reveals its lines of conspiracy all too directly. The effect flattens the tale. Here everything is ultimately identifiable. An ultimate cosmic conspiracy still haunts the novel—"the same people, the Real Ones, remained year in and year out, keeping what was desirable flowing their way" (276)—but the Real Ones all too easily appear to be Brock Vond and Richard Nixon, Hector Zuniga and Ronald Reagan. "An incoherent collection of souls . . . infiltrators and provocateurs of more than one political stripe" had participated in 24fps way back when, but the consequences are very coherent. When Frenesi worries that "the past was on her case forever, the zombie at her back" (71), we find out exactly why and how this came to be. "Pothead paranoia" (46) generates real paranoia, but when it is conveniently located in particular potheads of a particular time and place, the diffuse and therefore more unnerving paranoia of *Lot 49* and *Gravity's Rainbow* dissolves and disappears.

It is not the fact that Mark Twain's *Huckleberry Finn*, based supposedly on a real character, went and became a sheriff or that Moody Chastain, DL's abusive father, who was "a wild kid . . . ended up being that deputy sheriff" (120) that is so depressing but the fact that Pynchon spells out the reason why Chastain ended up the way he did. We can chart Chastain's progress because Pynchon has laid it out so clearly. Even his very apt feminist interpretation of the relationship between men, violence, derringers, and dicks strikes me as too pat and politically correct.

Takeshi, the man DL tries to assassinate, thinking he is Vond, and later, atoning, bonds with wishes "to make of his life a koan, or unsolvable Zen puzzle, that would send him purring into transcendence" (180). The koan resonates widely throughout *Gravity's Rainbow* and again in *Mason & Dixon*, but in *Vineland* Pynchon mentions rather than creates it. His eerie evocations of other worlds—the Thanatoids in Shade Creek, Van Meter's "searching all his life for transcendent chances" (223), God for Frenesi become an ultimate hacker for whom humanity lies beneath his notice, "a sunset that was the closest we get to seeing God's own jaundiced and bloodshot eyeball, looking back at us without much enthusiasm" (361)—are here reduced to occasional speeches, episodes, or almost throwaway scenes and one-liners. Ultimate mystery and ultimate visions of conspiracy collapse into cause-and-effect explanations.

Vineland may, in effect, be Pynchon's response to *The Crying of Lot 49*, 1964 as seen twenty years later in 1984. The Paranoids have now become a successful band "as revolution went blending into commerce" (308), and Wendell "Mucho" Mass, divorced amicably from Oedipa in 1967—did she finally go underground and create her own Tristero?—and now recoiling from his very lucrative reign as Count Drugula of Indolent Records, has become as virulent a spokesperson against drugs as Brock Vond. For him the only choice now is to renounce every pleasure before the state outlaws and eradicates all of them, determined to let television and pop culture mesmerize, infantilize, and numb the masses, which they seem to have succeeded in doing: "the green Free America of their childhoods even then was turning into . . . the heartless power of the scabland garrison state" (314). The state has re-established the fear of death that the acid trips of the 1960s blissfully avoided, and since that has been accomplished, all are now at the mercy of that ultimately realizable and recognizable conspiracy. It is not Pynchon's vision in *Vineland* that makes for such a listless performance but his naming names and transforming mystery into measured matters that do.

Although most reviewers praised *Mason & Dixon* for Pynchon's characterization of the spirited duo and proclaimed that the novel was his most humanistic and compassionate yet, the same assaults as those on *Gravity's Rainbow* reoccurred, perhaps best summarized by Michiko Kakutani's description of it as "dazzling and vexing, tiresome and amazing." The "wild tangents and sheer density" of this "sloppy monster" (Clerc 1983, 27, 16, 12) produce both bewilderment and excitement, dismay and delight. "You don't so much read it as tunnel through it" (30), remarked L. S. Klepp, although "you start the book bewildered, then slowly . . . " (22).

Charles Mason (1728–1786) and Jeremiah Dixon (1733–1779), who were brought to the United States from 1763 to 1767 to solve boundary disputes between the undefined royal land grants that became Pennsylvania and Maryland, provide Pynchon with a pair of opposite personalities, Mason who is "Gothickally depressive" and Dixon who becomes "Westeringly manic" (1997, 680). Mason the Anglican and Dixon the Quaker, Mason who dresses in neutral colors and Dixon in red, Mason the astronomer and Dixon the surveyor, the lover of the grain versus the lover of the grape; Mason who suffers from hyperthrenia, "excess in mourning" (25) because of his wife Rebekah's recent death and who talks with her ghost versus Dixon, the energetic bachelor who is always up for a good time: such polarized characters practically demand to be "postmodernly" deconstructed, as Pynchon slowly dismembers them and reveals Mason's lighter and Dixon's darker side. Opposites merge, as both men long for revelation of some kind. "Why mayn't there be Oracles, for us, in our time? Gateways to Futurity? That can't all have died with the ancient peoples," declares the melancholic Mason, unknowingly paraphrasing the transcendentalist Emerson's wish for "an original relation to the universe."

Although Michael Wood suggests that, unlike *Gravity's Rainbow*, "no overarching conspiracy, or even the steady suspicion of one, unites the unravelled strands of this book" (Clerc 2000, 36), conspiracy saturates the text from Dixon's wondering if he and Mason are being used by invisible forces to the bizarre tale that Eliza Fields spins about her capture by Jesuits and her induction into the Widows of Christ, a ring of Jesuit-sponsored prostitutes originating in Quebec. The pre-1776 world of the colonies bristled with intense conspiratorial anxieties on the eve of revolution, permeated by various threats and menace from the British government, the Native American presence and the uprising led by Pontiac, General Braddock's murder and defeat in 1755, and Pynchon's presentation of a Benjamin Franklin awash in intimations of a Sino-Jesuit plot. Coffee-Houses breed talk of conspiracy, making it "not only possible, but resultful as well" (1997, 305). Someone unnamed has tagged Dixon's dossier, "flagg'd in Yellow, which means, 'Caution,—may be connected dangerously'" (157). Mason begins to believe that his very project in America may be a plot rigged by his rival, the Reverend Dr. Nevil Maskelyne, the future Director of the Greenwich Observatory, to get him out of the way for Maskelyne's own ascension to the position of Royal Astronomer. In Cape Town, where Mason and Dixon chart the Transit of Venus on June 6, 1761, and which Pynchon incarnates as a colony rife with sexual intrigue plagued by the curse of slavery, Police Agent Bonk decides to flee to "the vast Hottentot Land beyond" in order to place himself "out of reach of the Company, who desire total Control over ev'ry moment of ev'ry Life here" (154). The German soldier Dieter on grim windswept St. Helena is convinced that the East India Company, which runs the place, has lied to him in order to get him to enlist: "The Company promis'd travel, adventure, dusky Maidens," but instead he feels that God "hath abandoned us. . . . We are spiritually ill here, deprav'd." Dixon, feeling himself forever under surveillance, wonders, "Why has ev'ry Observation site propos'd by the Royal Society prov'd to be a Factory, or Consulate, or other Agency of some royally Charter'd Company?" (252). In 1745 the Jacobites in league with the Scots rallied unsuccessfully against British power, and Jesuits, expelled from Europe, not only inhabit secret Papist tunnels but seem to be omnipotent and everywhere in league against the struggling colonies. Religious sects multiply and confront one another, and business is mysteriously manipulated by Adam Smith's invisible hand, an image that resurfaces in the strange tale of His and Ho: "Here must we answer to the Market, day upon day unending, for 'tis the inscrutable Power we serve, an invisible-Handed god without Mercy" (627). Even an inverted five-pointed star, the Sterloop, suggests the devil's sign since it mysteriously turns up on Dutch rifles in Cape Town, the rifles of slave mongers in America, and at a tavern in Lancaster, Pennsylvania, where the Paxton Boys massacred Indian men, women and children. "Perhaps these Occurrences . . . are invisibly connected" (429), muses Mason. "The Sign . . . has evil Powers" (681).

Mason & Dixon like *Gravity's Rainbow* is constructed like a conspiracy, the labyrinthine text presented to the reader in Pynchon's usual manner with its false leads, misleading trails, spontaneous and bizarre episodes, and his "passion for knowledge systems, alternative histories, crackpot sciences, mystical and cryptic occurrences that have been marginalized" (Clerc 1983, 123). It once again reveals Pynchon's vision of "the inadequacy of reason alone to explain the mystery that surrounds us. The haunted world, the suprareal, the ghostly, and the impossible have the same valence as the facts of history as we receive them" (Boyle 1997, 9). Snowballs fly their own arcs as if they themselves have created their own trajectories. Despite the Dickensian atmosphere of family, warmth, and comfort at Christmas in 1786, Pynchon hints at stranger worlds. Assonance lends a hypnotic quality to his prose—"brisk Wind," "slaps of Batter," "Fruits, Suet," "Pie-Spices," and if you look carefully at "a sinister and wonderful Card Table," you can be mesmerized by "an illusion of Depth into which for years children have gaz'd as into the illustrated Pages of Books" (1997, 5). Mason later muses on the patterns found in silks from Eastern lands, "damasks with epic-length Oriental tales woven into them, requiring hours of attentive gazing whilst the light at the window went changing so as to reveal newer and deeper labyrinths of event" (169).

It is always dangerous in Pynchon's fiction to pounce on an episode and seize it as emblematic of the entire novel, but it is difficult to resist Mason's strange revelations and epiphanies that occur throughout the text. It is "as if Gravity along the Visto [the eight-yard width of the Mason-Dixon Line] is become locally less important than Rapture" (651). "Mason's narrative is regularly blasted by strikingly intrusive moments of clarifying vision," suggests Joseph Dewey, "at right angles with Western thought" (2000, 126). His experience of hypnagogic states—"he seem'd one night to push through to the other side of something, some Membrane" (1997, 188)—of hallucinations—"I do not choose these moments, nor would I know how. They come upon me with no premonition" (434)—of "curious optical re-adjustment[s]"—a "rush both inward and away, and soon, quite soon, billowing out of control" (725)—hearkens back to his memory as a child in a wagon late at night with his parents, feeling "as if they liv'd at the edge of some great lighted Sky-Structure, with numberless Lanthorns hung and Shadows falling ev'rywhere, and pathways in, upon which once having ventur'd, he might account his life penetrated, and the rest of it claim'd" (653). Reason and Newtonian mechanics cannot account for these odd moments.

Such episodes speak to the strangeness of human experience, perhaps revealing what John Dewey describes as "a re-enchantment of the Earth as an animated creature and an overthrow of intellection, specifically the analytical system of oppositional logic" (Menand 2001, 128). That re-enchantment, however, can be filled with ominous signs and dark forebodings, particularly in two of Mason's most powerful epiphanies, the vortex he descends into that he understands as "a low rotating Loop . . . tangent to the Linear Path of what we imagine as Ordinary Time, but excluded from it" (555), the missing eleven days that had been removed from the calendar in the reform of 1752—in Britain September 2 gave way to September 14 to match the Gregorian Calendar on the continent, itself the possible incarnation of a conspiracy since it can be seen as a product of both Rome and Catholic France—and a final dream of a dark city of anarchy, "a City in Chaos. . . . The Monuments made no sense at all . . .

they bore no inscriptions" (750, 749). Such territories conjure up the haunted woodlands of Edgar Allan Poe and Nathaniel Hawthorne.

In the rotating vortex Mason feels as victimized as readers of Pynchon's fictions often do: "I myself did stumble, daz'd and unprepared, into that very Whirlpool in Time" (556). Everything remains uncertain; "all the Knowledge of Worlds civiliz'd and pagan, late and ancient, lay open to my Questions" (558); creatures in this twilight zone flit about in this "city of Gothickal Structures . . . I hop'd were only . . . Bats" (559). "Twas as if this Metropolis of British Reason [he finds himself in Oxford] had been abandon'd to the Occupancy of all that Reason would deny," he explains as he finds himself alone and at large in "A Carnival of Fear" (559). Dixon reacts by describing the episode as some embodiment of Faust's experience, to which Mason responds that "I was prevented from ever returning. Exil'd from the Knowledge. . . . the Keys and Seals of Gnosis within were too dangerous for me . . . I must hold out for the Promises of Holy Scripture, and forget about the Texts I'd imagin'd I'd seen [in the Bodleian Library at Oxford]" (560). Mason as a man of his times opts for deliverance from such a traumatic vision in the Christian Bible; he resists Gnosis, but his glimpse of Reason's inadequacy and sense that the world and human consciousness are stranger than he ever could have imagined never deserts him:

> Mason had seen in the Glass, unexpectedly, something beyond simple reflection,—outside of the world,—a procession of luminous Phantoms. . . . There may be found, within the malodorous Grotto of the Selves, a conscious Denial of all that Reason holds true . . . there are Beings who are . . . ever and implacably cruel, hiding, haunting, waiting . . . and any one who sees them out of Disguise are instantly pursued. . . . Spheres of Darkness, Darkness impure . . . of Spirits who dwell a little over the Line between its annihilation . . . between common safety and Ruin ever solitary. . . . (769)

One is reminded of the séances, the spirits and spirit voices in *Gravity's Rainbow*. This terrifying dark abyss yawns throughout Pynchon's fiction and may account for his assault on linear structures, cause and effect, and the optimistically enlightened faith in scientific and logical reason that inspire and plague his various characters. Here lies the black hole at the center of an ultimately cosmic conspiracy with its intimations of death, destruction, certain annihilation, and extinction. "Dreams, paranoia, phantasmagoria are all ways to resist 'modernization and rationalization'" (Clerc 1983, 20), Menand suggests, but they also spawn their own darker powers and forces that, in the words of Robert Lowell's narrative voice in "Skunk Hour," "will not scare."

Pynchon's West, that uncharted territory beyond Mason and Dixon's boundary line, underscores his sense of dreadful but mysteriously luminous forces, the kind of aura that infiltrates most religions and lost avenues of esoteric knowledge. The wilderness is a void "where quite another Presence reigns, undifferentiate,—That whichever *precedeth* Ghostliness . . ." (491). "Is it something in this Wilderness, something ancient, that waited for them, and infected their Souls when they came?" (347). Conspiracies surface here as well as mythic encounters of ancient peoples that precede even the Indians. Did a race of giants create enormous mounds? Are the layers of these mounds, like layers in an electrical battery, "a Sign of the intention to Accumulate Force" (599)? Is that why the "'Rap-ture de West,' Brother, / Sooner or later, / It's go-ing, to take ye . . ." (670)? Could the New World reveal "a secret Body of Knowledge,—meant to be studied with the same dedication as the Hebrew Kabbala" (487)? Is there something more to this "Unseen World" (469), this "savage Vacancy" (709)? Is that why "the Gospels of Reason [must denounce] all that once was Magic," and for the truth of the matter "one must turn to Gothick Fictions, folded acceptably between the covers of Books" (359)? Since in Christian tales wise men from the East travel in threes, who is the third surveyor that Captain Shelby asks about, "seen often in the Company of an Animal that most describe as a Dog . . . back at the edge of Visibility . . . a Figure . . . in these parts 'tis esteem'd a Wonder" (605)? Such speculations necessarily contribute to the "wild tangents and sheer density" of Pynchon's texts.

Strange beings, as usual, haunt *Mason & Dixon* from giant robed phantoms seen from St. Helena lurking at the edge of the horizon to talking dogs and clocks, huge cheeses run amuck, a single ear you can wish on but that must remain an anti-oracle since it can provide no wisdom, a mechanical duck in love with a French chef, a giant golem wandering in the woods, a dragonlike worm that surrounds a castle in England, an electric eel, and a hidden Indian valley that harbors giant vegetables. Strange sects,

America's splintered and virulent cults, also litter the landscape, such as the Illuminati, the Freemasons, mesmerists, many of them fearing Atheists, battling for each visionary prophecy in a land newly aroused by the Great Awakening in the 1740s. Peter Redzinger nearly drowns in a pit of hops and emerges converted, one more mad evangelical preacher to haunt the American countryside. "If Christ's Body could enter Bread, then what else might?—might it not be as easily haunted by ghosts less welcome?" (205), muses our narrator, the Reverend Mr. Wicks Cherrycoke.

Mason and Dixon's drawing their famous line, that "geometrick Scar" (1997, 257), intended to straighten out the unrealistically infinite land grants offered by James II, underlines the Age of Reason and its belief in right angles and mechanical traceries, haunted by visions of formless and ill-defined territories. The "notorious Wedge" at the northeast corner of Maryland fails to be included within Mason and Dixon's lines and thus remains "priz'd for its Ambiguity" (469), "beyond Resolution . . . an Unseen World" (470). Zhang, the Chinese prisoner of the Jesuit compound in Quebec, who escapes from there with the captive Eliza Fields—and from *The Ghastly Fop,* a popular series of tales that Cherrycoke expropriates for his own narrative, thus deliberately breaking the artificial boundaries of different texts—praises the practice of Feng-Shui, the Chinese adjustment to inhabited space and the environment, that looks upon all lines as "ill-omen'd" (692) and "conduit[s] for evil" (701). The boundary line slaughters trees and creates bad history as it moves forward, a predatory creature. True insight and wisdom, therefore, as embodied in Pynchon's tales, must discover "a Knowledge of Tunneling . . . as more of the Surface succumb'd to Enclosure, Sub-Division, and the simple Exhaustion of Space,—Down Below, where no property Lines existed, lay a World as yet untravers'd" (233), Pynchon's world and one that readers must "tunnel through . . . " (Clerc 1983, 30).

Mason & Dixon relies on history in a way that no other Pynchon novel has. The beginnings of paragraphs often set the time and place of the line's progress. The book parallels Mason and Dixon's travels, sandwiching the American assignment, as several critics have noticed, within two Transits of Venus, the first on June 6, 1761, and the second on June 3, 1769, from the two of them in Cape Town to Mason's in Donegal in Ireland and Dixon in Hammerfest, Norway. I have already tried to show how the structure of the novel continually undermines this linear trek as much as it relies on it for a framework and blueprint. At the same time Pynchon's eighteenth-century narrator is not only a minister, filled with his own musings and doubts about the role of Christian faith in the dawning era of enlightened science, but also one who has been arrested and sentenced to jail for having posted anonymous messages that reveal crimes "committed by the Stronger against the Weaker" (1997, 9). He also delights in spicing up his tale for his audience, especially the children, by telling them that he was sentenced to the Tower, when in reality he was sent to Ludgate. He has returned to Philadelphia in 1786 to attend Mason's funeral and first met the pair when sentenced to a voyage at sea aboard the ill-fated *Seahorse*, a remedy for those considered insane at the time, thus commencing "my Exile . . . for the best of Medical reasons" (10).

Several critics have commented on Pynchon's interest in religion and religious or metaphysical issues, and Cherrycoke provides his own battered Christian scrim to his tale. He admits his interest in Mason and Dixon because of his spiritual unease and discomfort. He would like to think that "History is the Dance of our Hunt for Christ. . . . If it is undeniably so that he rose from the Dead, then the Event is taken into History, and History is redeem'd" (75) and that America may yet prove to be "this object of hope that Miracles might yet occur, that God might yet return to Human Affairs" (353). His text reveals a religious dispensation with its sense of wonder, dread, and a haunted "otherness" but questions toward its conclusion, "Is it the Infinite that tempts us, or the Imp? Or is it merely our Vocational Habit, ancient as Kabbala, of seeking God there, among the Notation of these resonating Chains . . . " (721)? In Pynchon the pursuit persists while revelation merely tantalizes. Cherrycoke's text becomes his own test of faith, which is found wanting, since he acknowledges that "that inhuman Precision" (440), the new faith of the enlightened age, which he cannot believe in, is on the rise and becoming dominant. In his ideas of a plague on both houses, the "fall" of Christianity and the rise of the Age of Reason, he remains permanently adrift and exiled, ending his long-winded yarn with Mason's final revelation of the universe as "a great single Engine. . . . Not all the Connexions are made yet" (772) and Mason's ever hopeful vision of an America where one can touch the stars, "the Fish jump into your Arms [and] the Indians know Magick" (773).

History, asserts Ethelmer LeSpark in one of the few interruptions of Cherrycoke's narrative, "needs rather to be tended lovingly and honorably by fabulists and counterfeiters. Ballad-Mongers and Cranks of ev'ry Radius, Masters of Disguise . . . and Speech nimble enough to keep her beyond the Desires, or even the Curiosity, of Government" (350). It takes several lines to determine exactly who offers up this peroration, as if Pynchon wanted the description to stand forth on its own. The more practical Uncle Ives thinks that such madness is unfortunately found only in novels "that will not distinguish between fact and fancy" (351). Jeff Baker suggests that since literary realism, in effect, supports the status quo and can, therefore, be described as a state fiction, a government-supported vision of the world, Pynchon determinedly disassembles "realist narrative strategies [as] an act of narrative subversion that repudiates reality in favor of the monstrous possibilities of the irreal" (2000, 180). As Hawthorne and Faulkner before him, Pynchon would delight, I think, in being seen (or perceived, since of course he hasn't been seen in years) as "yet another damn'd Fabulator, such as ever haunt encampments, white or Indian, ev'ry night. Somewhere in this Continent" (1997, 552).

Mason & Dixon very clearly attacks slavery in all of its many variations from Cape Town and St. Helena to the newly emerging United States and the North Cape. This and the massacre of native populations from the Hereros in *Gravity's Rainbow* appall Pynchon. "The great worm of Slavery" (147) contributes to Cornelius Vroom's fears about "the coming Armageddon of the races" (63) in Cape Town. While there, Mason is propositioned by Astra, a slave woman, to impregnate her, because partly white babies are more valuable on the slave market. All the women in the Vroom family conspire to sexually arouse the befuddled and melancholy astronomer in order to drive him into Astra's inviting arms. As Mason realizes, "'tis the Slavery, not any form of Desire, that is of the essence" (68). At one heroic moment, even though it results in his having to flee from an unfriendly mob, Dixon seizes a whip from a slave driver who is striking his slaves, infuriated by "an old and melancholy History" (568). He recognizes that the famous line will divide slaveholders from opponents of slavery: "Where does it end? No matter where in it we go, shall we find all the World Tyrants and Slaves? America was the one place we should *not* have found them" (693).

Pynchon's own penchant for viewing the human race as plagued by submission and domination, by slaves and masters, culminates in his disgust with slavery as a social and historical institution. Tales of smallpox-infected blankets handed out to the Indians and the Lancaster Massacre permeate the text, as well as his recognition that everyone, including every member of the LeSpark clan, is somehow complicit with and involved in a society that perpetuates and underwrites that "peculiar institution." America, with its Native Americans and black slaves, has from the first "been long attended . . . by murder, slavery, and the poor fragments of a Magic irreparably broken . . . there is no Innocence" (612, 615). Even Cherrycoke joins the chorus, railing against "the inhuman ill-usage" (412) of slavery, the "Gothick Pursuit [of] Lords and Serfs" (275). Critics who chastise Pynchon for not taking moral stands on cultural and historical issues would do well to reconsider *Gravity's Rainbow* and the other novels in light of *Mason & Dixon's* incarnation of slavery.

"To imagine institutions as 'autonomous systems operating according to their own mysterious internal logic, to be fine-tuned only by experts' is . . . 'to opt for some kind of modern gnosticism that sees the world as controlled by the powers of darkness'" (142), charges Robert Bellah in *The Good Society* (1991). "Pynchon vividly dramatizes the view that bureaucracies are 'malevolent' entities that 'may crush us under their impersonal wheels'" (10, 144). Bellah joins several critics who adopt this assessment in their negative responses to Pynchon's and DeLillo's fictions. Pynchon's complex interactions between human submission and domination and the systems that both create and sustain them do not play out into the more simplistic notion of victim and persecutor, however, but they do explore the dark roots of humanity's compulsion to enslave, murder, and surrender to its perception of powerful forces. Even Dixon at one point admits to "the only time in my life I have felt that Surrender to Power, upon which, as I have learn'd after, to my Sorrow, all Government is founded" (1997, 312). As Cyrus R. K. Patell has explored, from his postmodern vision of the self, Pynchon opposes the self-reliant "methodological individualism" (2001, 29), the belief that all phenomena are grounded in the individual, which is the common denominator of all experience, that American mythology celebrates. From such a position, "all social groupings appear to the individual to be conspiracies" (30), and Pynchon views the institution of slavery as the ultimate trope for all forms of domination. His own fascination with conspiracy and paranoia does not undermine his anti-slavery position, even when it appears in tales that do not attack racial slavery directly. Bellah's interpretation is correct, but he doesn't extend it far enough, perhaps aware of the larger fact of poststructuralism's failure "to undermine the ideological persuasiveness of individualism" (169–70) in contemporary American society.

Patell insists that Pynchon struggles with the disconnection in American culture between its trumpeting the separate individual self (what he describes as "freedom from") and at the same time praising the benefits of community (the "freedom to"). "The official narrative of United States individualism," Patell concludes, "thus encompasses a complex structure of contradiction held in abeyance" (2001, 32), as if the experience of the radically situated and isolated self were merely the present experience of what will eventually become a thriving and interdependent community. The gap occurs in the future between self-reliance and community values, a yawning chasm bridged by the belief that the first will eventually lead to the second. Pynchon drives his narratives right into and through this impasse, and the structure of his fiction presents in all its stark and surreal contours this disconnected and disrupted landscape. Paranoia fills that impasse, and individual conspiracies provide a kind of comfort in trying to bridge it. Such a broad perspective connects Pynchon to Toni Morrison's vision of slavery and race in American society, since both create postmodernist "fractured narratives" (29) that express that similar perspective.

Pynchon continues to tower over postmodern novelists in our contemporary era. His novels create a fictional landscape as recognizable and as initially foreign and strange as Faulkner's South or DeLillo's futuristic worlds. His use of language and structure, tone and diction, nightmarish episode and disturbing incident meticulously incarnates the conspiratorial fears and paranoid powers of his age. We really cannot understand one without the other. Yes, he is mesmerized by the same conspiratorial visions and perceptions he continually undermines and eviscerates, and he pays tribute to their unsettling seductiveness and persuasiveness. His remains, however, *the* postmodern vision above all others, difficult, quirky, incalculably strange and, at times, off-putting and tedious, but it is a vision that inhabits the characters of the western lands he surveys and explores, characters who are continuously drawn to a functioning conspiratorial outlook, which produces and performs the very apocalyptic paranoia that has all too easily seeped into the mainstream, become a part of our lives, and points in the harrowing direction of the postmodern sublime.

7
Toni Morrison's Trilogy of Obsession
"Something Rogue" and Conspiracy's Comeuppance

From the mutual interdependence between postmodernism, conspiracy theory, and the postmodern sublime, conspiracy emerges as a restrictive vision, a basically irrational but highly analytical perception of the world based on the fear of and resistance to postmodern instability, radical skepticism, and the elusive but seductive allure of the postmodern sublime. Conspiracy theorists wish to establish an authority figure or group that they can oppose, relying on confrontation and opposition to make sense of the world around them. In *Paradise* Toni Morrison explores the ramifications of conspiracy, linking it to patriarchal traditions and generational anxieties, and then goes on to suggest a possible remedy or divergent view, which relies heavily on the Brazilian syncretic religion of Candomble. In fact when in Brazil she heard the tale of a convent of black nuns who practiced Candomble and were murdered by men. The story turned out not to be true, but its general narrative framework and plot may have conjured up the images and patterns she usually seeks in order to write fiction.

Morrison also examines the ideology and psychology of various cults and cabals in *Paradise,* exploring fundamentalist missions and the conspiracies that are perceived as threatening them. The novel tackles conspiracy as conspiracy from the patriarchal traditionalists of Ruby to the more synthetic religious perspectives of the Convent. *Paradise* epitomizes the various views of and use for conspiracy theory that we have been pursuing, an issue that continues to plague contemporary American culture, fiction, and politics.

The stigma of black identity, a product of white society, forever haunts Morrison's world in the shape of Beloved, Wild, and Dorcas, as she follows her characters from Kentucky to Ohio, Virginia to New York City, from

Haven to Ruby and the Convent, ever mindful of escape and liberation but also of displacement, alienation, depression, isolation, and what used to be called in student-abroad programs "culture shock." In time the past invades the present; neither can escape the other. What Sethe calls "re-memory," a vision that suggests that memories live outside and beyond us and can be seen and experienced by others, interpenetrates all of Morrison's world, generating the terrifying necessity of facing backward as one staggers forward. In her texts from succinct facts and incidents she creates a wider, more conscious web of psychological oppression, speculation, interpretation, and comprehension, all of which contribute to a quest for identity that remains as provisional, relational, uncertain, and ambiguous as postmodern identity itself. Such is the nature of the postmodern sublime in Morrison's fiction. These historical realities, this epic metanarrative, is forever present in every act and thought, even though her style and structure do not replicate the linear metanarratives of the past.

American culture usually generates confrontation and showdowns in an apocalyptic manner, the saved vs. the damned, good vs. evil, believers vs. demonic Others. Morrison knows this territory well, the utopian hopes that come with it, and clearly stages a similar conflict between the men of Ruby and the women at the Convent. "The isolation, the separateness, is always a part of any utopia," she acknowledges, in our culture that can be traced from the Branch Davidians of Waco, Texas, to the single-minded crusade of Timothy McVeigh. "And [*Paradise*] was my meditation . . . and interrogation of the whole idea of paradise, the safe place, the place full of bounty, where no one can harm you. But, in addition to that, it's based on the notion of exclusivity. All paradises, all utopias are designed by who is not there, by the people who are not allowed in" (Farnsworth 2001, 21). Morrison's idea clearly underscores the vision behind the towns of Haven and Ruby and, to a lesser degree, the Convent. "Isolation . . . carries the seeds of its own destruction" (29), she maintains, an insight that *Paradise* embodies again and again. She adds, "I wanted . . . to move [the idea of paradise] from its pedestal of exclusion and to make it more accessible to everybody" (Timehost 2001, 61), which is why she objected to the capitalization of the word at the very end of the novel. She prefers the final line to read: "Now they will rest before shouldering the endless work they were created to do down here in paradise" (1998, 318).

Critics brought in split decisions about the novel, torn between its realistic and allegorical elements, at times finding it too schematic and too much of a gender-infused confrontation. For me the inclusion of many characters, complete with their different idiosyncrasies, qualities, and perspectives, helps to soften the allegorical elements and works to focus the reader on individual destinies as well as the final showdown. The controlling story of the founding of Haven and Ruby often strains for allegorical significance, but Morrison demonstrates how these hallowed signs and traditional signifiers shift and change over the course of several years. Allegory becomes part of a historical context, not some free-floating transcendent signified that resists time and human complicity.

For instance, the significance of the words on the oven that men carry and reassemble once they have completed the trek from Haven to Ruby depends on who is interpreting it. Younger men like Destry Beauchamp oppose the word "Beware," which is supposed to be the first word in the phrase, "Beware the Furrow of His Brow." Destry thinks it is meant to be read as "*Be* the Furrow of His Brow," interpreting it to mean that "We'll be his Voice" (87), not mere servants to the fear implied in "Beware." The older men, especially Steward Morgan, in whose prodigious memory rests the entire traditional story of the town, oppose the revision and demand that things be left exactly as they are or else. He is supported in this interpretation by others but especially the Reverend Mr. Pulliam, a fiery apocalypse-hurling Methodist of the New Zion Church. The Reverend Mr. Richard Misner of the Mount Cavalry Baptist Church, a more moderate man who believes in the power of open discussion, opposes Pulliam's view and reads the inscription as he finds it, incomplete: " . . . the 'Furrow of His Brow.' " Dovey Morgan, Steward's wife, believes that " 'Furrow of His Brow' alone was enough. . . . Specifying it, particularizing it, nailing its meaning down, was futile" (93).

Later in the novel we learn that the author of the phrase, Zechariah Morgan, one of the founding patriarchs and named for an Old Testament prophet, meant the original message as a threat, a way to instill fear and obedience in his people and uphold the rule of his own patriarchal leadership. Not for nothing is his son named Rector and his twin grandsons named Steward and Deacon, titles derived from the New Testament. In fact Zechariah expected that obedience to God coincided with obedience to him; it is his own brow he celebrated. At one point graffiti mars the

oven with the line, "*We Are* the Furrow of His Brow," one more generational thrust against the old order.

Of course the primal tale of Ruby's founding bristles with parallels to
the founding myths of the Hebrews, the Mormons, and the early Puritans,
a very American narrative: "the Old Fathers recited the stories of that journey: the signs God gave to guide them" (14). It becomes a litany to protect
the African Americans from "Out There where every cluster of whitemen
looked like a posse" (16) and thereby extends Morrison's focus on love and
obsession from *Beloved* and *Jazz.* The story transforms the utility of the
oven into a shrine and comes complete with a mysterious satchel-carrying
stranger who leads Zechariah to the very spot where Ruby will take root.
The conspiracy of tradition enacts a rigid prophecy and fulfillment that
cannot be changed, that is literally writ in stone. Even at the annual Christmas Pageant, the tale of Mary, Joseph, and the Inn reflects the exodus of
the Ruby founders, a darker part of the legend in which the lighter-
skinned residents of Fairly, Oklahoma, would not allow them to stay. This
assumed mythic proportions as "The Disallowing" and underscored Ruby's
petrified insistence on remaining isolated and separate from the rest of the
world. No wonder in this novel that creates, explores, and dismantles the
polarizations of tradition and change, men and women, dark-skinned
blacks and lighter-skinned blacks, Ruby and the Convent, the narrative
begins and ends with conspiratorial perspectives, the men of Ruby assuming that their apocalyptic attack on the Convent will usher in a new era:
"God at their side, the men take aim. For Ruby" (18).

Meticulously Morrison examines the reasons and compulsions that mo-
tivate the men of Ruby to murder the women in the Convent. The Ruby
renegades wish to "expose its filth" (1); they attack at dawn, seeing "how
the mansion floated, dark and malevolently disconnected from God's
earth" (8). The giddiness of their mission propels them toward "the female
malice that hides there" (4). They discover strange objects—a letter in
blood, an astrological chart, baby booties—and assume the worst, viewing
the Convent as the FBI and the media viewed the Branch Davidians: a
sanctuary for "revolting sex, deceit and the sly torture of children" (8).
"Graven idols were worshipped here [by] bodacious black Eves unredeemed by Mary" (9, 18), a rhetoric of religious crusade that permeates
their assault. They meet secretly to plan their attack, contemplating "the

sheer destructive power" of the Convent, which they hold responsible for all the anguish and anxiety in Ruby, generational and otherwise: "The one thing that connected all these catastrophes was in the Convent. And in the Convent were those women" (17, 11). "They managed to call into question the value of almost every woman [they] knew" (8), an apocalyptic vision that Fairy DuPres, a midwife in Ruby, sums up succinctly: "Men scared of us, always will be. To them we're death's handmaiden" (272). In their eyes the helpful, harmless retreat that Morrison creates at the Convent can only be the flimsiest façade for lies, demonic rites, and venomous behavior.

Morrison builds her vision of the Ruby conspiracy carefully, revealing ideas and feelings that underscore all the conspiracies we have been examining up to this point. The men "mapped [their] defense . . . and honed evidence . . . till each piece fit an already polished groove" (275). They see themselves as "invaders preparing for slaughter . . . to execute the mission" (280). Opposition escalates: "I know they got powers. Question is whose power is stronger. . . . Bitches. More like witches. . . . They don't need men and they don't need God" (275–76). Lone DuPres, Fairy's daughter and also a midwife, makes the obvious linguistic connection, for the men see "not a convent but a coven" (276). Insists one, "Before those heifers came to town this was a peaceable kingdom" (176).

Evidence, of course, also appears in great and gathering abundance. The women from the Convent scandalize the wedding of Arnette Fleetwood and K. D. Morgan, the Morgan twins' nephew and only heir, by kissing, dancing, and fighting afterward. Of course when Arnette got pregnant awhile back and beat herself, among other things, to try and kill the child, she took herself to the Convent, where the women oversaw the birth of the damaged boy who lived only a few days. The Convent women poison Sweetie's opinion of her lot, a mother of four permanently damaged children and wife of Jeff Fleetwood. People have heard babies crying at the Convent and declared, "It ain't natural." "Something's going on out there" (276), a character exclaims, as more incidents pile up: the women drink like fish; they have something to do with a white family who got lost in their car in a blizzard and died, not very far from the Convent; and they constantly meddle in individual affairs, maiming all they come in contact with.

Morrison also interrogates the men who are involved in the final cataclysm. Sargeant covets the land the old Convent occupies. Wisdom Poole can no longer control his brothers and sisters, two of whom fight over the love of Billie Delia Best, who loves them both. That certainly ain't natural. Jeff Fleetwood and his father Arnold need to blame someone for Sweetie's deformed children. Menus, who wanted to marry a light-skinned woman but was forced by the Ruby hierarchy to give her up, took to drink, often dried out at the Convent, but now can't wait to raid it. K. D. had a torrid affair with Gigi (Grace) who lives out there and condemns her for demonically possessing him sexually. Deacon Morgan, Steward's brother, had a torrid, short-lived affair with Connie, the head of the Convent after Mary Magna died. And Connie had to have "seduced" Soane, his wife, who actually went there to have an abortion and sought consolation. Yet they remain incredulous and stunned: "How could so clean and blessed a mission devour itself and become the world they had escaped?" (292). How, indeed!

The effects of the conspiracy that kills the Convent women overwhelm Ruby at first, reinforcing Morrison's sad comment: "How exquisitely human was the wish for permanent happiness, and how thin human imagination became trying to achieve it" (306). "Something seismic had happened since July" (296), since the massacre in Ruby. Slowly two official stories emerge, one closer to the truth that brands all nine men guilty as charged, another that suggests only five of the men went on a rampage; the other four tried to stop them. Yet each did it because the women were "impure . . . unholy . . . and because they *could*" (297). Each changes his story, leaving many unanswered questions, especially when the dead bodies of the women mysteriously vanish. Only Deacon Morgan changes, turns quiet and against his twin brother Steward, who remains "insolent and unapologetic" (299), unforgiving, obstinate, inflexible, and proud. Walking barefoot to the Rev. Misner's house, he confesses to the minister, recognizing that he has become as much of a judge and destroyer as was his founding father Zechariah. Zechariah's checkered past emerges in a manner far different from the official story, abandoning his brother for dancing before white men and accused of "malfeasance in office" (302). Misner feels that the Ruby men betrayed their heritage or at least the better part of it: "How can they hold it together . . . this hard-won heaven defined only by the absence of the unsaved, the unworthy and the strange? Who will protect them from their leaders?" (306). Such questions target every cult and every conspiratorial cabal, imagined or otherwise. Billie

Delia, branded as a slut when she is still a virgin, who decides to leave Ruby once and for all, calls the place a prison, "a backward noplace ruled by men whose power to control was out of control" in their version of "the mutiny of the mares" (308).

The religious politics of Ruby enlarge and underscore the bipolarities of the missionaries' conspiracy and the victims' coven. On the one hand the Methodist Pulliam insists that his people can never be good enough for God. His fiery rhetoric condemns humanity as worthless and sinful, and he pumps his poison into the ears of the faithful. His Calvinist rage displays "a ravenous appetite for vengeance" (160) and stokes the fires of Ruby's revenge. His railing against women, pleasure, and sin prompts one character to describe all Methodists as "repressed rednecks, too scared to have wet dreams" (63). The Baptist Misner on the other hand at one point responds to one of Pulliam's tirades by marching down the aisle at K. D.'s and Arnette's wedding silently carrying the cross. He came to Ruby from a church in which "covert meetings" took place often "to stir folks up" (56) and discovers the same approach in Pulliam. For Misner God does not oppose humanity; "they did not have to beg for respect; it was already in them, and they needed only to display it" (209).

I have emphasized the conspiracy and polarizing aspects of *Paradise* to reveal Morrison's astuteness and concerns about such issues and as a way of summarizing the thrust of this book. The novel, of course, does not read so schematically and starkly, organized as it is around individual lives and such social ceremonies as the Morgan-Fleetwood wedding, Christmas in 1974, and Save-Marie's funeral at the end, one of Sweetie Fleetwood's damaged children. In doing so I have purposely left out the traumas and horrors that the women who arrive at the Convent have undergone— Mavis, Grace, Seneca, and Pallas—from the smothering and abandonment of their children to civil rights marches, sexual slavery, sexual betrayal, and abusive men. These are as individually explored as are the complex and interwoven lives of the people of Ruby and their problematic heritage: Steward and Dovey Morgan, Deacon and Soane Morgan (Dovey and Soane are also siblings); Anna Flood's and Pat Best's love for the Rev. Misner; the Bests, the Fleetwoods; the founding of Ruby and its suspicions of outsiders as revolutionary pioneers become rabid reactionaries; the racism between dark-skinned and light-skinned African Americans (Violet in *Jazz* always thought that Joe left her because Dorcas was light-skinned, a damaged self-image she had carried with her for years, based on her grandmother's devotion to the beautifully blonde Golden Gray); and the various problems of the younger souls of Ruby—Arnette, Menus, Billie Delia, and K. D.

Morrison provides an alternative to the conspiratorial vision. Consolata, kidnapped as a child from the abject poverty of a Latin American city by Mary Magna and brought back to the Convent, takes over the Convent after Mary Magna dies. However, she attacks herself for having kept Magna alive by embracing her and filling her with a strange interior glow: "She knew it was anathema . . . yoking the sin of pride to witchcraft . . . knowing [Mary's] life was prolonged by evil" (247). At fifty-four Connie is crushed by her actions, takes to drink, moves into the basement, and allows the Convent to run itself no matter whoever should stumble on it and decide to move in. Raised as a Catholic, she condemns herself for her use of the gift, of "stepping in" or "seeing in." At times she despises Mavis, Gigi, and the rest, but they see her as a "sweet, unthreatening old lady who seemed to love each of them best; who never criticized . . . accepted each as she was" (262). Morrison has always had a penchant for healers, and slowly Connie begins to occupy that role, "much more in touch with the magic and the mystery and things of the body" (78). "It seems to me that the most respectable person is that woman who is a healer and understands plants and stones and yet they live in the world. . . . Sometimes people call these people spirits, feminine spirits . . . 'gathering women . . . '" (Koenan 1980, 82, 81).

Connie initiates the "Loud Dreaming," a kind of exorcism in which the women whirl and sing and shriek, where Connie exclaims, "Hear me, listen. Never break them in two. Never put one over the other. Eve is Mary's Mother. Mary is the daughter of Eve" (263). What is this but Morrison's response to the men of Ruby's vision of the Convent women as "bodacious Eves unredeemed by Mary" (18). Connie transcends apocalyptic-generating, conspiracy-producing polarities by jettisoning the cramped rationality and bipolar language of English and becomes the Convent's new Reverend Mother. She and the Convent women are, indeed, witches of healing, and the men of Ruby should fear their harmonious and unifying vision. It is not for nothing that "the whole house felt permeated with a blessed malelessness, like a protected domain . . . an unbridled, authentic self" (177). Men must penetrate such female enclaves, aroused by their very conspiratorial natures and venomous missionary positions. Steward Morgan, we learn, kills the first woman.

Before the cataclysm the Convent women with shaved heads dance in the rain, and Connie sings the songs of Piedade, a female goddess or spirit whose name in Portuguese suggests compassion, pity, piety. "Piedade had songs that could still a wave," Connie tells her disciples. "Travelers refused to board homebound ships while she sang" (285). At the very end of *Paradise,* Piedade sings anew, evoking visions "of reaching age in the company of the other; of speech shared and divided bread smoking from the fire; the unambivalent bliss of going home to be at home—the ease of coming back to love begun" (318). Such an ending rivals the end of *Jazz* with the singer/the writer in love with her own art, praising her voice and including the reader within it. Paradise, if it exists at all, exists "down here" on this Earth and in these bodies. No wonder "women dragged their sorrow up and down the road between Ruby and the Convent" (270).

In Brazil Candomble, a religion in which African gods and Catholic saints masquerade as and are interchangeable with one another, speaks to a mingling of religious rites and vision that Morrison celebrates. Worshippers whirl in trances, possessed by the various gods and goddesses, overseen by a single female leader, the mother-of-the-spirits or the mother-of-the-saints. Women when initiated shave their heads. The world of Brazilian spirits exists equally on material and spiritual planes; neither one can be separate from the other.

Hidden away in the depths of the baroque carvings and statues high up on the cavernous ceilings of churches in Ouro Preto, the beautifully restored old colonial mining town in the interior Brazilian province of Minas Gerais, lurk black saints. The African slaves brought to Brazil by their Portuguese overlords often worked on the construction of such cathedral-like buildings and managed to include images of themselves amid the Catholic saints and prophets that look down on the parishioners. Salvation for these slaves may have existed in both their guile and their artistry.

Morrison admired that distant, barely visible black face that day in Ouro Preto in 1991 where, by sheer luck, both of us had been driven for the day. Suffused with her own religious sensibility and outlook, not in a dogmatic but in an expansive manner, like one standing before mysteries and legends you could not ever hope to understand but warmly appreciated both for their own power and the power African Brazilians nursed and cultivated in order to sustain themselves, Morrison spoke of herself as bearing witness to the rich and tragic experience of black people, a task and vision that permeate her fiction and criticism.

In that church in Ouro Preto where Morrison looked up to find the black spirit-saint hidden away in the far corner of the high ceiling, she described her interest in Candomble, perceiving it at its most syncretic in which separate "races" eventually become one, another destructive polarity overcome. At the end of *Paradise,* as filled with images of reconciliation as *Jazz,* as *Beloved* is with its images of loneliness and loss, focused on the possibilities of a very human paradise "down there" in place of *Beloved*'s darker depths, Piedade's song encompasses the strange, otherworldly incidents of reconciliation that precede it: Gigi is reunited with her father; Dee Dee, "Divine," paints her daughter Pallas's portrait; Sally finds her mother Mavis, and only Jean, who long ago abandoned Seneca, remains empty-handed.

Morrison's "supernatural" world invades our natural one, although she would never describe these common circumstances, embedded in her own African American culture and family stories, as an "invasion." Instead it happens naturally: the bodies of the Convent women vanish; there are no traces of the crime; and future reconciliations between these abused women and remnants of their families are possible. At the scene of the massacre Anna Flood sees a door, "or sensed it, rather, for there was nothing to see" (305), but her husband-to-be, the Rev. Misner, sees a window. "Whether through a door needing to be opened or a beckoning window already raised, what would happen if you entered? What would be on the other side? What *on earth* would it be? What *on earth*?" (italics mine, 305).

Perhaps a permissible, elusive human paradise on Earth is what Morrison envisions at the end of the novel, where Piedade continues to sing, and we can experience "the ease of coming back to love begun" (318). It is a fiction, but it is a craftily designed fiction to override the polarities of conspiracy and paranoia, those driving forces behind America's fascination with and seemingly untamed lust for its demise. Morrison attempts to heal that great divide by using her own postmodern techniques and structures, not neglecting at all the darker side of her own and our culture. She recognizes the rampant and festering ambiguities in her titles—*Beloved, Jazz, Paradise*—but she also recognizes the power of art, of fiction: "Look. How lovely it is, this thing we have done—together" (1994, 30).

"My complaint about letters now would be the state of criticism," Morrison complained in 1981. "It's following post-modern fiction into self-consciousness, talking about itself as though it were the work of art. Fine for the critic, but not helpful for the writer" (LeClair 1981, 127). At the height of literary theory, theories did infuse, co-opt, and digest one another, but even now such self-consciousness, particularly in Morrison's art, continues to thrive. Her fiction talks about itself all the time, as if it were in the talking that the work of art takes shape, and slowly dismantles conspiracy theories in its postmodern, fragmented structure, opening avenues to experience the wider, more fluid possibilities of the postmodern sublime.

After all our wrestlings and struggles with postmodern theory, fundamentalist faiths, apocalyptic visions, and the conspiratorial nature of language itself, underscored and abetted by American politics and culture over the last thirty years or so, Morrison's trilogy of tragic obsessions and demonic devotions—*Beloved, Jazz, Paradise*—strike me as a consummation and revelation of such things. For instance the character, if we can call her that, of Beloved shimmers as the perfect postmodern icon that remains ontologically uncertain, both fact and figment, ghost and girl who mesmerizes and possesses all those who come into intimate contact with her. As Morrison has described her, "She is a spirit on one hand, literally she is what Sethe thinks she is, her child returned to her from the dead [and] a survivor from the true, factual slave ship . . . because the language of both experiences—death and the Middle Passage—is the same" (Darling 1988, 247). She is also an assault on language's capability of trying to claim her, trying to render her significance complete and understandable. Her elusive existence conjures up the problems with the subatomic world, with quantum theories of light as particle and/or wave. Do we find it impossible to contain her because she is uncontainable, which suggests the truth of the uncanny, the unfathomable, and the incomprehensible, or because we haven't yet been able to find the means to contain and explain her? As postmodern readers we are stymied and stunned by what Marianne DeKoven has called "the uncontainable, apocalyptic excess Beloved represents" (1997, 8).

The conspiracies and effects of slavery and racism permeate Morrison's fictional realm, most conspicuously in the final novel of the trilogy, *Paradise*, which makes full use of conspiracy both in form and structure and in the furies unleashed within and those that contribute to the events that occur. In every case she despises "the reduction of the individual into a bloc, monolithic," defining one of her tasks as a writer, in a talk in Belo Horizonte, "to resist as much as possible the generalization." For her, as is well known, "a dark, abiding, signing Africanist presence" (1992, *Playing*, 5) defines and underscores white American freedoms: "The distinguishing features of the not-Americans were their slave status, their social status— and their color. . . . Africanism is the vehicle by which the American self knows itself as not enslaved, but free" (48, 52). She would agree, I think, with K. Anthony Appiah and Amy Gutmann that "we make up selves from a tool kit of options made available by our culture and society [and that] every major part of the cultural heritage of the United States is similarly changeable and contingent. And every major group's identity is culturally plural, not singular. Black and white Americans are multicultural" (1996, 96, 175). Our "visibility has made the prejudices last longer," Morrison asserts (Ruas 1981, 117), but she also explores the reality that race is a social construct, that, as Appiah and Gutmann conclude, "nobody has a race" (1996, 37). Of course, as they maintain, "if . . . you understand the sociohistorical process of construction of the race, you'll see that the label works despite the absence of an essence," but finally we must "live with fractured identities; engage in identity play; find solidarity, yes, but recognize contingency, and, above all, practice irony . . . the proposals of a banal 'postmodernism' " (81, 104).

J. Brooks Bouson carefully explores the conspiracy of silence, of self-denial that results from the trauma and shame Morrison's characters encounter. They "experience the inarticulateness and emotional paralysis of intense shame. Morrison dramatizes the painful sense of exposure that accompanies the single shame event and also the devastating effect of chronic shame on her characters' sense of individual and social identity, describing their self-loathing and self-contempt, their feelings that they are, in some essential way, inferior, flawed, and/or dirty . . . being ashamed about shame in an endless, and paralyzing, spiral of feelings" (2000, 4). Trauma drives such shame—social, individual, racial in the sense of slavery, personal prejudice, and institutionalized racism—and leads to conspiratorial narratives, secrets that slowly appear as if someone were about to confess or reveal some long lost curse or horror. Morrison often uses the phrase, "quiet as it's kept," to set up the revelation of a secret as she circles it, broods on it, and probes it. Here her narratives expose the conspiracies of slavery and racism, the curse and traumatic history of her characters' perceptions and consciousness. Accepting the living "with fractured identities" and engaging "in identity play" cannot begin to happen at all, until the horrors are faced and the "apocalyptic excess" of the African American experience in America acknowledged.

In *Jazz* Morrison questions and practically dismantles the authority of narrator and narrative, projecting herself as struggling with the same linguistic and conceptual difficulties that Sethe, Paul D., and Denver have wrestled with in *Beloved*. She recognizes the ease with which language, particularly in its Western "enlightened" and analytical manner, creates binary opposites, committing hierarchical sins by disguising them as logical equivalents: male and female, black and white, good and evil. She assaults this way of looking at the world, much as Derrida does, creating fictions that rely on oral traditions, different voices, multiple perspectives, the call-and-return structure of African American church services, and the breaks and riffs of jazz. Dismantling such simplistic, either/or categories also becomes a very effective way of dismantling racist categories and dichotomies.

"The fact is," Morrison explains, "that the stories look as though they come from people who are not even authors. No author tells these stories. They are just told—meanderingly—as though they are going in several directions at the same time. . . . The stories are constantly being retold, constantly being imagined within a framework. And I hook into this like a life-support system" (McKay 1983, 152, 153). As Philip Page contends, Morrison's novels are "quintessentially postmodern, American, and African-American. They are postmodern, not in the sense of extreme self-referentiality or in the mockery of narration, but in their privileging of polyvocalism, stretched boundaries, open-endedness, and unraveled binary oppositions" (1995, 9, 34). Rachel C. Lee views Morrison as "attempting a redefinition or respecifying of postmodernism's general emphasis on the instability of meaning" (2000, 8), that redefinition most likely originating from Morrison's proceeding "from one vision to the next," as Wendy Harding and Jacky Martin maintain. "The finished narrative is an attempt to connect the important scenes in her novels through chains of imagery that, weaving into one another, recreate the complexity of the original impression" (1994, 151). That complexity like the figure of Beloved remains ultimately ungraspable, incomprehensible, and consistently unstable, but the pursuit and process of the narrative underscore the necessary quests of the individual characters and narrator.

In all of her novels Morrison consistently marginalizes the marginal-ized, creating characters who must operate in extreme circumstances, pushed beyond the "mere" binaries that racism underwrites. "The norm itself becomes abnormal because of its inordinate pressure on individuals," Harding maintains, since "abnormality becomes the norm of the op-pressed" (1994, 16, 19). Morrison forces her characters beyond the institu-tionalized abnormalities of the system because of her interest in outlaws and pariahs, marginalized characters inhabiting the already marginalized world of their background. "All the books I have written deal with char-acters placed deliberately under enormous duress in order to see of what they are made," she explains (McKay 1983, 143), most likely because "my inclination is in the tragic direction" (125). Individual tragedy can rein-force cultural and social tragedies and reveal how racism not only deforms both blacks and whites involved within it but also forces many African Americans to react in more extreme and disturbing ways.

The outlaw attracts Morrison, a character type rendered in starker di-mensions because of the racist system within which she and her culture operate. "It's the complexity of how people behave under duress that is of interest to me," she explains, "the qualities they show at the end of an event when their backs are up against the wall" (McKay 1983, 1, 145). "It is always a push towards the abyss somewhere to see what is remarkable, because that's the way I find out what is heroic . . . models from Greek tragedy [seem] to me extremely sympathetic to Black culture and in some ways to African culture" (180–81, 2). Morrison insists on this vision: "In the stories, I place the characters on a cliff. I push them as far as I can to see what they are made of" (268, 2). The culture marginalizes the African American whom Morrison then marginalizes within that realm to test them, pursue them, play out the way they act and react because of their marginalized existence to begin with: "Living totally by the law and sur-rendering completely to it without questioning anything sometimes makes it impossible to know anything about yourself. . . . Many men [were] outlaws. . . . They were, oh, I don't know, episodic; they were adventures. They felt that they had been dealt a bad hand, and they just made up other rules" (14, 182). "These are not your normal everyday lives" (180–81), but neither is the culture that helps to produce them "normal." Or the language that often entraps and imprisons them. Or the spectators who often define them only to encircle and crush them. "It's a kind of self-flagellant resistance to certain kinds of control, which is fascinating," Morrison admits. "Opposed to accepted notions of progress, the lock-step life, they live in the world unreconstructed and that's it. . . . There are several levels of the pariah figure working in my writing. The black community is a pariah community. Black people are pariahs. The civilization of black people that lives apart from but in juxtaposition to other civilizations is a pariah relationship" (165, 168). It is akin to Ahab's "madness maddened," a kind of romantic exaggeration and enlargement of life that links Morrison's work to the best of the Hawthorne-Melville-Faulkner-Ellison tradition, though she would insist on this comment's being one more attempt on the part of the white community to co-opt and incarcerate her work.

The apocalyptic strain and vision in league with and perhaps a product of gothic fiction's fascination with haunted houses, traumatic repetition, the curse of the past and the doom of the present, permeate Morrison's work as well. She attacks the "old order," presses for individual and social renewal, pushes her characters often to the brink of insanity and breakdown, positing this as a kind of *via negativa* toward possible redemption and reconciliation. In doing so, in her attempt to unveil present circumstances and complexities, Morrison according to Susan Bowers reverses the expectations of white American apocalypse by viewing apocalypse as "repeatable and survivable," a West African sense of cyclical time as opposed to the white American vision of a linear trajectory toward some cataclysmic climax in the future that will cleanse the world as we presently know it (Bowers 1997, 212). Lift the veil and generate change. As Bowers continues, "the concentration on the horrors of the past and present is characteristic of apocalyptic writing," but for Morrison "apocalypse is not a synonym for disaster or cataclysm; it is linked to revelation" (214, 224). Morrison's apocalyptic moments—Bowers cites the arrival of Schoolteacher along with the four horseman in Cincinnati to take Sethe and her children back to Sweet Home in *Beloved*—reveal that the moral agency is human; there exists no "invisible presence of a god" to judge and rescue (221). Her characters, as well as the narrator in *Jazz*, must pursue those revelations no matter where they will lead and, in doing so, recognize the often painful and profound necessity of change and altered consciousness. African Americans can overcome their trauma, shame, and guilt, but it will continue to be a traumatic and apocalyptic process. They must discover and recognize the horrors—"no one tells the story about himself or herself unless forced. They don't want to talk, they don't want to remember" (248)—before being able to do anything about or with them and from there move toward a less oppressive revelation of human possibility and apocalyptic hope. But so must all of us, as we readers become participants in Morrison's texts.

The theory of emergence suggests that more complex beings and concepts emerge from the bottom up, not from the top down, and this idea can be seen as a way to grapple with Morrison's deployment of voices, tales, legends, and yarns, perhaps the best antidote to conspiracy-freighted perspectives and paranoia-inducing scenarios. Morrison's fiction, I suggest, operates in a similar manner, leaving many of her novels open-ended and multiply suggestive. As Gay Wilentz explains, "Certain genres of African orature, particularly the dilemma tales, have unresolved endings which call for community response" (1997, 115). Whether cultural product or stylistic process and, in Morrison's case, essentially both, she has always said that she knows the endings of her fictions before they begin "because that's part of the idea, part of the theme," but "it doesn't shut, or stop there. That's why the endings are multiple endings. That's where the horror is. That's where the meaning rests; that's where the novel rests" (Ruas 1981, 101). For her "the open-ended quality that is sometimes a problematic in the novel form reminds me of the uses to which stories are put in the black community" (153). The stories continue, are reshaped, reimagined, remade as the community reworks its relationship to its own past and its individual responses to that past. Morrison seeks no resolution to a mystery in the sense of revealing the culprit or spelling out solutions: "There is a resolution of a sort but there are always possibilities—choices. . . . And in that sense it is Greek in the sense that the best you can hope for is some realization and that, you know, a certain amount of suffering is not just anxiety. It's also information" (177). Characters pursue knowledge not necessarily answers, and the open-ended endings allow both them and readers to follow that pursuit beyond the final words on the final page.

At their best, stories and language for Morrison produce not a post-modernist radical skepticism or a worldview made vertiginously fluid by a sense of ultimate relativity but a cosmos and vision that is more relational, contingent, communicative, and inclusive. Things become interconnected and are mutually constructed. The "dumb, predatory, sentimental" qualities of official language that is meant to dominate and demand obeisance—binary oppositions, racism—must be shattered, Morrison proclaimed in her Nobel lecture, for "language alone protects us from the scariness of things with no names. Language alone is meditation" (1994, 14, 28). True, language is a system, ossified and regulated by its own signs and scrawls, but it can also be "a living thing over which one has control." It is an agent that produces "an act with consequences." Therefore "narrative is radical, creating us at the very moment it is being created." As Morrison stated in *Playing in the Dark,* in her talk with Belo Horizonte in 1991, she works to reproduce "the music of the sound of the speaking text . . . for the sound of the sentence, [perceiving the] text as a score. . . . When it's going very well, I can hear it."

Language creates the stories that bind and empower, articulate and evoke. "The point was to tell the same story again and again. . . . People who are listening comment on it and make it up, too, as it goes along" (1994, 105–6). Such tellings and re-tellings "[create] interdependence, an intersubjectivity that exists not only among but also within every member of the community" (103). To narrate is to speak, to address, to connect, recover, and attempt to possess. It demands "the head-on encounter with . . . historical forces and the contradictions inherent in them, [promising] not escape but entanglement" (1992, *Playing,* 36, 37).

Morrison's postmodern vision emerges from this engagement, one that opposes the modernist sense of a self braving alien entanglements, a subject attempting to dominate the objects of the world and of the Other but of a self mired in the world, entangled and webbed within it, aware of its own relational contingency and fragile culpabilities. Morrison's is what Louise M. Rosenblatt would call a transactional vision, "freeing us from the old separation between the human creature and the world, [that] reveals the individual consciousness as a continuing self-ordering, self-creating process, shaped by and shaping a network of interrelationships with its environing social and natural matrix. Out of such transactions flowers the author's text, an utterance awaiting the readers whose participation will consummate the speech act" (1978, 172, 73).

This vision dovetails with Morrison's sense of the supernatural and ghost stories: "I want my books to reflect the imaginative combination of the real world, the very practical, shrewd, day to day functioning that black people must do, while at the same time they encompass some great supernatural element. We know that it does not bother them one bit to do something practical and have visions at the same time" (153). Morrison grew up with ghost stories, especially her father's, in a culture in which ghosts and visions were as prevalent as the most mundane of ordinary objects or events: "Black people believe in magic. Once a woman asked me, 'Do you believe in ghosts?' I said, 'Yes. Do you believe in germs?' It's part of our heritage" (46). The postmodern sense of being possessed, being controlled by outside forces, for Morrison appears as part and parcel of her overall perspective: "While we watch the world, the world watches us. [All my novels are] open to animism and anthropomorphism" (110). "It's an animated world in which trees can be outraged and hurt, and in which the presence or absence of birds is meaningful" (100).

> Spiritual forces [are] the reality. I mean, it's not as though it's a thing you do on Sunday morning in church, it's not a tiny, entertaining aspect of one's life—it's what *informs* your sensibility. I grew up in a house in which people talked about their dreams with the same authority that they talked about what "really" happened. They had visitations and did not find that fact shocking and they had some sweet, intimate connection with things that were not empirically verifiable. It not only made them for me the most interesting people in the world—it was an enormous resource. (226)

Such an inclusive vision, in combination with Christian theology, left Morrison aware of "something larger and coherent, and benevolent . . . " (Taylor-Guthrie 1994, 178).

Morrison's fictions move from conspiracy to community, from feud to family, from race typecast by white culture as an essence to race as a lived, complex, socially constructed experience in America. From an initial crime—Sethe's murder of Beloved, Joe's murder of Dorcas, the Ruby vigilantes' murder of the Convent women, from aggressor and victimizer to victim—she writes herself into more complex and communal interconnections where victims can become aggressors, women can triumph, and men can begin to heal. Morrison's trilogy develops sinuous tales that dismantle binary compulsions and stereotypically cultural perspectives, creating elaborate narratives that entangle and enmesh both characters and readers.

This narrative trajectory toward reconciliation and connection is certainly true, but it also remains fragile and ambiguous. Sethe and Paul D. may seem reconciled to each other, but *Beloved* ends with ominous comments on the still-elusive Beloved, an enormous presence-as-absence that cannot be entirely circumvented or forgotten. *Jazz* ends with the narrator's revelations about her doubts and uncertainties, hoping that by speaking to readers directly and acknowledging that in holding the book they are connecting directly with her, she and they may be able to transcend the lingering shadows that still hover around the fact of Dorcas's death. The different stories that surface after the attack on the Convent in *Paradise* may somewhat soothe the remaining doubts about the men of Ruby, and Morrison does create a kind of wish-fulfilling ending of reconciliation and redemption, but the gaps between these narrative strategies and the horrific murders of the Convent women do not close so easily. The path from conspiracy to community exists, but it remains ambivalent, uncertain, and ephemeral. This may figure into the overly simplistic fictional and binary-bookended route from trauma to triumph that Morrison works to dismantle and thus be part of her genuine ambiguity and complexity, but in her own comments and in those of several critics, the rush to reconciliation seems more pronounced outside the novels than within.

Beloved completes a circle in much the same way that *The Scarlet Letter* does. Forgoing the simplistic connections critics have made between Hester Prynne and Sethe, we can still see that both books begin with the title and end with it. In each the major focus, Beloved and the letter itself, remain ultimately unfathomable icons, a subject and object so riddled with multiple interpretations and speculations that they suggest only more such possibilities, ultimately eluding writer and reader in the scope of signification that surrounds them. They continue to mesmerize, fester, and appall, images that have performed in certain ceremonies that at the novels' end go right on performing, right on suggesting, uncannily luminous with further meanings and darker designs. They function like the images in nightmares that terrorize and hypnotize their spectators, involving them to participate in rites that can only be repeated, never fully comprehended. As Sally Keenan suggests, "*Beloved* is a story that revolves around contradiction: a story of an infanticide motivated by the mother's fierce love, a story that is itself about a preoccupation with storytelling" (1998, 121). Like *The Scarlet Letter* before it, *Beloved* "presents these patterns of ambiguous circularity but also enacts them"; in effect "it reworks the postmodern condition" (140, 158).

The confusion at the beginning of the novel never entirely disappears at the conclusion. Morrison has remarked how she shortened the opening sentences to create a more jagged, staccato effect, so that the reader would be both entirely ensnared and confused. We begin with spite and venom, the flight of Sethe's sons, ominous signs of shattered mirrors and handprints in cakes, Baby Suggs's illness and her sense that both past and present are "intolerable" (1987, 4). At the end we are left with the kind of "loneliness that roams. No rocking can hold it down. . . . Remembering seemed unwise. . . . So they forgot her" (274, 275). But "sometimes the photograph of a close friend or relative—looked at too long [like the scarlet letter; the gaze invests the object with hypnotic powers to the point at which it seems the letter demonically possesses the mind and soul of the spectator whose obsession curdles all too easily into trance]—shifts, and something more familiar than the dear face itself moves there" (275). All traces of Beloved may vanish, but the people must compel themselves to forget, fearing to remember "what it is down there." The last word is the title, embodied phantom and book that, however eager we are not to pass them on, to let them die, yet suggests that we will be unable to do so.

Beloved remains the perfect postmodern icon, the "thing" that language cannot subdue or explain, epistemologically and ontologically adrift, a signified whose many signifiers will never catch up to her fleeting, fleeing absence. She becomes an embodied ghost, a ghostly embodiment, succubus, vampire, demon, daughter. In Morrison's African American realm the supernatural and the natural mingle and mix; they are not at all mutually exclusive but part of some wider, more mysterious cosmos. She shimmers just beyond human attempts to render her symbolic and thereby capture her within the skein of language. She remains untranslatable, unspeakable, a creature always in transition from ghost to baby to adolescent to adult to would-be mother. Her story as Jean Wyatt posits "continues to haunt the borders of a symbolic order that excludes it" (1993, 249). Caroline Rody describes her as "an eruption of powerful, physical female desire that radically threatens the distinction between past and present" (2000, 103), a voracious past desiring to overtake the present and imbue it with Beloved's own wants and needs. She shines, and she ruptures, exorcised by the Cincinnati women who come to the house at 124 and literally shout her into nonexistence.

Throughout *Beloved* Morrison concentrates on the shifting alliances and betrayals of various relationships between Sethe, Paul D., Denver, and Beloved. Each of these characters develops into a postmodern self, which becomes contingent, relational, and provisional. At one time, for instance, Denver delights in Beloved's existence and vows to protect her from Sethe; at another she devotes herself to protecting Sethe from Beloved. In each case Morrison creates a thickening web of fluid relationships, ever changing, always in transition. This emerges most dramatically in the three monologues of the three women. Each claims that the other belongs to her. Sethe claims a daughter, Denver a sister, Beloved a mother and a kind of alternate or mutual self. Sethe turns on Paul D. Denver, fearing her mother's violence, remembers her grandmother, Baby Suggs, and praises Suggs's advice that "the ghost was after Ma'am and her too for not doing anything to stop it. But it would never hurt me" (1987, 209).

Much has been written about Beloved's tortuous monologue with its gaps and fissures, as if her very presence threatens all language and every attempt to try and explain her existence. Pronouns stumble into one another, so that Beloved, Sethe's mother, and Sethe become one and the same. It is a postmodern reverie with a vengeance, as unstable and uncertain as language can be and still suggest a vague aura of coherence and rationality with its references to slave ships, slave auctions, bridges, suicides, water, urine, rain, diamonds, and iron circles. One need only re-read the Quentin Compson section of Faulkner's *The Sound and the Fury* to see how much more conceptually lucid Quentin's monologue is than Beloved's. He, too, is virtually a ghost, but the male urge to analyze and conceptualize, to define and separate dominates his diatribe. Beloved wishes demonically to possess, join, become one whole instead of one singular, become another's face, "a hot thing" (213).

This rises to a crescendo in the final spare dialogues between Beloved and Sethe, Beloved and Denver, Denver and Sethe in the final pages of this strange, remarkably haunting section. Language collapses into chant, into stasis, into numbing obsessive repetition: "You are mine You are mine You are mine" (217). Separate selves slide into a vacuous, language-stunning unity and identity, a kind of maternal embrace run amuck, a horrible transcendence of the postmodern self that can only leave most of the page of text blank. The ghost story becomes the ghost of narrative, reaching that still point of silence and space that can only be radically overcome by Morrison's swift shift to Paul D. in the basement of the Church of the Holy Redeemer, remembering his Kentucky past and Beloved's seemingly calculated campaign to move him out of Sethe's house.

Morrison achieves a perilous balance between past and present, memory and action that are so interfused one with the other that each continually breaks into the other's realm. At one point Paul D. exclaims, "It made him dizzy. At first he thought it was [Sethe's] spinning. Circling him the way she was circling the subject" (161).

Sethe defines the process as "rememory," a condition that results in the materialization of memory itself. If she remembers something—an image, an incident, an odor, a glimpse—it achieves its own presence "out there," so that if you were to revisit the place you can remember, you would come upon the memory intact and visible. It waits for you. "What I remember," Sethe muses, "is a picture floating around out there outside my head. I mean, even if I don't think it, even if I die, the picture of what I did, or knew, or saw is still out there. Right in the place where it happened" (36). You can even "bump into a rememory that belongs to somebody else." This description reflects Morrison's own process of writing: "The approach that's most productive and most trustworthy for me is the recollection that moves from the image to the text. Not from the text to the image" (Plasa 1998, 47). Sethe's "rememorying" parallels Morrison's, which involves the reader in a similar process, a postmodern layering of images and incidents that float in and out of focus and bind us to the text in the same possessively aggressive manner that memory haunts and nearly eviscerates Sethe and, by analogy, her creator.

What start out as separate places or spaces—the past and the present, memory and action—turn out to become one sumptuously interwoven process that reiterates the choral horrors of "You are mine You are mine You are mine" (1987, 217), as we are Morrison's readers as well. Morrison's narrative performs actions similar to Beloved's demonic urge to join, possess, and embody, entangling the reader in the epistemological and ontological postmodern puzzles and mysteries of Morrison's text. Text metamorphoses into web, language into chant, narrative into seductive performance that can lead only to its final enigmatic end: "Beloved."

"What makes one write anyway," Morrison has said, "is something in the past that is haunting, that is not explained or wasn't clear so that you are almost constantly rediscovering the past. I am geared toward the past, I think, because it is important to me; it is living history" (Jones and Vinson 1985, 171). She has also stated, "I am very happy to hear that my books haunt. That is what I work hard for, and for me it is an achievement when they haunt readers. . . . I think it is a corollary, or parallel, or an outgrowth of what the oral tradition was" (146). For Morrison, then, the past haunts her in such a way that she wishes to convey that process and experience of haunting in novels that are themselves haunted and haunting. She links this vision directly to the oral tradition, since characters can then witness their own hauntings and pass them on, their tales to be continued and reinvigorated by others who follow them in a persistent and continuous condition of hauntedness. The problem, of course, is that such hauntings can immobilize more than they redeem, but for Morrison the haunting and the possible redemption, collectively participated in, are flip sides of the same coin. Thus as Paul D. recognizes about Sethe, "Her story was bearable because it was his as well—to tell, to refine and tell again . . . the things neither had word-shapes for—well, it would come in time" (1987, 99). The telling and re-telling provide their own ghostly presence or aura of hope. In time, well, things will be told, and redemption may surface.

Morrison has described the oral tradition as a peasant one: "Peasant stories don't pass any judgments. The village participates in the story and makes it whatever it is. So that accounts for the structure, the sort of call-and-response thing that goes on" (Wilson 1981, 132). That participation may account for her mingling of historical lore with generic gothic devices—the haunted house, the haunted self, the deep dark secret that because it gets repressed, must explode into the open later on. The African American tradition of oral participation also participates in a kind of psychological unthawing or communal exorcism, a necessary product of slavery and racism. The apocalyptic flavoring and aura derive from this process of persistent unveiling, an interior as well as an exterior process, the horror revealed in the circular chant that envelops and articulates it. Once made visible or audible, the horror loses some of its hidden horrific aura, and the more communal process of healing can begin.

In theory this reveals the trajectory of *Beloved*'s narrative, although the actual process remains far more ambivalent and uncertain, participating and reinforcing Beloved's own inchoate compulsions and desires. In such a way the text does not so much heal as it possesses and overpowers both Sethe and the reader, thereby not so much transcending the horrors of history but immersing itself—and us—in them. Thus, as Andrew Schopp asserts, "Morrison's text demonizes the very processes of cultural narration, [since she] constructs a narrative that is highly complicit with what it seeks to challenge" (2000, 227). *Beloved* performs the postmodern process that seduces, subverts, and mesmerizes, leaving the reader as affected by text as Sethe is by memory, the both of us victimized by the elusive, demanding presence/absence of Beloved.

"Freeing yourself was one thing," Paul D. thinks as slavery has been outlawed and dismantled. "Claiming ownership of that freed self was another" (1987, 95). Therein lies the complex psychology of *Beloved* with its focus on mother love, infanticide, overwhelming human suffering, and their residual effects on the survivors. One can never "own" the postmodern self—one is reminded of Jack Barnes's comment to Brett Ashley at the end of *The Sun Also Rises:* "Isn't it pretty to think so?"—but it is the process toward that remote possibility that intrigues Morrison. At the same time characters long "to get to a place where you could love anything you chose—not to need permission for desire—well now, *that* was freedom" (162). Baby Suggs's sermons direct desire to one's flesh, to love and cherish it beyond and despite the way it has been marked, marred, and marketed by slavery, thus focusing attention on the self as body, the self as desire for and of itself. That message contradicts the desire to keep the haunting haunted, which argues in its textual embodiment against an ultimate freedom. Ownership and desire may be the qualities of an ultimate human freedom, but the text never quite achieves this. If it does not or cannot, at the very least it propels us forward toward the moment when Paul D. tells Sethe, "You your best thing" and longs "to put his story next to hers" (273).

The complex relationship between reconciliation and ongoing "haunts" continues long after *Beloved* ends. It enters the postmodern realm of instability and uncertainty, the postmodern sublime having emerged from the postmodern text. "It's not over just because it stops," Morrison explains. "It lingers and it's passed on. It's passed on ["This is not a story to pass on" (1987, 275)] and somebody else can alter it later. You may even end it if you want. It has a moment beyond which it doesn't go, but the ending is never like in a Western folktale where they all drop dead or live happily ever after" (Darling 1988, 253). Baby Suggs's idea of possible grace collapses after Sethe's murder of Beloved: "There is no bad luck in the world but whitefolks" (1987, 89), and Sethe learns early "that anybody white could take your whole self for anything that came to mind" (251). Such black-white fears need no explanation, but one wonders if Morrison by histori-cally situating this grimly comprehensible "racism" in some ways perpetu-ates it. At one point she stated that if she had not tried to write *Beloved*, she would have allowed slaveholders to win: "You have to take the au-thority back; you realign where the power is. So I wanted to *take* the power. They were very inventive and imaginative with cruelty, so I have to take it back, in a way that I can tell. And that is the satisfaction" (Caldwell 1987, 245). She has acknowledged that "we are all of us, in some measure, *victims* of *something*" (40), and yet like the complicated novel itself, we can continue to wonder what is being reconciled, what is being left as a haunting history, and what is being perpetuated. Her perspective, however, remains clear: "There was this ad hoc nature of everyday life. For black people, anybody might do anything at any moment. Two miles in any direction, you may run into Quakers who feed you or Klansmen who kill you—you don't know" (258).

Beloved remains powerful and open-ended, a postmodern text on so many levels that it continues to haunt and taunt the reader. The pain ren-dered here does not lead to a kind of redemptive Christian suffering. In-stead it undercuts all attempts at discovering and holding onto whatever sense of self can be salvaged from the wreckage of Sweet Home, the fires, the murders, the tortures, the rapes, and the visceral humiliations and trau-mas. As does Beloved, the elusive, fascinating and terrifying postmodern icon that will not scare. She remains "down there . . . the breath of the disremembered and unaccounted for. . . .

"Beloved" (275).

Beloved appears in a similar guise in *Jazz* as the wild woman in the woods, naked and pregnant, whom Golden Gray stumbles on. "Every-thing about her is violent," Gray thinks, but his biggest fear is "that an exposed woman will explode in his arms, or worse, that he will, in hers" (1992, *Jazz*, 153). Gray has just learned that however blonde his hair and light his skin, he is black, the illegitimate son of Vera Louise Gray and her parents' slave, Henry LesTroy/LeStory, also known as Hunters Hunter. Outraged, Gray has gone in search of his father to kill him, and it is then in the wet forest that he comes across a naked, pregnant, black woman who is so disheveled that at first he thinks she might be a vision. Gray is repulsed and confused, eager to be off and pass her by, but he finally relents as if his good manners kick in and save the day, according to the narrator. If we press the issue, we could make the case that Joe, who names the woman "Wild" and goes on to become the husband of Violet and lover of Dorcas, could be the son of Beloved and Paul D., thus linking *Jazz* to *Beloved*, to the "black, liquid female" (145) of "unmothering" (167): "Wild was always on his mind. . . . [She was] everywhere and nowhere. . . . A wild woman is the worst of all" (176, 179, 165). As the narrator admits, she can never be sure if Joe's tears "were for more than Dorcas. . . . I thought he was looking for her, not Wild's chamber of gold" (221).

The narrator's relationship to Wild becomes one of the more interesting facets of *Jazz*, as she (the narrator) meticulously undermines the authority of her own narration, another postmodern phenomenon, which Morrison raises to new heights in the second novel of her trilogy. Let us first take a step back, however, to see the broader implications of the narrator and the narrative before exploring them in greater detail.

In 1985 Morrison told Gloria Naylor about a photograph she had seen and a story she had read. James Van der Zee's collection of pictures, *The Harlem Book of the Dead*, had been published by Camille Billops, and Billops related the tale about Van der Zee's remembering "everybody he had photographed":

In one picture, there was a young girl lying in a coffin and he says that she was eighteen years old and she had gone to a party and that she was dancing and suddenly she slumped and they noticed there was blood on her and they said, "What happened to you?" And she said, "I'll tell you tomorrow. I'll tell you tomorrow." That's all she would say. And apparently her ex-boyfriend or somebody who was jealous had come into the party with a gun and a silencer and shot her. And she kept saying, "I'll tell you tomorrow" because she

wanted him to get away. And he did, I guess; anyway, she died.
(Naylor 1985, 207)

Morrison was fascinated with this story because it was one of those apoc-
ryphal tales like the story of Margaret Garner in 1851 who became the
prototype for Sethe: "A woman loved something other than herself so
much. She had placed all of the value of her life in something outside
herself" (Naylor 1985, 207). Morrison told Naylor: "It's peculiar to women
. . . because the best thing that is in us is also the thing that makes us
sabotage ourselves, sabotage in the sense that our life is not as worthy . . .
[what is it] that really compels a good woman to displace the self, her self"
(208)?

In *Beloved* Beloved returns to try and find out her own answers to that
complicated question, and Morrison decided "to extend her life . . . her
search, her quest, all the way through as long as I care to go, into the
twenties where it switches to this other girl. Therefore, I have a New York
uptown-Harlem milieu in which to put this love story, but Beloved will
be there also" (Naylor 1985, 208). In an analogous manner Dorcas embodies Sethe's role in her relation to Beloved, and Wild plays a kind of displaced Beloved in relation to Dorcas. Whereas Sethe wishes to protect
Beloved by killing her, Dorcas wishes to protect Joe by letting herself die.
As Morrison continued, "So what I started doing and thinking about for
a year was to project the self not into the way we say 'yourself,' but to put
a space between those words, as though the self were really a *twin* or
a thirst or a friend or something that sits right next to you and watches
you . . . " (208). The idea of the twin underscores the structure of Morrison's paired characters—Sethe and Beloved, Dorcas and Wild, Joe and
Dorcas, Paul D. and Sethe—that binary opposition, which Morrison then
dismantles.

In Dorcas's actual death scene in *Jazz,* which we observe both from her
point of view (as related by the narrator) and from her friend Felice's, as
Felice reveals Dorcas's dying words to the Traces, Dorcas refuses to divulge
Joe's name, but at the same time she has left him for a younger man Acton,
whom she aggressively pursues, and told Joe that he makes her sick. She
feels that Joe may be coming for her, but "if he does he will look and see
how close me and Acton dance" (1992, 190). At the party where Joe shoots
her, she is in love with the room and the music: "This is the market where

gesture is all. . . . This is not the place for old men; this is the place for romance" (192). Felice is asking her who shot her, but Dorcas thinks, as she slowly sinks into unconsciousness, "They want me to say his name. Say it in public at last" (192). All the while she focuses on Acton and her own dying. It isn't love that stops her but a sense of glamour and power. She remembers Joe's sample case of cosmetics and that "the world rocked from a stick beneath my hand" (193), a very different impression from the story Morrison told Naylor about Van der Zee's photograph. The narrator of *Jazz* views Dorcas as Felice sees her, aggressive, superficial, and driven to enjoy life—"Joe didn't care what kind of woman I was. He should have. I cared. I wanted to have a personality and with Acton I'm getting one. I have a look now" (190)—a perspective that helps to undermine the image of Joe as a crazed, vengeful, and violent man.

When speaking to the Traces, perhaps hoping to ease their pain and quiet desperation, especially Joe's, Felice explains, "Dorcas let herself die. . . . 'Don't let them call nobody,' she said. 'No ambulance; no police, no nobody.' I thought she didn't want her aunt, Mrs. Manfred, to know. Where she was and all. . . . She bled to death . . . " (209–10). And she adds: "Dorcas cold. . . . I never saw her shed a tear about anything" (212). It may be true of Dorcas that she "loved something other than herself. . . . She had placed all of the value of her life in something outside herself" (207), but that something suggests more her pursuit of Acton and her "look" than it does any love for Joe. As we will see, the narrator views the city as the great instigator and generator of such behavior, and perhaps Dorcas in such a context, especially with the horrible deaths of her parents and the strict aunt she lives with, can choose no other course, but she might also have decided to throw in the towel and given up the ghost once and for all. Felice's perspective scorns the fickle but manipulative Dorcas, but the narrator also aids and abets it.

Several critics have rightly pointed out that what the narrator predicts will happen doesn't. The narrator thinks that Violet will probably kill Joe, believing in a cycle of violence that must be obeyed and satiated. The convergence of Violet, Joe, and Felice can lead only to another triangle of bloodshed: "Violet invited her [Felice] in to examine the record and that's how that scandalizing threesome on Lenox Avenue began. What turned out different was who shot whom" (6). No one shot anyone, and the "scandalizing" exists only in the narrator's mind. She prides herself on knowing Joe's true character—"I was never deceived . . . his hat had to be just so. . . . Look out for a faithful man near fifty . . . free to do something wild" (119, 120)—and later in the novel upbraids the spoiled blonde Golden Gray as well, but at the conclusion, she realizes her mistake: "I was sure one would kill the other. I waited for it so I could describe it" (220).

As Morrison assaults her own believability and authority as a narrator (I am calling the narrator "Morrison" for convenience's sake, when she just as easily could be and is one more character in the tale, the lively gossip monger feeding on rumor, innuendo, and half-truths, although she does slip into the third-person omniscient point of view, thereby problematizing the narrator's voice as both inside and outside the narrative), she at the same time performs her role as a participatory voice in the story. As she upbraids her own conceits and strategies and distances herself from the characters' motives and conscious plans, she leaves them intact as seemingly "factual" as the crimes revealed in the first paragraph of the novel. Harding concurs: "The narrative seemingly disintegrates in order to celebrate its narratively constructed referent. Instead of reducing the novel to optical diffractions, Morrison altogether dismisses the machinery of the novel as a fundamentally deficient means of representing the inaccessible humanity of its subject" (1994, 168). And yet she wonders, "What would I be without a few brilliant spots of blood to ponder? Without aching words that set, then miss, the mark?" (219). For her, violence and the act of writing reflect each other as she admits her own complicity in the bloody tale she has just conjured up.

Convinced "that the past was an abused record with no choice but to repeat itself," she recognizes "how shabbily my know-it-all self covered helplessness. That when I invented stories about [other characters] . . . I was completely in their hands, managed without mercy" (220). By creating broken lives, she can then mend them: "I was so sure, and they danced and walked all over me" (220). In criticizing herself and revealing her penchant for violence and possible reconciliation, Morrison suggests the postmodern position that does not deny the existence of the past but only our inability to know and master it. The instability of truth lies not in the record of past events, of specific incidents, but in our interpretation and understanding of them. In that sense there is nothing outside the text, as Derrida proclaims, because texts provide the only evidence of what happened, and each and every one of them bristles with personal perceptions and conceptual choices. In *Jazz* Morrison has made this process more visible and, therefore, wonderfully problematic. The narrator becomes the predictable character, not her characters: "Now it's clear why they contradicted me at every turn: they knew me all along" (220).

Which brings us back to Wild, the possible (re)incarnation of Beloved in the wet woods. Much of the underlying narrators' strategies and compulsions of *Beloved* lie in their attempt to come to grips with the elusive, persistent "loneliness that roams. . . . It is alive, on its own. A dry and spreading thing . . . " (274). That untranslatable, uncanny, unfathomable presence participates in the stigma of black identity, in its supposed wildness, sexuality, and lawlessness. Morrison locates much of that wildness in black men, in the male urge to dominate and flee. Men "don't talk about the vulnerable 'me,'" she has explained. "It must be hard for men to confide in one another. . . . That's hard for them. Because they are trained out of it so early in life. . . . Only when they get very much older, then they can stop posturing. . . . It's a terrible burden" (193). She admits to finding that sense of flight and adventure "attractive" (27) and maleness a kind of outlaw and rogue quality and condition: "They have an enormous responsibility to be *men*. There's something very large in that word. Men define their masculinity by other men" (7). Hunters Hunter tells his son Golden Gray, "Be what you want—white or black. Choose. But if you choose black, you got to act black, meaning draw your manhood up—quicklike, and don't bring me no whiteboy sass" (173). Joe in his own view reinvents himself seven times, choosing various roles and possibilities, as if it were only a matter of individual will: "I sell trust. I make things easy. . . . You could say I've been a new Negro all my life" (122, 129). His fear of Wild and his loss of Dorcas compel him to act, but he prefers seeing himself as the self-made man, the autonomous individual who, being male, can call the shots.

But it is the black woman in whom Morrison puts most of her faith and hope. "They were the culture bearers," she maintains (McKay 1983, 140). "Aggression is not as new to black women as it is to white women. Black women seem able to combine the nest and the adventure" (Tate 1983, 161). For her, the black woman "had nothing to fall back upon: not maleness, not whiteness, not ladyhood, not anything. And out of the profound desolation of her reality she may very well have invented herself" (62–63). "What's the world for if you can't make it up the way you want it?" Violet asks Felice. "Don't you want it to be something more than what it is?" (1992, 208). Black women for Morrison "have held, have been given, you know, the cross. They don't walk near it. They're often on it. And they've borne that, I think, extremely well" (Stepto 1976, 17).

For the narrator of *Jazz* to embrace Wild and reveal her feelings of identification with her totally implicates her in all the horrors and dangerous delights of black identity in a white society, and that abiding sense of identity precedes and transcends the city she loves so much. The narrator feels safe and snug in Wild's "chamber of gold" but also "wide open": "I am touched by her. Released in secret. Now I know" (1992, 221). Joe's search for Wild and later for Dorcas parallels the narrator's search for her own selfhood, that self-identification she must link to Beloved and Wild: "We have a lot of rage, a lot of violence; it comes too easily to us. The amazing thing to me is that there is so much love also" (41). Morrison's characters are not the only ones caught in extreme circumstances with tragic implications, and the narrator of *Jazz* recognizes this as she moves from her gossipy opening line—"Sth I know that woman" (3)—to "they knew me all along" (220).

New York City in the 1920s, before she considers and recognizes deeper, more underground and inner revelations, dazzles and seduces the narrator, deranges and distorts, enlivens and compels. She surrenders herself to all of its sumptuous and lascivious offerings as if it embodies inexhaustible desire, complete in and of itself with no thought to imminent demise. Surrendering to such a lavish and seemingly omnipotent desire, explosively embodied in the Harlem of 1926, she celebrates surrender in others: Joe to Violet, Vera Louise Gray to Hunters Hunter, Golden Gray to Henry Les-Troy, True Belle and Violet to the image of Golden Gray, Dorcas to Acton, birds to music, men and women to jazz, "something rogue" that she cannot explain, "something else you have to figure in before you can figure it out" (228). "I'm crazy about this City" (7), she exclaims but then has to admit that "It was loving the City that distracted me and gave me ideas. Made me think I could speak its loud voice and make that sound human. I missed the people altogether" (220).

The narrator's romance with the city as an environment and magical landscape of unrelenting and unquenchable desire underscores her sense of self: "I'm strong. Alone, yes, but topnotch and indestructible—like the City in 1926" (7). The downside of this perilous but energizing infatuation, however, bothers her early on but not enough to destroy it: "I lived a long time, maybe too much, in my own mind. People say I should come out more" (9). She marches on, celebrating and strutting her vision: "Here comes the new. Look out. There goes the sad stuff. . . . History is over, you all" (7), and in doing so expresses the hopes and elation of African Americans migrating from the South to this glorious Xanadu: "I like the way the City makes people think they can do what they want and get away with it . . . it's all laid out for you" (8, 9). In such a magic kingdom how else can people live? Joe's love for Dorcas? "He *knew* wrong wasn't right, and did it anyway" (74). "That's the way the City spins you. Makes you do what it wants" (120). Morrison's Whitmanic sense of abundance overpowers any doubts as the narrator waxes eloquently about the sky seen from the city, the satisfaction of Thursday men, the colors and aromas of spring, and the young men on the rooftops with their clarinets and brass and jazz: "You would have thought everything had been forgiven the way they played. . . . Sure of themselves, sure they were holy, [they] lifted those horns straight up and joined the light just as pure and steady and kind of kind" (196, 197).

The narrator's recognition that her ecstatic vision of the city has blinded her from other truths and human possibilities eventually catches up with her. She describes dark omens, darker possibilities, "something evil . . . underneath the good times . . . nothing was safe—not even the dead" (9). Felice's father knows the racist landscape all too well. There are two kinds of whites, "the ones that feel sorry for you and the ones that don't. And both amount to the same thing. Nowhere in between is respect" (204). Violet admits that "before I came North I made sense and so did the world. We didn't have nothing but we didn't miss it" (207). The narrator calculates the risk, recognizes that when people abandon their pasts, for whatever reason, and throw themselves into the hedonistic revelries of the big city, they are suddenly on their own: "Little of that makes for love, but it does pump desire" (34). Alice Manfred, Dorcas's strict aunt, voices her disapproval in no uncertain tones; for her jazz embodies "the lowdown stuff that signaled Imminent Demise" (56). That "dirty, get-on-down music . . . made you do unwise disorderly things. Just hearing it was like violating the law" (58). She can celebrate the bitter and steady drums of a parade to remember those killed in the East St. Louis Riots, where Dorcas's father died, but not jazz which celebrates only the body, sex, and sensual pleasures. She may have contributed to Dorcas's eagerness to escape from her and take up with Joe.

The narrator also reveals gaps and fissures in her perceptions of Golden Gray. "I see him in a two-seat phaeton," she begins. "I like to think of him that way" (143, 150) on his quest to find and kill his father, smug, self-righteous, spoiled, certain in his sense of racist vengeance, raised rich. She admits it is "risky, I'd say, trying to figure out anybody's state of mind. But worth the trouble if you're like me—curious, inventive and well-informed" (137), and continues to assemble her psychological portrait of the blonde god. Coming upon Wild, he worries more about ruining his clothes than her. He first tries to avoid her, looking out only for his horse, but then rescues her and carries her to what turns out to be his father's shack. "I know he is a hypocrite" (154), the narrator carps, who sees himself as chivalrous, doing the right thing whether he wants to or not, the correct rescue: "He thinks his story is wonderful . . . that he is shaping a story for himself to tell somebody. . . . But I know better. He wants to brag about the encounter, like a knight errant . . . " (154). Yet she backs off: "I don't hate him much anymore. . . . Aw, but he is young, young and he is hurting, so I forgive him his self-deception, and his grand, fake gestures . . . he is a boy after all" (154, 155). In a way the narrator backs off from her inherent racism as well, maligning the man for passing as white and growing up rich. She seems to be agreeing with True Belle, Gray's "mammy," who tells him, "It don't matter if you do find him or not; it's the going that counts" (159). The narrator restructures several scenes of entrance and exit, remarking that "I have to alter things. . . . I want him to stand next to a well" (161). The fact that Violet's mother killed herself by throwing herself down a well juxtaposes this particular scene cleverly, presenting the white man's casual acceptance of things in relation to the black woman's ultimate despair.

The vivid postmodern techniques and vision of *Jazz* reveal their roots in African American storytelling, in the improvisatory nature of the music, and in modernist traces that suggest an ontologically recognizable cosmos —Harlem, 1926, the murder of Dorcas, African American displacement and alienation—within multiple points of view with their different epistemological perspectives. Once again Morrison leads off with a crime, complete with Violet's stabbing Dorcas's face at the funeral parlor, a kind of apocalyptic act that generates the whole novel and leads to horrific tales of suicide, migration, poverty, secret identities, damaged mothers, and night-marish gestures. Yet Violet more or less forgives Joe and befriends Alice Manfred, Dorcas's aunt. No one else gets shot: "It's nice when grown people whisper to each other under the covers. Their ecstasy is more leaf-sigh than bray and the body is the vehicle, not the point" (228).

Every one of Morrison's characters is a compulsive talker, ready with their interpretations, speculations, rumors, and innuendos. Each grasps in-stinctively Morrison's sense of African American storytelling, in which the speakers revise previous tales and pass them on in a more communal and collective manner, creating community and a sense of self as they do so. At the same time the novel mimics the improvisation of jazz with its breaks and riffs, its solos and asides. As Morrison explains, "Classical mu-sic satisfies and closes. Black music does not do that. Jazz always keeps you on the edge. There is no final chord. There may be a long chord, but no final chord. And it agitates you" (McKay 1983, 155). Her references to mu-sic, to guitars, clarinets, and horns throughout the novel only underscore its postmodern connections with the structure of jazz.

Bouson believes that Morrison has aestheticized Dorcas's murder, that in letting Joe off the hook and not seeing him as just another man "caught up in the classic rejection-humiliation-revenge sequence," she has backed off from the violence he has committed in order to turn the murder "into a kind of jazzy-bluesy performance" (2000, 180, 189). While there may be some truth to this idea—by emphasizing Dorcas's aggression at the end of the narrative, Morrison seems to be laying the foundation for Violet to forgive Joe, thereby, in her usual manner, muddying the more dichoto-mous distinctions between victim and aggressor—I think that Morrison, in many ways here like Hawthorne, is more interested in the reverberations and effects of a particular crime and in its antecedent causes or contribu-tions to it than she is in the stark horror of it. She does not deny the violence or turn away from the blood but uses them to stalk a deeper perpetrator—the past, the city, racism, the northern migrations, slavery—that elaborate web of complicity and complexity, including the narrator's own, that hones in on shame, trauma, displacement, and the African American experience in America. Morrison does not deny Dorcas's death; she explores the roots and the reverberations of it.

Finally, the narrator, having pulled back from her fascination with the city, her own racism in regard to Golden Gray, her own predictable outcome of the scandalous trio at Lenox Avenue and revealed her own "loneliness that roams" and her links to Wild and bloodshed, admits that human motive and compulsion still elude her: "I started out believing that life was made just so the world would have some way to think about itself, but that it had gone awry with humans because flesh, pinioned by misery, hangs on to it with pleasure. . . . I don't believe that anymore. Something is missing. Something rogue" (227–28). She disrupts her various surrenderings to her characters and theirs to one another, as if signaling the end to inexhaustible desire and settling for some cooler, grayer apprehension of her own imminent demise. Yet she regroups, returns to herself as a writer, and in splendid postmodern fashion offers herself up to the reader of her book, as absent as she is present, by elegantly creating a voice, marks on a page that can suggest the possibility of a hovering ghost, captured at the very moment the reader is turning her pages, an ultimate beloved that can only be experienced and never fully comprehended or identified. Morrison proclaims her love for the reader reading, having "*surrendered my whole self reckless to you and nobody else*" (229). Like Joe, like Violet, and akin to Dorcas and the others, she has heretofore clutched that love in secret: "I can't say that aloud." Italics become the secret voice revealed, linked to "something rogue" that undermines the more constricted concepts of conspiracy and paranoia. It is her embodiment of the postmodern sublime. She continues: "If I were able to say it. Say make me, remake me. You are free to do it and I am free to let you because look, look. Look where your hands are. Now."

Epilogue
No Mo' Po Mo? Persistent Post-Millennial Misgivings and the Postmodern Sublime

The millennium has come and gone, but the American fascination with and participation in debates on postmodernism, fundamentalist faiths and furies, apocalyptic visions, and conspiracy theories continue, exposed and dramatized by various media. The shock of the attacks on the World Trade Center towers on September 11, 2001, still resonates, and the demonization of Islamic terrorists and Saddam Hussein, only one of the trio that make up President George W. Bush's "axis of evil," re-enacts yet again America's polarized view of itself and the world in apocalyptic, not to mention apoplectic, terms. Our enemy remains and should continue to remain Al Qaeda and all of its associates and offshoots, but amplifying this necessary and rightful task into a "War on Terrorism" suggests that our fundamentalist, conspiracist roots are very much alive and thriving.

Postmodernist space, as interpreted by pundits and cultural critics, threatens many Americans. At least 30 percent of them have reacted viscerally against it and cling to fundamentalist texts and apocalyptic visions, while many more re-invent conspiracies that lead back to the Illuminati, aliens in Sumer, the military-industrial complex, or faceless bureaucrats in Washington, D.C.[1] None of this is new, but our best novelists in recent years—Thomas Pynchon, Toni Morrison, Don DeLillo, Joan Didion, Robert Stone, and others—have chosen to grapple with its contemporary incarnation in complicit and critical ways, intrigued by cultural plots that help to illuminate the way we live now. "Everything is connected," bemoaned a Pynchon character in *Gravity's Rainbow* and another in DeLillo's *Underworld,* a far cry from E. M. Forster's "Only connect."

Where exactly are we in terms of the state of postmodernism both as a critique of our present state and as a reflection of it? Is postmodernism, or "Po-Mo" as some lively pundits have nicknamed it, a thing of the past?

Have we entered a new era in which it has been replaced at the end of an age of irony by what Joan Didion has disparagingly described as "moral clarity"?

Certainly the academic community has absorbed postmodern theory as capitalism commodifies and fetishizes all goods and services, making one wonder what happens to such a vision once it becomes institutionalized, transformed into a critical apparatus that is used to analyze style and structure, much in the manner that deconstruction has been co-opted by many American critics, including me. Does this signal a loss of elasticity and enigma, relegating postmodern theory to just one more academic "game"?

Physicist Alan Sokal in his famous parody of postmodern jargon and concepts, "Transgressing the Boundaries: Toward a Transformative Hermeneutics of Quantum Gravity," took on the postmodern "establishment" in order to skewer what he sees as the "radical version of social constructivism [and its belief] that physical reality (and not merely our ideas about it) is 'at bottom a social and linguistic construct'" (Sokal and Bricmont 1998, 259). He pounces on the subjective writings and interpretations of Werner Heisenberg and Niels Bohr, insisting that postmodern critics confuse the everyday meanings of such words as "uncertainty" and "discontinuity" with their more technical manifestations. With the eye of a mordant satirist, he makes fun of jargon-ridden quotations from the likes of Jacques Lacan, Julia Kristeva, Thomas Kuhn, Gilles Deleuze, Luce Irigaray, and Jean Baudrillard, a not particularly difficult thing to do, and proclaims that they have abused and misused genuine scientific ideas and concepts (in these quotes if not entirely in their works), failed to explicate fully the logical precise arguments that support these ideas, and spawned an epistemological relativism that can only lead to a voracious and virtually unassailable radical doubt. Postmodern thinkers confuse "facts with *assertions* of fact. . . . a 'fact' is a situation in the external world that exists irrespective of the knowledge we have (or don't have) of it . . . there exist facts independent of our claims" (102, 103). Science appears only as a narrative, a social and cultural construction and a myth "if one does not also take into account the empirical aspects" (197) of it.

Sokal suggests, and rightly so, that it is practically impossible to refute radical skepticism. From his perspective "we do not see any fundamental difference between the epistemology of science and the rational attitude in everyday life" (Sokal and Bricmont 1998, 91–92). Like Samuel Johnson he might kick a rock with his foot and, in feeling its resistance, claim to undermine all idealistic philosophy with a single blow. Specific evidence, "a respect for the clarity and logical coherence of theories, and for the confrontation of theories with empirical evidence" (193), underscores his point of view, as he castigates the postmodernists for jumping to erroneous conclusions from inadequate proofs.

Sokal's perspective remains problematic, however. First of all he asserts that he is assaulting only the more radical elements of postmodernism, a position not many critics would disagree with. He upbraids these writers' "fascination with obscure discourses [with its] emphasis on discourse and language as opposed to the facts to which those discourses refer (or, worse, the rejection of the very idea that facts exist or that one may refer to them" (Sokal and Bricmont 1998, 183). He continues: "Let us start by recognizing that many 'postmodern' ideas, expressed in a moderate form, provide a needed correction to naïve modernism (belief in indefinite and continuous progress, scientism, cultural Eurocentrism, etc.)" (183). Fair enough, but in attacking the "radical fringe," underscoring it with the odd quotes that he unearths and making it appear to be mainstream postmodernism, he de-rails his own argument. As Linda Hutcheon, a clear voice for moderation and logic, writes, "Past events are given meaning, not existence, by their representation in history"; she readily warns against "the 'ontological re-duction' of history to text" (1988, 41). This begs the issue somewhat, since, as Derrida suggests, texts may be all that we have of history to look at and in a perilous sleight of hand, ontological reduction and epistemological speculations may often appear to be one and the same thing.

One other issue I find particularly troublesome concerns Sokal's assess-ment of analogy. Of course similar words are used differently in a techni-cal as opposed to an everyday context: "What we are criticizing is some postmodernists' tendency to *confuse* their sense of the word with the mathematical one, and to draw conclusions with chaos that are not sup-ported by any valid argument" (Sokal and Bricmont 1998, 144). What is wrong with using chaos or emergence theory as an analogy to describe something entirely different from its specific scientific use and proof? Why cannot one use scientific theories generally as metaphor, provided that you clearly reveal your particular use of them? Analogies as such have always been used by writers and do not require an entire argument to underscore them. The physicists' use of particularly precise words in their discipline and discourse, such as "uncertainty" and "discontinuity," does not automatically prevent the literary and/or cultural critic from using them as well. Analogy is a legitimate linguistic device or technique, which most moderate postmodernists and their readers recognize. Sokal attacks the nature of language when it does not conform to his more rigid sense of argument and proof, thus complicating his attitude toward his more stereotypical and one-dimensional sense of "radical postmodernism" and its very obvious failings.

The more immediate battle over postmodernism and what it means erupted soon after 9/11 when Edward Rothstein wrote a piece in the *New York Times* in September, 2001, "Attacks on U.S. Challenge the Perspectives of Postmodern True Believers." I would have thought that the attacks would have challenged everyone, but Rothstein has a certain ax to grind. He argues that postmodernism asserts that there can be no objective validity to truth and ethical judgments, that the 9/11 attacks cry out for a transcendent vision of polarization between "democracies and absolutist societies," and that postmodernism, eviscerated by its sweeping sense of "ethically perverse" (A17) relativism in all things and rejection of values and ideals, leaves the befuddled postmodernist guiltily passive in the wake of terrorism.

Rothstein confuses specific actions with philosophical arguments. Reactions to the terrorists' attacks, of course, are very different from debating concepts of "reality" and ideal positions. At the same time he seems to be relying on Samuel Huntington's clash-of-cultures thesis (that Cold War vision of the West versus Islam that oversimplifies actual historical differences and circumstances) when he links the terrorists to "absolutist societies," as if they were one and the same. Rothstein rides the old either/or hobbyhorse, the polarized argument, which excludes the very middle in which most discussions of postmodernism and most other "isms" take place. When attacked, we fight: no contest, no problem, but the human condition itself remains far from the simplistic polarization Rothstein offers, riddled as it must be with paradox, contradiction, compromise, and complicity. Robert Stone in *Dog Soldiers* describes an attitude that one of his characters "had not experienced for years and never thoroughly understood. It was the attitude in which people acted on coherent ethical apprehensions that seemed real to them. He had observed that people in the

grip of this attitude did things which were quite as confused and ultimately ineffectual as the things other people did; nevertheless he held
them in a certain—perhaps merely superstitious—esteem" (1997, 261).

Stanley Fish roared back in July 2002, in "Postmodern Warfare: The
Ignorance of Our Warrior Intellectuals" in *Harper's*. He quarreled with
Rothstein's definition of "objective," suggesting that there are such univer-
sals that people do believe in, but none of these standards can ever be
"independent of any historically emergent and therefore revisable system
of thought and practice" (33). He, therefore, does not "deny the category
of true belief, just the possibility of identifying it uncontroversially" (37).
Right and wrong exist and direct our individual actions, "rooted in a
strong sense of values, priorities, [and] goals," but they do not exist in such
a way "*that no one would dispute and everyone accepts*" (34). We believe in
universal truths; we just cannot prove that they are universal.

Fundamentalists of all stripes seek to locate that independent validation
in a sacred book, an authority figure, historical and cultural practices, and
certain sacred narratives. From my point of view that validation restricts
life's possibilities as it seeks to ground and harness them once and for all.
For me validation exists in the ongoing and open-ended pursuit for ultimate validation, which, of course, will never be discovered, hence my pro-
motion in this book of the postmodern sublime. Choices, values, and possibilities always remain since we are human seekers, not gods. Things can
shift, amaze, baffle, and satisfy and then do the same thing all over again.
The nature of the human condition will always be conflict. Unity and
harmony lie just beyond our ability to reach and enact them.

Fish stands on slipperier ground when he suggests that "postmodernism
is a series of arguments, not a way of life or a recipe for action" (2002, 34).
The statement is true when we separate philosophical debate from the
hurly-burly and conflicts of everyday life, but it would be very difficult to
prove that our philosophical perspectives in no way influence our actions.
Experience is muddier, more contradictory and paradoxical than that. We
surely make allowances for different kinds, different levels and realms in
which abstract argument and concrete actions remain separate from each
other, but in our experience they both transpire in a more complicated and
interpenetrating way. At the very least the postmodernist remains alert to
and wary of fundamentalist and conspiracist arguments that brook no re-
buttal or debate.

"Are we living in a golden age of conspiracy theory?" asks Darrin M. McMahon in the *Boston Globe* on February 1, 2004. Conspiracy lives on, undaunted and undeterred, as evidenced by the existence of the Web site www.conspiracy-net.com, as rampant in our culture as in our politics or, more particularly, in the culture of politics and the politics of culture. In the cover story of the *New York Times Magazine* in August 2002, "Coincidence in an Age of Conspiracy," the very title defining the era and thereby contributing to the aura of conspiracy that hovers everywhere about us, Lisa Belkin surveys the deaths of eleven men purported to be connected "to the world of bioterror and germ warfare" while insisting, "*In paranoid times like these,* people see connections where there aren't any" (italics mine, 32). The media reports the rumors that get transformed "into the specter of conspiracy as they circulated first on the Internet and then in the mainstream media" (34). Of course "much religious faith is based on the idea that almost nothing is coincidence," a notion that need not surprise us. But as Bradley Efron, a professor of statistics at Stanford, maintains, "We can never say for a fact that something isn't a conspiracy. We can just point out the odds that it isn't" (quoted in Belkin 2002, 34–35). Not a particularly comforting idea for a people versed in "religious faith" living "in paranoid times like these." As others commented on "The Deadly Curse of the Bioresearchers," "It is possible that nothing connects this string of events, but . . . it offers ample fodder for the conspiracy theorist or thriller writer. . . . We're all natural storytellers, and conspiracy theorists are just frustrated novelists" (Belkin 2002, 58); "In another political climate I don't think anyone would have noticed" (61). Comments yet another in Belkin's article: "You become paranoid. You have to be" (61).

Perhaps Jane Kramer's informative and elegant *Lone Patriot* best summarizes our current era, particularly with her emphasis on *Lone.* She recounts the paranoid journey of John Pitner, once the self-declared leader of the Washington State Militia. She also discovers a fanatical group of Dutch dairy farmers who are so fiercely Calvinist that they believe "that sex might *lead* to dancing" (2002, 137). Conspiracy theorists thrived in the woods and trailers of Whatcom County, fundamentalist to the core: "John believed in his documents and his info and his intel the way a fundamentalist . . . believed in the Bible . . . as the Word, absolute, incontrovertible, not open to discussion" (24). At the same time "John understood that in millennial America the idea of making good had become so fatally confused with the idea of getting saved that the choice for the failed and the poor was either to believe that they were damned themselves or else, like John, to believe that they were victims of a great conspiracy of the damned against them" (35). As Kramer concludes, noting the politics of the era, "they were not a community until the propagandists of the radical right and the salesmen of the armed right and the crusaders of the Christian right turned some of them into a constituency that thought a militia was a perfectly reasonable 'American' addition to the neighborhood" (139). Pitner's sister Susan admitted that the saddest part of her brother's crusade finally was that "the only person who believed him was the F.B.I." (256).

Was it ever thus? Of course millennial fevers stoked such apocalyptic flames, but the fire has never really gone out in American culture. It may be as Kramer suggests that the ferocious "right" to bear arms and protect property, even and especially if you decide to secede from the United States, really underscores "the propaganda of expansion. . . . You could find this same odd synergy of American pathology and American mythology, this entitlement to whatever 'space' you chose to inhabit" (2002, 136), even if the very existence of that space in terms of land and water had been made possible by a federal government.

Lone patriots will continue to thrive, and the lure of the conspiracy, the secret cabal, the ultimately rational and organized group within a persistently postmodern and irrationally fragmented world, will as well. As a character in *Gravity's Rainbow* explains, the Second World War came about "just to keep the people distracted . . . secretly, it was being dictated instead by the needs of technology . . . by a conspiracy between human beings and techniques . . . " (Pynchon 1973, 521). That vision and variations of it doggedly persist.

I would like to conclude by suggesting that the postmodern sublime will outlive postmodern but not conspiracy theory. First of all the vision and experience of the sublime itself reveal a distinguished pedigree and historical-aesthetic background that precedes postmodernism. It has always involved the suggestion of "design but no designer," a "web of relations" that suggests but never leads to a definitive "underlying agency" (Pillow 2000, 310). It has always been rooted in a fear of the unknown, which encourages and generates the self-preservative act of thought and aesthetic response, as well as contingency, contradiction, enigma, and ambiguity. It remains more performative than descriptive, more intuitive than conceptual and as such questions all epistemological perspectives and the very grounds of ontological being. As Stathis Gourgouris suggests in *Does Literature Think? Literature as Theory for an Antimythical Era,* "in a world of time (in history) nothing has ontological permanence as such, except as a figure of endlessly deferrable actualization. Ontological permanence is true only as potential" (2003, 138).

In discussing the Enlightenment faith in reason and rational argument, Gourgouris adds, "The Enlightenment's relation to the mystery of existence, understood in dialectical terms, is grounded equally in the aim to abolish mystery in the name of rational knowledge and in the desire that draws one toward the mystery, the desire for decipherment, which necessitates one's surrender to the mysterious experience itself" (2003, 177). Conspiracy seeks refuge in abolishing mystery. The postmodern sublime pursues and performs it, imbued with radical skepticism and anti-authoritarianism at the same time it celebrates the pursuit and the performance themselves. Its faith in a possible future presence, neither theological nor transcendent but still to be performed, dialectically participates in postmodernism's faith in present absence. Each performs the other, and literature performs them both. As Gourgouris concludes, "literature becomes theory, which is not to say that it becomes something other than literature but that it occupies the space where imagination and contemplation become one" (245). For me the postmodern sublime continues to exist and thrive, occupying and haunting that fluid, ever-changing, always open-ended space.

Notes

CHAPTER 1

1. Two recent examples include Bruns (1999) and Eagleton (2003, *After Theory*).

2. In "Vietnam Mythology and the Rise of Public Cynicism," Appy and Bloom (2002) meticulously dismantle the myths that the war helped create. Just to name a few of them suggests the thrust of his arguments: "The Myth of South Vietnamese Nationhood," "The Myth of 'External Aggression,'" "The Myth of South Vietnamese 'Freedom and Democracy,'" "The Myth of Progress or 'There's Light at the End of the Tunnel,'" "The Myth of Withdrawal and Vietnamization," and "The Myth of 'Peace with Honor.'" These writers conclude: "When the war ended, public trust in the government had plummeted, from a high of seventy-six percent in 1964 to a low of thirty-seven percent. Attitudes about government duplicity with regard to Vietnam were compounded by a sense of betrayal around other key events, most notably Watergate."

Vietnam and Watergate also revealed the elaborate web of conspiracy at the heart of the Nixon presidency. As White (1975) suggested, "The idea *of ever present conspiracy* blurred and merged always in [Nixon's] political thinking with the political issues which his ideological enemies thrust at him" (330). "No administration before Nixon's can have lent itself so readily to a conspiratorial view of government," declared Mary McCarthy, " . . . as he drew closer to the notion (unnamed by him, of course) of forming a conspiratorial nucleus within his own government" (155).

Schell (1975) spelled it out: "The Nixon men used the language of the theatre —'scenario,' 'script,' 'players,' 'orchestration'—to describe the way they ran the country"; "President Nixon was setting himself up as the scriptwriter of the whole of American political life . . . in subordinating the full range of policymaking to the requirements of public-relations scenarios" (332–33, 227, 223). Nixon had completely mastered Jean Baudrillard's simulacra, "in which images consistently took precedence over substance" (259).

Language itself must inevitably suffer from such an approach, as Nixon and company planned that it would. In speaking of one of the conspirators, H. R. Haldeman replied, "I could tell that he was back-pedaling fast. That he was now in the process of uninvolving himself," lines that Higgins (1975) describes as "a semantic coinage suggestive of the inner circle solipsism which made real what the sovereign declared real" (175).

In his acceptance of Gerald Ford's pardon on September 8, 1974, Nixon wrote, "I know that many fair-minded believe that my motivation and actions . . . were intentionally self-serving and illegal. I now understand how my own mistakes and misjudgments have contributed to that belief and seemed to support it" (White 1975, 343). White describes these self-serving remarks as a breach of faith: "He still had not really learned the way America works" (343). But Higgins (1975) in *The Friends of Richard Nixon*, after "self-serving and illegal," adds, "Felonious, as a matter of fact, vicious, unprincipled, deceitful, corrupt, malicious, spiteful, vengeful and dead wrong" (210). He characterizes the matter of "my own mistakes and misjudgments" as "surely the most delicate phraseology ever employed by a President of the United States to *describe a conspiracy* to obstruct justice" and lands squarely on Nixon's "seemed to support it" with his own, "*Seemed, my lord?* If this is seeming, what the hell is fact?" (210–11). Is there any wonder that deconstruction and postmodernism began their conquest in academe at about, to quote another favorite Nixon phrase, "this point in time"?

In his *Watergate in American Memory*, Schudson (1992) quotes Frances Fitzgerald's view "that textbooks operate by the 'natural-disaster theory of history'" (144). Problems exist as either natural disasters or the results from some systemic difficulty. "This natural-disaster theory of 'authorless crimes,'" she suggests, is the pervasive, governing explanation of Watergate" (145). Richard Nixon gets some of the blame, but the script itself seems to be at fault—a triumph, ultimately, for Nixon.

Schudson goes on to explore the ways in which the past resists present analysis and how memory can be "mobilized," "contested," "mythologized," and "contained." His is ultimately an open-ended postmodern "take" on a thoroughly deconstructed but still festering problem of interpretation. With Watergate did the system fail, or did it function? If it worked, then reform was unnecessary. If it didn't, reform became mandatory, and several reforms, such as ethics rules, financial disclosure forms, limits on political contributions, donor and campaign expenditure reports, campaign spending limits, taxpayer campaign funding, and special prosecutors, were passed, although several have been either overridden or allowed to expire since then.

Watergate, Schudson explains, can also be seen as an attempt to forget Vietnam with one media spectacle replacing the other, aware as he is of the postmodern notion that "every memory is necessarily also a forgetting" (1992, 220). He opposes "the radical, relativist constructionist, who believes that there is only discourse and no independent world" (218), but he also recognizes that "all stories can be read in more than one way . . . every story contains its own alternative readings. Narratives are ambiguous or, to use a fancier term, polysemic" (216). Such a description lies at the heart of Jacques Derrida's deconstruction and constitutes a further deconstructing of the Watergate legacy, the events of which, within the Nixon White House, are visibly deconstructed, reconstructed, and deconstructed again in the transcripts of the tapes.

When I visited the Nixon Library in Yorba Linda, California, in August 2000, strange postmodern juxtapositions struck me yet again. Designers were festooning the building with ribbons and banners in preparation for an Indian wedding. A huge figure of Ganesh, the Hindu elephant fertility god with several legs, blocked the wall upon which the names of major contributors to the library were inscribed. A life-sized cardboard figure of Nixon shaking hands with Elvis Presley overwhelmed the doorway of the gift shop. Rows of identical Barbie dolls displayed the inaugural gowns of First Ladies. It was the only time I have seen Barbara Bush's pearls hang straight down.

But beyond the Nixon exhibits and celebratory artifacts lies a dark corridor within which photographs and newspaper headlines document Watergate. On one of the small cards words describe the infamous "Smoking Gun" tape that led to Nixon's resignation: "These six minutes in the conversation *were and are the only evidence* which *suggests* that President Nixon *tried* to curtail the investigation into Watergate to *protect* his people" (italics mine). The cover-up continues.

3. Even though Norris in *Deconstruction* (2000) believes that "deconstruction stands very firmly apart from postmodernism" (45), in his attempt to dissociate Derrida from the more wildly relativistic critiques of the likes of Thomas Kuhn, Willard Quine, Paul de Man, and Michel Foucault, many literary critics associate Jacques Derrida and deconstruction in particular with postmodernism in general. In the American "crisis conversions" of critics to deconstruction in the 1970s, Derrida's elusive dogma took on a decidedly relativistic and decisively pessimistic point of view, as we shall see below. "I believe it has an absolutely new and original dimension in the United States," Derrida wrote in *Glas*, as quoted by Rapaport (2001). "I don't think that there is something like *one* deconstruction" (37). America is the "historical space which today, in all its dimensions and through all its power plays, reveals itself as being undeniably the most sensitive, receptive, or responsive space of all to the themes and effects of deconstruction" (34). Rapaport adds, "Derrida was almost certainly thinking, too, of America as the home of postmodernism. . . . America is the home of not only a willingness to continually deconstruct the immediate past but to continually construct immediate futures" (35).

Most of these critics also transformed a highly speculative body of work into an analytical tool, a system for analyzing texts that others believed corrupted and to some extent undermined Derrida's initial philosophical speculations. Postmodernism also prides itself on its response to modernism but in doing so necessarily limits and reduces the old New Criticism, that modernist tool of analyzing texts and disconnecting them from their cultural and social milieu, to a parody of its actual practices. In general critics have argued that the dilemma is both an epistemological and an ontological one, that modernists wrestled with the relativity of human perception and the "how" of knowing, whereas postmodernists struggle with the "what" that can possibly be known in the first place, if anything.

4. Melley, in writing about paranoia avows, "It is remarkably difficult to separate interpretation from 'normal' interpretive practices" and goes on to explore "how much Freud's description of paranoia has in common with paranoia itself. . . . To be 'paranoid' may only be to reject the normalizing ideology of the powerful" (2000, 17, 18). Extremism, fundamentalism, and the reactionary right have emerged so vividly and querulously within the cultural mainstream that Melley insists, "We can in fact hypothesize that paranoia is a defense of—perhaps even a component of—liberal individualism. . . . [The paranoid] retain[s] the liberal notion that intentions are the supreme causes of events in the world" (25). We have come a great distance from Richard Hofstadter's marginal and pathologically assailed paranoids to Melley's celebration of paranoia that lies at the heart of the American myth of the liberal and autonomous individual.

5. There are several critics who view postmodernism and deconstruction as less than radical, as extensions of the modernist agenda in literature and the arts, and as essentially part of an interregnum between what has been and what is yet to come. These critics are not as much negative as they are neutral and descriptive and can offer us an exploration of the issues in a calmer and less self-threatening manner.

For instance Chabot (1988), acknowledging that postmodernism is probably an essentially American phenomenon, along with Alan Wilde, Todd Gitlin, David Simpson, and others, has decided that "no satisfactory and widely accepted account of postmodernism now exists [and] that much of what is called postmodernism in fact derives directly from modernism" (37). Postmodernism as a particular philosophical concept remains decidedly confused and arbitrary. For him modernism is one of those blanket terms that spans a particular era in literature and the arts. It cannot be defined succinctly since it has been used to cover everything from architecture to poetry, and postmodernism just continues the process of fragmentation, spatial rearrangements, and psychological disruption that modernism had introduced.

In effect Chabot suggests that we have entered a mannerist period in the arts that always follows a more heroic one, or, as Sypher (1960) has indicated, "occurring whenever a so-called classic art disintegrates or is revised" (156). For Sypher mannerism emerges "as a symptom of unrest and experiment, not as a legitimate style" (158). It is the result of "technical ingenuities, deliberate deviations [with] a consuming interest in aesthetic theory [and in] strange psychological effects" (158, 157). It is basically negative since it is essentially "a revolt against a prevailing style, or a reformulating of style" (158). Sypher describes mannerism as the inevitable follow-up to a "classical" period, from Faulkner to Vonnegut or Hemingway to Pynchon, say, in American literature. Writers such as Toni Morrison, Robert Stone, and others may build upon modernist traditions, but the general aesthetic smolders with sparks of doubt, distortion, disruption, and dis-ease. It is also interesting to see that Sypher, like Chabot, treats this aesthetic shift as inevitable, not as a threat or an assault on art in general. "A sense of malaise [and] the rejection of outworn official canons" (160) accompanies such a mannerist shift, but it is neither virulent nor predatory in its final incarnations.

Gitlin (1989) would agree, describing postmodernism as "an intermission" (76), a sequel to and continuance of modernism. As yet it remains incomplete and has produced that sense of general irony and indifferent attitude, "whatever," "an experience of aftermath, privatization [and] weightlessness" (74) that the political failures or the social and cultural disruptions of the 1960s have left us with. He adds that "postmodernism is born in the U.S.A. because juxtaposition is one of the things we do best" (76). Baudrillard (1988) would concur, though he would embrace Eagleton's political approach more directly and sees postmodernism more negatively as a cynical hedonism that emerges from the over-consumption of the 1980s.

CHAPTER 2

1. One way that the vision of conspiracy and its counterpart, religious fundamentalism, have invaded in no small manner the contemporary American mind is to look at national polls. While not entirely accurate and often contradictory, these polls do give us a sense of the American public at large and what they are feeling and thinking about religion generally. In a nationwide survey of Americans in May 2000, 48 percent agreed that religion played a big role in their lives; 31 percent responded, "Some role" (*New York Times Magazine* 2000, 67). 81 percent believed in some form of an afterlife, and 72 percent believed that the religious practices they follow are absolutely authentic. Asked whether or not one agreed or disagreed with the statement, "The best religion would be one that borrowed from all religions," 42 percent agreed, and 45 percent disagreed (84). At the same time 53 percent agreed with the statement, "I still feel guilty about a thing or two I did when I was young"; 47 percent disagreed (96).

When we look more closely at other polls, the number of self-described fundamentalist believers hovers at about the 30 percent mark. In 1990, for instance, according to Boyer (1992), 40 percent of adult Americans believed that the Bible incarnated the actual word of God, while 31 percent believed in the literal word of God. 80 percent feel that they will appear before God on Judgment Day, report Strozier and Flynn (1997), and 53 percent in 1992, according to Weber (1999), "expected the imminent return of Jesus Christ and the fulfillment of Biblical prophecies about a cataclysmic destruction of evil" (209). That premillennial vision we will look at in further detail below. In an October 30, 1999, *New York Times* poll 33 percent believed in ghosts, which was three times as many than in the 1970s, and 25 percent in witches, a doubling of the number since that time. 40 percent believed in Armageddon, the ultimate battle to be fought at history's end between Christ and Satan, and 68 percent admitted that they would probably go to heaven after they died. 39 percent believed that fire in biblical prophecies clearly predicts nuclear holocaust, according to a 1984 Yankelovic Poll. 22 percent declared themselves Evangelical Christians in a 1978–79 Princeton poll, and that figure had risen to 32 percent in 1986 during the Reagan Restoration.

About 1,600 religions and denominations existed in the United States in 1997, but of that 1,600, 800 were founded since 1965. In 1974 nine religious TV stations existed; in 1996, that had increased to 257. 58 percent of the 38 percent who support conservative political organizations believe that Jews must convert to Christianity. The Assemblies of God, another fundamentalist sect, grew by 95 percent from 1973 to 1988 with 2.1 million members. 60 percent of Americans, however, could not name the person who delivered the Sermon on the Mount, 54 percent could not name the authors of the four gospels, an amazing 63 percent did not know what a gospel was, and 19 percent believed that Joan of Arc was Noah's wife (*New York Times Magazine,* 1997, 61). Interestingly enough, Pipes (1997) confirms that 56 percent in 1991 believed that there was a conspiracy behind the assassination of Kennedy (15).

2. Ronald Reagan declared Vietnam "a noble cause" in his 1980 presidential campaign, but by the 1980s the number of suicides of Vietnam veterans equaled the number of battlefield deaths in Vietnam. Alexander Bloom (Appy and Bloom 2002) has discovered that "if there is a common phrase that binds all the [presidential] campaigns since 1976 it is 'restore.' . . . It is not possible to find another period in American history when this has been the central political concept of an era" (7). Restoration included the rewriting of the past along with the Cold War–reincarnation of the "Evil Empire." It included the reassertion of manhood on a mythic scale from Sylvester Stallone to Arnold Schwarzenegger in the movies, a cultural phenomenon that also contributed to the rise of paramilitary groups in the conspiracy-riddled culture of the 1980s and 1990s.

The process, begun during the Reagan Restoration, accelerated in the 1990s. In that decade conservative churches grew much faster than mainline, more liberal ones. Between 1990 and 2000 the Church of Jesus Christ of Latter Day Saints grew by 19.3 percent to 4.2 million members. Similarly the Assemblies of God, a Pentecostal denomination, grew by 18.5 percent to 2.5 million members, and the Churches of Christ grew by 18.6 percent to 1.4 million members.

Clifton (2002) reveals in great detail how brilliantly the Christian Right has employed grass-roots organization, all aspects of the modern media, lobbying, and carefully crafted policy statements to infiltrate the Republican Party. Such interest groups as the Christian Coalition, the Family Research Council, and Focus on the Family, led by such articulate spokespersons and meticulous organizers as Pat Robertson, Ralph Reed, Gary Bauer, and James Dobson, have mastered the art of grass-roots policy mobilization, swamping congressional offices with phone calls, e-mail, and postcards at critical junctures; mobilized their electorate to vote; infiltrated local and state party organizations; provided carefully selected and clearly defined policy statements for their voters; and lobbied members of Congress incessantly.

As Clifton makes clear, the 1994 Republican "Revolution," in which the Republicans for the first time in recent memory earned majorities in both the House and the Senate in the Congress (the demonization of Clinton, yet another instance of the polarization of such evangelical points of view, didn't hurt the Republican cause), energized the Christian Right. They gave 72 percent of their votes in primaries to Republican candidates for the House, and in 2000, 80 percent voted for George W. Bush. The statistics overwhelmingly reveal how successfully the Christian Right has been shaped into a distinct political constituency with such specific goals as gutting pro-abortion legislation, upholding "family values," and passing the Defense of Marriage Act. Their very terms—the generic "pro-life" and "family values" slogans, the "Moral Majority" coalition (did that mean all opponents were, therefore, members of the Immoral Minority?)—reveal how well they were able to package their far-right agenda. Concludes Clifton, at one point, "Until Pat Robertson organized them, [religious conservatives] had been dismissed as irrelevant to the political process" (2002, Chap. 5, p. 6).

As described by the reactionary reverend Tim LeHaye, secular humanism, the corrosive vision behind all of American decline and decay, advocated "amorality, evolution and atheism" (in Bennett 1995, 378). Dr. James C. Dobson, founder of the evangelical Focus on the Family, declared, "We are engaged at this time in an enormous civil war of values [in which] the Judeo-Christian, biblical prescriptions we trust [confront] the humanistic, avant-garde point of view that there are no absolutes" (in Bennett 1995, 426). Trumpeted Paul Weyrich, political organizer of the rightist Heritage Foundation, "This is really the most significant battle of the age-old conflict between good and evil, between the forces of God and the forces against God, that we have seen in our country" (in Bennett 1995, 427).

In many ways postmodernism and deconstruction in the academy contributed to this right-wing and reactionary surge. As Marcus (1999) suggests, "The specifically postmodern version of a contemporary crisis of representation as the opportunity for the proliferation of [the] paranoid mode of social thought . . . [in] the novels of Don DeLillo, [evokes] a contemporary atmosphere of institutions and systems sustained by powerful, invisible conspiracies" (4). The attack on certainty and authority of all kinds exacerbated the rigid beliefs of fundamentalists and certain politicians. The fundamentalists preached with tongues of fire that intellectuals, always a suspicious group and one of the first to be assailed in times of American crusades, were undermining America's faith in itself, detonating our traditional and mythic values of self-reliance and self-willed independence, and exposing our children's minds to the dangerous ravings of Nietzsche and Heidegger, a vision querulously documented by Allan Bloom (1987). In 1987 Bloom railed against the German invasion in the academy, the attack on the American self, the masturbatory features of rock music, the spread of sexual license, and the "social solitaries" (118) of our increasingly nomadic and disconnected society. "The dualism in contemporary American intellectual life that keeps recurring in these pages and is their unifying theme" (189)—nature vs. culture, economy vs. culture, the American self vs. Nietzschean relativism and will to power—turns out to be precisely what postmodernism and deconstruction undertook to interrogate and problematize.

3. Wills (1999) helps to define the anti–federal government ethos of American culture, particularly in western states. The idea that one must surrender personal liberty to government bondage strikes Wills as a simplistic and dangerous notion, particularly when such fundamentalist believers rely on it so faithfully: "When real history conflicts with symbolic history, the former is subsumed within the latter" (41). He makes the very strong case that an increase of power does not automatically mean a corresponding loss of rights and meticulously investigates the myths of the free market versus the federal government, of individualism and the ownership of guns—according to Wills, there existed only one gun for every ten people in the American Colonies, and none of them was reliable—of states' rights, and of the misinterpretations of the Second Amendment. The idea that the West was founded by individual gunslingers crumbles in the wake of his careful eye: "It expresses the desire for self-sufficiency that is at odds with government control" (242), when in fact most western states could not have existed or survived without federal assistance in terms of land grants and water rights. The real victims of such anti-government positions are not the Timothy McVeighs of the far right but the poor: "Better for them to starve than to be enslaved by 'big government.' That is the real cost of anti-government values" (21). Of course the Reagan Restoration saluted those sentiments. As Wills concludes, "Only paranoia can turn [the real problems of bad government with its penchant for secrecy and unaccountability] into a belief that government is in itself a necessary evil" (316).

4. Writers such as Wójcik (1997) and Weber (1999), among others, have described and analyzed the apocalyptic vision carefully and, like fundamentalism, have found similar characteristics. The world, lurching from one crisis-generating eruption to another, reveals only the impossibility of human agency in attempting to fix anything or stem the tide. The master plan or divine design hovers at the core of history and can be unearthed only through the persistent hunting for signs and symbols. This Ahab-like quest for when the final battle between Christ and Satan will occur, and where, drives the select few, that conspiratorial elitist cabal, who alone have discovered the truth and can reveal it. The entire drama plays out in narrative form, just as in the Bible, with its beginning and its destined end, and true believers, knowing this and seeking their roles in it, empower themselves with ultimate hope and preordained direction.

Everything takes on a cosmic significance; nothing remains coincidental or trivial. As Weber suggests, "By defining human suffering in cosmic terms, as part of a cosmic order that contains an issue, catastrophe is dignified, endowed with meaning, and hence made bearable" (1999, 235). Unbelievers will perish; only true believers will see the light. Robinson (1985) adds, "The very idea of America in history is apocalyptic, arising as it did out of the historicizing of apocalyptic hopes in the Protestant Reformation" (xi, 226). History leads to the end of history; prophecy predicts the ultimate conflagration and deliverance; believers submit themselves to the cosmic struggle knowing that they will eventually triumph. The apocalyptic narrative clearly parallels the conspiratorial mode of thought, and vice versa.

Cohn (1970), who has written several books over the years about millennial visions and apocalyptic scenarios—his most influential would be *The Pursuit of the Millennium*—traces the Judeo-Christian view of apocalypse back to ancient times to the combat myths of ancient civilizations, the struggles between men and monsters, gods and gorgons. In these myths the forces of good and evil fought it out, but in doing so the world remained unchanged, static, and fixed. It was Zoroaster who transformed these combat myths into an apocalyptic faith, an idea I have come upon again and again when tracing Manichaeism and its influences on Western culture, watching it frame the Calvinist vision and darkly smoldering in the fictions of, among others, Nathaniel Hawthorne, Herman Melville, Harriet Beecher Stowe, and William Styron. Zoroaster replaced a static world with a vision of future triumph, the deadly dualistic battle resulting in ultimate victory for the forces of good, thereby transforming the world and saving mankind. Individuals could exercise their free choice to believe or not to believe, but Armageddon would take place in any case. All would be changed and the cosmic battle won. Until that time, however, the deadly dualism between the two opposing gods would continue.

In his primer on doomsday texts from William L. Pierce's *The Turner Diaries* (1978) to the Branch Davidians, the Montana Freemen, and Heaven's Gate, Daniels (1999) links apocalyptic cults to political conspiracies: both seek to overthrow the status quo because of its abuse of power and imagine a determined future in which power will be redistributed, either in terms of salvation or revolution. Dellamora (1995) views apocalypse in postmodern culture as part of its very tone and style, as an attitude that assaults all levels and categories of authority and power. Postmodernism, he suggests, has aestheticized apocalypse as a textual phenomenon, although it has always been this, so that it permeates various postmodern theories and expectations. Of course texts cannot possibly represent or incorporate an actual apocalypse; they can only appropriate its tone and attitude, reducing it to a style, a narrative, and the process of continuous unveiling and stripping away, a process that can never end, since if the apocalypse actually existed, texts would self-destruct. Postmodernism, as Baudrillard describes it in his imagistic, over-the-top style, filled with its apocalyptic bursts and sudden epiphanies, celebrates a virtual apocalypse, since the "real one" will always exceed whatever representations of it we try to fabricate.

The list of apocalyptic cults and beliefs grows longer each year. Kaminer, in *Sleeping with Extra-Terrestrials* (1999), and Heard, in the also wonderfully titled *Apocalypse Pretty Soon* (1999), have interviewed various cult members from the archangels Uriel and Raphiel of the Unarius Academy of Science in El Cajon, California, to Stephen M. Greer who seeks encounters with friendly aliens. Both grapple with such texts as Herb Bowie's *Why Die?: A Beginner's Guide to Living*

Forever (Scottsdale, AZ: PowerSurge Publishing, 1998) and Chet Fleming's *If We Can Keep a Severed Head Alive* (St. Louis: Polinym Press, 1987). Heard views such apocalyptic and millennial visions as "a way of living on the edge of apocalypse forever, and never losing the twin thrills—the pang of impending disaster, the anticipatory joy of ultimate redemption—that can make millennialism terrible and enjoyable at the same time" (122). Kaminer explains, "It's worth noting that the loonier conspiracy theories that circulated in the 1990s combined mistrust of government with belief in the supernatural" (13). In both cases faith trumps knowledge, and the apocalyptic narratives begin the predestined journey to salvation.

Kermode (1967) treated such religious literalism with much disdain in his book *The Sense of an Ending,* because to assume a specific end to something became dangerously self-fulfilling. In fiction this functions well, but in religion or myth it freezes out any other possibilities and makes a certain path of prophecy and prediction inevitable and fatal. If we think in terms of perpetual crisis, as the anxious postmodern era does so easily and readily, or in the mythic terms of apocalypse and the necessity for bloodshed, there is a strong chance that crisis and bloodshed will prevail. Of crisis and transition, Kermode insists, "We can think of them as fictions, as useful. If we treat them as something other than they are we are yielding to irrationalism." In 1967 he was writing from a faith in modernist narrative forms and the blessed rage for order, and such forms do reveal "a paradigmatic aspect, and can be studied in historical depth," but he had no way of knowing how powerful and "mainstreamed" such apocalyptic visions would become. "Apocalypse is part of the modern Absurd," he mused authoritatively. He approved of Henry James's notion that "Really, universally, relations stop nowhere, and the exquisite problem of the artist is eternally to draw, by a geometry of his own, the circle in which they shall happily appear to do so" (103, 123, 176), but Lindsey (1970) works to tighten the circle so that there will never be a loose end.

5. In *American Extremists: Militias, Supremacists, Klansmen, Communists & Others,* ed. George and Wilcox (1996), David Robson lists the characteristics and traits of those who, in their rhetoric and propaganda, view the world around them as a conspiracy against which they have positioned themselves. Their extremist vision "tends to be 'feeling-based' rather than 'evidence-based.' . . . They try to discourage critical examination of their beliefs by a variety of means, usually by false logic, rhetorical trickery, or some kind of censorship, intimidation, or repression" (60, 61). They may also be leading and promoting their cause from "motives they themselves do not recognize" (61). They emphasize the omnipotence and omnipresence of the enemy—enemies are all around us and may not be recognizable at first glance—they view the world in starkly Manichean terms—Good vs. Evil, the Legions of Light vs. the Forces of Darkness; they use any means to justify their ends, usually in a self-righteous and morally superior manner; and they often resort to sweeping generalities and assertions, demanding that you accept their views on faith but that we must prove ours. If they happen to be reli-

gious extremists or zealots, they can always rely on a supernatural divine design or designer, literally confirmed in the text of their choice as interpreted and understood by them. In either case the believer in conspiracies searches for signs wherever he or she goes or looks in a relentlessly unending pursuit for the final clue, the ultimate revelation. As Stewart (1999) points out, "Conspiracy theory is a skeptical, paranoid, obsessive practice of scanning for signs and sifting through bits of evidence for the missing link. . . . The moment of seduction is the moment when the puzzle is almost solved but there is always something more you need, the missing piece" (14).

6. Thompson (1996) heard Zecharia Sitchin give a talk on *The Twelfth Planet* at the Harvard Club in New York City: "I never before had heard anyone who was so totally like his book" (72). Sitchin spoke in a soft voice in a methodical manner: "Everything was sane, sober, gentlemanly. . . . It was only when Sitchin began to discuss the Gulf War that his mania appeared" (72). Evidently Sitchin was determined to link the dawn of Sumerian civilization to the Gulf War: "The recent battle became part of a grand conspiracy theory about ancient titanic forces that clash by night" (72). Thompson concludes that Sitchin sees himself as the ultimate code-breaker, as do most conspiracy theorists and cult figures: "He can read the secret conspiratorial code that holds it all together . . . in a classic maniacal narrative of cosmic synthesis" (73).

Thompson discusses Sitchin's theory in his chapter "Weird Myths about Human Origins," suggesting that Sitchin takes things literally. He literalizes the imagination or in this case biblical mythology and ancient Sumerian texts about Sumerian gods. The distinctions between historical fact and myths of origin do not exist. According to Thompson, "The literalism of the Mormons, or of Zecharia Sitchin, comes about precisely because they do not understand the nature of psyche and the imagination and always seek to literalize, to concretize in a *simple and idolatrous fundamentalism*. . . . Sitchin has the *simple and idolatrous mind* of a peasant—not that peasants are bad—but the peasant's imagination, as opposed to the poet's, is a literalist one. For Sitchin, technology is the idol . . . and that's all there is to it" (italics mine, 1996, 77, 89). Even the technology is wrong, Thompson continues, for Sitchin's tales of space and space aliens resemble "cheap 1950s B movie rockets and space suits. . . . What Sitchin sees is what he needs for his theory" (75). For Thompson the imagination remains forever fluid, "polysemic, complex, and multidimensional; it is never simple, linear, fundamentalist, and literal" (84). For Sitchin cause diffuses mystery, icons master enigma, and the origins of human civilization could only have come from somewhere other than our own fragile and precarious humanity and earth.

CHAPTER 3

1. John Saul, interview with the author.

EPILOGUE

1. Fundamentalist fulminations and furies continue. In "The Opening of the Evangelical Mind," Wolfe (2000) tries to make the case that intellectually starved evangelical students and teachers are reaching out, trying to transcend their restrictive and intellectually limited traditions of biblical literalism and anti-Catholic prejudices. While Wolfe's presentation catalogues more than it convinces, it acknowledges the fact that in 1996 "29% of Americans could be described as conservative Protestants, with roughly equal numbers of evangelicals and fundamentalists, making them the largest religious group in America" (58). They continue to "shift back and forth from the rejection of authority to the imposition of authority [which] mirrors perfectly the combination of populism and authoritarianism that has characterized the history of fundamentalist churches in America" (73–74).

More interesting for our purposes are the connections that Wolfe finds between evangelicals and postmodernism. Both assault authority and power; both are very skeptical about science and its explanations of the cosmos; both are wary of progress; and both rely on a kind of radical anti-humanism that attacks the enlightened notion "of the knowing self, a direct slap at God's authority" (Wolfe 2000, "Opening"; *New York Times Magazine* 2000, 69). They both feel "that secular rationality does not have all the answers to life's mysteries" (69), although I would argue that postmodernism's disagreement is with the kinds of rational arguments that are constructed, not with rationality itself. In either case Wolfe concludes that evangelicals are drawn to postmodernists like Stanley Fish because of "his general hostility toward liberalism" (74), although he also makes it clear that Fish has taught in institutions, which allow open-ended debate in a way that evangelicals do not. The fundamentalists also have not rejected their literal interpretation of the Bible "because they believe that the Bible is the greatest meta-narrative ever written," but then Wolfe adds that "everything else about postmodernism appeals to them" (69). That strikes me as a pretty big "but," just as "although" does in his sentence that begins, "Although postmodernism's suspicion of textual certainty is the very opposite of fundamentalist literalism. . . . " (73). Wolfe may have discovered a yearning on the part of the "evangelical mind," but the opening of it, as discussed here, is open to question.

In his article "The Pursuit of Autonomy," Wolfe (2000) summarizes the results of the *New York Times'* "The Way We Live Now Poll" of the American people: "No strong God. No strong rules. No strong superiors, moral or otherwise. The Way We Live Now poll finds that most Americans want to decide for themselves what is right, good and meaningful" (53). Americans like to choose their own religions, and "no one should ever underestimate Americans' faith in faith. . . . Americans are inveterate optimists; 75 percent believe in the intrinsic goodness of people, which suggests, whether they fully realize it or not, that they no longer subscribe to the Judeo-Christian notion of original sin" (54). 79 percent believe that religion has played a big or some role "in making you who you are," while 85 percent "believe it is possible in America to pretty much be who you want to be" (2000, 67).

And yet in a poll taken in 1997 and reported in the *New York Times Magazine,* 65 percent of Americans believed in Satan, 73 percent in hell (although only 6 percent think they'll end up there), and 94 percent believed "they have a fair-to-excellent chance of going to heaven" (1997, 61). Over the last thirty years mainline religions have lost a fair number of their church-going members, especially Episcopalians and Methodists, but evangelical and fundamentalist sects have increased remarkably: Jehovah's Witnesses +119 (as a proportion of the U.S. population, in percentages); Assemblies of God +211; and Church of God in Christ +863.

Evangelicals seemed to have turned in two directions. In its splashy cover of July 2001, *Newsweek* shows a group of shouting, upbeat teenagers, arms and thumbs raised, smiles at the breaking point, under the headline, "JESUS ROCKS! Christian Entertainment Makes a Joyful Noise." The first Christian alternative-rock tour, Festival Con Dios, explodes inside the magazine, bands and fans having expropriated the look and flailing style of rock concerts, except when they are praying. They clutch their crosses instead of their crotches. Music, videos, movies, events, and books with Christian themes have exploded across the country as well, adding up to nearly $3-billion worth of merchandise. Promoters have moved in on the faithful, transforming evangelical proselytizing into a multi-media event: "The largely evangelical industry has created its own parallel world anyway, a place where popular art and culture are filtered through a conservative Christian lens and infused with messages of faith" (41).

Withdrawal and retreat, however, have also emerged in the fundamentalist quarrel with our optimistic, do-it-yourself, be-all-that-you-can-be culture. The family has become its own cult, not hidden away in some 1840s commune but rigorously policing its children from the evil effects of contemporary lifestyles. At the same time such families express their disillusion with politics as the headier religious-right revelries of the Reagan years have dissipated and run out of steam.

Ohio, Georgia, and Kansas are still wrestling with issues that concern Darwin's theory of evolution with certain people trying to secure equal footing for "intelligent design," that is, "creationism," in science classes. In 1961 at Wheaton College in Illinois, as reported by Salamon (2001) in her review of the PBS series *Evolution,* a biochemist named Walter Hearn remarked "that the same chemical processes that bring humans into existence today could have produced Adam and Eve." An angry mother, her voice as shrill as many others, "worrying about her daughter's response to Professor Hearn's comments, wrote, 'If her faith should be shattered or even shaken, I'd rather see her dead'" (E5). In 1999 Kansas school board members voted to delete evolution from the state's science curriculum and standardized tests. The members who voted for that action lost in the next election, but the issue has risen again (Clines 2002, "In Ohio School Hearing," A14). In Ohio believers in an intelligent designer argued that evolutionary science is elitist and unfairly "inhibits theism," and later at an open hearing by the State Board of Education another tried to make the case that challenges the legitimacy of Darwin's theory as a matter of "a growing scientific controversy" (Clines 2002, "Ohio Board Hears Debate," A16). Others challenged this view, stating that support "for intelligent design was nonexistent among the vast majority of scientists" (A16). At this writing Ohio has yet to vote, but in Cobb County, Georgia, they did, requiring "teachers to give a 'balanced education' about the origin of life, giving equal weight to evolution and biblical interpretations." "To deny there is a God is to stand on a building and deny there is a building," exclaimed Russell Brock, "who described himself as an insurance salesman and a minister." These incidents underline the fact that such controversies exist and that the mainstream press continues to follow it, revealing its persistent potency and the continuing fundamentalist force that is still "out there."

Did you hear the one about the mayor of the Florida town who banned Satan? Carolyn Risher, mayor of Inglis, Florida, claims to have never seen him, "but I have felt his works," she insists, on the front page of the *New York Times* (Bragg 2002, A1). By official proclamation she banned Satan from the Inglis city limits, aided and abetted by the Rev. Richard Moore, pastor of the Yankeetown Church of God, who advised her to cleanse the town "by installing four hollowed-out wooden posts at the four entrances to town. In the hollow of each post would be a prayer." The mayor installed her proclamation in the posts: "Satan is hereby declared powerless, no longer ruling over, nor influencing, our citizens. In the past, Satan has caused division, animosity, hate, confusion, ungodly acts on our youth and discord among our friends and loved ones. No longer!" Proof involved a reputed rise in drug use, spousal and child abuse, and young people who continued to paint their faces black even when Halloween was over. Further proof may include the perpetrator or perpetrators who stole the posts. Mayor Risher reinstalled them, "sunk in reinforced concrete" (A22). Satan has not yet been seen in Inglis according to the latest reports.

"Tax Revolt Takes Aim at Rural County's Libraries" declares the headline, again on the front page of the *New York Times* (August 20, 2002, A1). Who is taking the aim in Kettle Falls, Washington? Retirees for one who oppose taxes in general and "small but persistent groups of people who are strongly antigovernment, even some militia supporters" (A12). Dave Sitler, another supporter, is also a member of the American Heritage Party, which calls for an end to all property taxes and for a government based on biblical tenets.

One group sued the University of North Carolina at Chapel Hill for assigning the book *Approaching the Qur'an: The Early Revelations,* to all incoming first-year students (Zernike, "Assigned Reading on Koran in Chapel Hill Raises Hackles," 2002, A1). The issue was thrown out of court, but the Family Policy Network in Virginia, the "conservative Christian group" which charged that reading the book would be tantamount to "forced Islamic indoctrination," argued "that the assignment violated Constitutional provisions against state-sponsored religion." More chilling, perhaps, was the revelation that the thirty-two-member board of governors of the university, wary of upsetting the legislature with its hand on the university's budget, "refused to support a resolution . . . proclaiming the importance of academic freedom."

The quiet rural town of St. Marys, Kansas, once interrogated for its possible connections to Timothy McVeigh and Terry Nichols, who had traveled in the area before the Oklahoma City bombing, prides itself on being "the last civilized stop on the Oregon Trail" (Thomas 1998, A16). At St. Mary's Academy, founded twenty years ago by the Society of St. Pius X, a conservative Roman Catholic group that still uses the Latin Mass, "only boys can play high school sports. 'It doesn't help form the feminine nature,'" quoth Denise Petit, mother of ten. The town began as a Jesuit mission for the Potawatomi tribe who were driven out of Indiana and then into Oklahoma. Writes Jo Thomas, "the decline of small family farms, with its consequent population and anger, is the backdrop for the rise of radical right-wing groups." Leonard Zeskind, president of the Institute for Research and Education on Human Rights in Kansas City, Missouri, disagrees. "The shift in the nation's political climate" has caused the swing to the right, he maintains, "in which the issue of 'Who is an American?' is much more up for grabs. It used to be that Americans were the people who were not Communists. Now Communism isn't around to differentiate ourselves. Who are we now?" (A16).

The events of 9/11 added new zest to America's love affair with apocalyptic visions. "Apocalyptic Theology Revitalized by Attacks: Calling 9/11 a Harbinger of the End Times" shrieked the headline on November 23, 2001, in the article by Kevin Sack in the New York Times (A17). "I'm settled on the fact that this happened for a reason," exclaimed twenty-three-year-old, middle-school teacher Aaron M. Hopper at the Family Christian Store in Gainesville, Georgia, "that God was trying to get our attention. The Bible says there will be great sorrow before the end times, and what happened on Sept. 11 is just an example" (A17). The Evangelical Christian Publishers Association noted a 71 percent increase in nonfiction books about prophecy in a survey of 500 bookstores during the eight weeks after September 11. Asserted Doug R. Ross, president of the association, "A cataclysmic event like Sept. 11 and the unsettledness in the Middle East cause people to say, 'Is this the war to end all wars?'" One Web site features a "Rapture Index" that "ostensibly measures the velocity of movement toward the Rapture, when Christians supposedly will vanish before a seven-year apocalypse led by the anti-Christ. The total score of 182 recorded on September 24 was the highest ever, "a particular feat since any score over 145 suggests you should 'fasten your seat belt.'"

Apocalyptic visions even find their way into Wilson's The Future of Life (2002), the Pulitzer Prize–winning biologist's view of current environmental disasters, in which "Nature's Last Stand" is part of nature's being a victim of humanity as the "serial killer of the biosphere" (94). In his opening prologue, a letter to Thoreau,

Wilson states grimly, "An Armageddon is approaching at the beginning of the third millennium. But it is not the cosmic war and fiery collapse of mankind foretold in sacred scripture. It is the wreckage of the planet by an exuberantly plentiful and ingenious humanity" (xxiii).

Even *Time* magazine got into the act with its fiery cover of July 1, 2002, complete with a white cross on which is written in red and black, "THE BIBLE & THE APOCALYPSE: Why more Americans are reading and talking about THE END OF THE WORLD." According to Nancy Gibbs, who wrote the article, "36% of Americans believe that the Bible is the word of God and is to be taken literally," and "59% believe the prophecies in the Book of Revelation will come true" (42–43). States Gibbs, "interest in the End Times is no fringe phenomenon . . . one-third of Americans say they are paying more attention now to how the news might relate to the end of the world . . . and nearly one-quarter think the Bible predicted the Sept. 11 attack" (42). She continues: "The growing audience for apocalyptic literature extends even into mainline Protestantism. . . . It took the shocking events of the last mid-century to draw apocalyptic thinking off the Fundamentalist margins and into the mainstream" (45). Of course Gibbs does not mention the fact that *Time* is also drawing apocalyptic visions directly into the mainstream by featuring her particular cover story. Someone was even quoted as being "joyful," since for True Believers the End Time heralds the Rapture and their own ultimate redemption. Photographs march one by one across the bottom of two pages and feature in succession the atom bomb, the creation of Israel, the Gulf War in 1991, the millennium, and the September 11 attacks. Before the first picture words in purple against a black background proclaim: "COUNT-DOWN."

Four pages on the two men who created and wrote the *Left Behind* novels about the Rapture, Tim LaHaye and Jerry B. Jenkins, follow after the covers of all ten novels are pictured with the number of copies sold (Gibbs 2002, 44–45). "The future is settled, and not open to change" (51), LeHaye insists, an evangelical Christian minister whose Christian Unified Schools of San Diego, only one of his many successful projects, "now sprawls across three campuses" (52). A man unvisited by doubt, LeHaye also believes that Catholicism is a "false religion . . . that witchcraft is real [and that] a 'secret order' called the Illuminati . . . has carried out a 'conspiracy on the church, our government, media, and the public schools' for more than 300 years" (52, 53). Sound familiar?

A full-page ad appeared in the *New York Times* on December 5, 2002. In huge black letters, the ad with the cover of Michael Drosnin's *Bible Code II: The Countdown*, proclaims: "IT STARTS WITH 9/11 AND COUNTS DOWN TO ARMAGEDDON." Circles, diamonds, and squares enclose certain Hebrew letters that supposedly refer to "Twin," "Towers," and "Airplane" (A19). There is no end in sight to the proclaiming of the end that is to come.

Works Cited

Altemeyer, Bob. 1996. *The Authoritarian Specter*. Cambridge: Harvard University Press.

Anderson, Perry. 1998. *The Origins of Postmodernity*. London: Verso.

Appiah, K. Anthony, and Amy Gutmann. 1996. *Color Conscious: The Political Morality of Race*. Princeton: Princeton University Press.

Appy, Christian, and Alexander Bloom. 2002. "Vietnam Mythology and the Rise of Public Cynicism." Unpublished essay.

Attridge, Derek, Geoff Bennington, and Robert Young. 1987. *Post-Structuralism and the Question of History*. Cambridge: Cambridge University Press.

Auster, Paul. 1985. *City of Glass*. New York: Penguin.

Baker, Jeff. 2000. "Plucking the American Albatross: Pynchon's Irrealism in *Mason & Dixon*." In *Pynchon and* Mason & Dixon, ed. Brooke Horvath and Irving Malin. Newark: University of Delaware Press.

Barkun, Michael. 1974. *Disaster and the Millennium*. New Haven: Yale University Press.

———. 1986. *Crucible of the Millennium: The Burned-Over District of New York in the 1840s*. Syracuse: Syracuse University Press.

———. 1997. *Religion and the Racist Right: The Origins of the Christian Identity Movement*. Chapel Hill: University of North Carolina Press.

Baudrillard, Jean. 1988. *America*. London: Verso.

Bauerlein, Mark. 1997. *Literary Criticism: An Autopsy*. Philadelphia: University of Pennsylvania Press.

Begley, Adam. n.d. "Case of the Brooklyn Symbolist," *Intellectual Design*. Online at http://www.nytimes.com/books/99/06/02/specials/auster-92mag.html.

———. 2001. "Ghostbuster." Review of *The Body Artist. New York Review of Books*, February 4, 12.

Beidler, Philip D. 1982. *American Literature and the Experience of Vietnam*. Athens: University of Georgia Press.

Belkin, Lisa. 2002. "Coincidence in an Age of Conspiracy." *New York Times Magazine,* August 11, 32–37, 46, 58–61.

Bellah, Robert. 1991. *The Good Society*. New York: Knopf.

Beller, Mara. 1999. *Quantum Dialogue: The Making of a Revolution*. Chicago: University of Chicago Press.

Benjamin, Walter. 1935. "The Work of Art in the Age of Mechanical Reproduction." Online at http://www.jahsonic.com/WAAMR.html.

Bennett, David H. 1995. *The Party of Fear: The American Far Right from Nativism to the Militia Movement*, rev. and updated. New York: Vintage.

Berger, John. 1972. *Ways of Seeing*. New York: Penguin Books.

Berlin, Isaiah. 1998. "My Intellectual Path." *New York Review of Books*, May 14, 53–60.

———. 1999. *The Roots of Romanticism*. Princeton: Princeton University Press.

Bernstein, Jeremy. 1993. *Cranks, Quarks, and the Cosmos: Writings on Science*. New York: Basic Books.

Berressem, Hanjo. 1993. *Pynchon's Poetics: Interfacing Theory and Text*. Urbana: University of Illinois Press.

Best, Steven, and Douglas Kellner. 1997. *The Postmodern Turn*. New York: The Guilford Press.

Billops, Camille, Owen Dodson, and James Van Der Zee. 1978. *The Harlem Book of the Dead*, foreword by Toni Morrison. Dobbs Ferry, NY: Morgan and Morgan.

Bloom, Allan. 1987. *The Closing of the American Mind: How Higher Education Has Failed Democracy and Impoverished the Souls of Today's Students*. New York: Simon and Schuster.

Bloom, Harold. 1992. *The American Religion: The Emergence of the Post-Christian Nation*. New York: Simon and Schuster.

———. 1996. *Omens of Millennium: The Gnosis of Angels, Dreams, and Resurrection*. New York: Riverhead.

Bonnycastle, Stephen. 1997. *In Search of Authority: An Introductory Guide to Literary Theory*, 2nd ed. Peterborough, ON, Canada: Broadview Press.

Bouson, J. Brooks. 2000. *Quiet as It's Kept: Shame, Trauma, and Race in the Novels of Toni Morrison*. Albany: State University of New York Press.

Bowers, Susan. 1997. "*Beloved* and the New Apocalypse." In *Toni Morrison's Fiction: Contemporary Criticism*, ed. David L. Middleton. New York: Garland, 209–30.

Boyer, Paul. 1992. *When Time Shall Be No More: Prophecy Belief in Modern American Culture*. Cambridge: Harvard University Press.

Boyle, T. Coraghessan. 1997. "New World Disorder: In *Mason & Dixon*, Pynchon Realigns American History." *New York Times Book Review*, May 18, 9.

Bragg, Rick. 1995. "In Shock, Loathing, Denial: 'This Doesn't Happen Here.'" *New York Times*, April 20, A1, B9.

———. 2002. "Florida Town Finds Satan an Offense Unto It." *New York Times*, March 14, A1, A22.

Brodhead, Richard H. 1986. *The School of Hawthorne*. New York: Oxford University Press.

Brown, Dan. 2003. *The Da Vinci Code*. New York: Doubleday.

Bruns, Gerald L. 1999. *Tragic Thoughts at the End of Philosophy: Language, Literature, and Ethical Theory*. Evanston, IL: Northwestern University Press.

Caldwell, Gail. 1987. "Author Toni Morrison Discusses Her Latest Novel *Beloved.*" In *Conversations with Toni Morrison,* ed. Danille Taylor-Guthrie. Jackson: University Press of Mississippi, 1994, 239–45.

Carmichael, Virginia. 1993. *Framing History: The Rosenberg Story and the Cold War.* Minneapolis: University of Minnesota Press.

Caserio, Robert L. 1979. *Plot, Story, and the Novel: From Dickens and Poe to the Modern Period.* Princeton: Princeton University Press.

Casey, David. 2001. "Didion as Postmodernist." Unpublished seminar paper, Wheaton College, Norton, MA.

Chabot, C. Barry. 1988. "The Problem of the Postmodern." *New Literary History* 20, no. 1 (Autumn): 11–17. Reprinted in Ingeborg Hoesterey, ed., *Zeitgeist in Babel: The Postmodernist Controversy.* 1991. Bloomington: Indiana University Press, 31–36.

Chambers, Judith. 1992. *Thomas Pynchon.* New York: Twayne.

Clerc, Charles, ed. 1983. *Approaches to* Gravity's Rainbow. Columbus: Ohio State University Press.

———. 2000. Mason & Dixon *& Pynchon.* Lanham, MD: University Press of America.

Clifton, Brett. 2002. Rousing the Faithful to Seek the Promised Land: Analyzing the Christian Right's Penetration of the Republican Party. PhD thesis, Brown University.

Clines, Francis X. 2002. "In Ohio School Hearing, a New Theory Will Seek a Place Alongside Evolution." *New York Times,* February 2, A14.

———. 2002. "Ohio Board Hears Debate on an Alternative to Darwinism: 'Intelligent Design' Seeks Place in Class." *New York Times,* March 12, A16.

Cloud, Jon. 2002. "Meet the Prophet." *Time,* July 1, 50–53.

Cohn, Norman. 1970. *The Pursuit of the Millennium: Revolutionary Millenarians and Mystical Anarchists of the Middle Ages.* New York: Oxford University Press.

———. 1993. *Cosmos, Chaos, and the World to Come: The Ancient Roots of Apocalyptic Faith.* New Haven: Yale University Press.

Conner, Marc C., ed. 2000. *The Aesthetics of Toni Morrison: Speaking the Unspeakable.* Jackson: University Press of Mississippi.

Connor, Steven. 1997. *Postmodernist Culture: An Introduction to Theories of the Contemporary,* 2nd ed. Oxford: Blackwell.

Cooper, Peter L. 1983. *Signs and Symptoms: Thomas Pynchon and the Contemporary World.* Berkeley: University of California Press.

Cowart, David. 2002. *Don DeLillo: The Physics of Language.* Athens: University of Georgia Press.

Daniels, Ted, ed. 1999. *A Doomsday Reader: Prophets, Predictors, and Hucksters of Salvation.* New York: New York University Press.

Darling, Marsha. 1988. "In the Realm of Responsibility: A Conversation with Toni Morrison." In *Conversations with Toni Morrison,* ed. Danille Taylor-Guthrie. Jackson: University Press of Mississippi, 1994, 246–54.

Dasenbrock, Reed Way. 2001. *Truth and Consequences: Intentions, Conventions, and the New Thematics.* University Park: Pennsylvania State University Press.

Davis, David Brion, ed. 1971. *The Fear of Conspiracy: Images of Un-American Subversion from the Revolution to the Present.* Ithaca: Cornell University Press.

DeCurtis, Anthony. 1991. "'An Outsider in This Society': An Interview with Don DeLillo." In *Introducing Don DeLillo,* ed. Frank Lentricchia. Durham, NC: Duke University Press, 43–66.

DeKoven, Marianne. 1997. "Postmodernism and Post-Utopian Desire in Toni Morrison and E. L. Doctorow." In *Toni Morrison: Critical and Theoretical Approaches,* ed. Nancy J. Peterson. Baltimore: Johns Hopkins University Press, 111–30.

Delbanco, Andrew, 2000. "The Decline and Fall of Literature." *New York Review of Books,* January 21, 32–38.

DeLillo, Don. 1977. *Players.* New York: Knopf.

———. 1978. *Running Dog.* New York: Vintage.

———. 1982. *The Names.* New York: Knopf.

———. 1983. "American Blood: A Journey through the Labyrinth of Dallas and JFK." *Rolling Stone,* December 8, 21–28, 74.

———. 1988. *Libra.* New York: Viking.

———. 1991. *Mao II.* New York: Viking.

———. 1997. "The Power of History." *New York Times Magazine,* September 7, 60–63.

———. 1997. *Underworld.* New York: Scribner.

———. 2001. *The Body Artist.* New York: Scribner.

Dellamora, Richard, ed. 1995. *Postmodern Apocalypse: Theory and Cultural Practice at the End.* Philadelphia: University of Pennsylvania Press.

de Man, Paul. 1984. *The Rhetoric of Romanticism.* New York: Columbia University Press.

Denby, David. 1996. *Great Books: My Adventures with Homer, Rousseau, Woolf, and Other Indestructible Writers of the Western World.* New York: Simon and Schuster.

de Tocqueville, Alexis. 1945 [1840]. *Democracy in America,* vol. 2. New York: Vintage.

Dewey, Joseph. 2000. "The Sound of One Man Mapping: Wicks Cherrycoke and the Eastern (Re)solution." In *Pynchon and Mason & Dixon,* ed. Brooke Horvath and Irving Malin. Newark: University of Delaware Press, 112–31.

Didion, Joan. 1968. *Slouching Towards Bethlehem.* New York: Simon and Schuster.

———. 1978. *A Book of Common Prayer.* New York: Pocket Books.

———. 1978. *Play It As It Lays.* New York: Pocket Books.

———. 1979. *The White Album.* New York: Pocket Books.

———. 1983. *Salvador.* New York: Washington Square Press.

———. 1984. *Democracy.* New York: Simon and Schuster.

———. 1987. *Miami.* New York: Simon and Schuster.

——. 1996. *The Last Thing He Wanted*. New York: Knopf.

——. 2001. *Political Fictions*. New York: Knopf.

——. 2003. "Fixed Opinions, or The Hinge of History." *New York Review of Books,* January 16, 54.

Dryden, Edgar A. 1988. *The Form of American Romance*. Baltimore: Johns Hopkins University Press.

Duvall, John N. 2000. *The Identifying Fictions of Toni Morrison: Modernist Authenticity and Postmodern Blackness*. New York: Palgrave.

Eagleton, Terry. 1983. *Literary Theory: An Introduction*. Minneapolis: University of Minnesota Press.

——. 1990. *The Ideology of the Aesthetic*. Oxford: Blackwell.

——. 1990. *The Significance of Theory*. Oxford: Blackwell.

——. 1997. *The Illusions of Postmodernism*. Oxford: Blackwell.

——. 2000. *The Idea of Culture*. Oxford: Blackwell.

——. 2003. *After Theory*. New York: Basic Books.

——. 2003. *Sweet Violence: The Idea of the Tragic*. Oxford: Blackwell.

Eddins, Dwight. 1990. *The Gnostic Pynchon*. Bloomington: Indiana University Press.

Edmundson, Mark. 1997. *Nightmare on Main Street: Angels, Sadomasochism, and the Culture of Gothic*. Cambridge: Harvard University Press.

Egan, Timothy. 2002. "Tax Revolt Takes Aim at Rural County's Libraries." *New York Times,* August 20, A1.

Eggers, David. n.d. "The Salon Interview: Joan Didion." Online at http://www.salon.com/oct96/didion961028.html.

Eliot, T. S. 1962. *The Waste Land and Other Poems*. New York: Harvest Books.

Ellroy, James. 1995. *American Tabloid*. New York: Knopf.

Falck, Colin. 1989. *Myth, Truth and Literature: Towards a True Post-Modernism*. Cambridge: Cambridge University Press.

Farnsworth, Elizabeth. 2001. *Toni Morrison's* Paradise. In Kelly Reames, *Toni Morrison's* Paradise: *A Reader's Guide*. New York: Continuum, 29. Online at *The NewsHour with Jim Lehrer Transcript,* http://www.pbs.org/newshour/bb/entertainment/jan-june98/morrison_3-9.html.

Fenster, Mark. 1999. *Conspiracy Theories: Secrecy and Power in American Culture*. Minneapolis: University of Minnesota Press.

Fischer, David Hackett. 1970. *Historians' Fallacies: Toward a Logic of Historical Thought*. New York: Harper and Row.

Fish, Stanley. 2002. "Postmodern Warfare: The Ignorance of Our Warrior Intellectuals." *Harper's,* July, 33–40.

Fowler, Douglas. 1980. *A Reader's Guide to Gravity's Rainbow*. Ann Arbor, MI: Ardia.

Garis, Leslie. 1987. "Didion & Dunne: The Rewards of a Literary Marriage." *New York Times Magazine,* February 8, 18–65.

Gediman, Paul. 1997. "Visions of the American Berserk." *Boston Review* (October/November): 46–48.

George, John, and Laird Wilcox. 1996. *American Extremists: Militias, Supremacists, Klansmen, Communists, and Others*. Amherst, NY: Prometheus Books.

Gibbs, Nancy. 2002. "Apocalypse Now." *Time*, July 1, 40–48.

Gitlin, Todd. 1989. "The Postmodern Predicament." *Wilson Quarterly* (Summer): 67–76.

Glassner, Barry. 1999. *The Culture of Fear: Why Americans Are Afraid of the Wrong Things*. New York: Basic Books.

Goddu, Teresa. 1997. *Gothic America: Narrative, History, and Nation*. New York: Columbia University Press.

Goldberg, Robert Alan. 2001. *Enemies Within: The Culture of Conspiracy in Modern America*. New Haven: Yale University Press.

Goodheart, Eugene. 1991. "Some Speculations on Don DeLillo and the Cinematic Road." In *Introducing Don DeLillo*, ed. Frank Lentricchia. Durham NC: Duke University Press.

Goodman, Walter. 1995. "From the Networks, Desperate Rescues, Crying Babies and Talking Heads." *New York Times*, April 20, B10.

Gopnik, Adam. 1998. "American Studies." *New Yorker*, September 28, 39–42.

Gourgouris, Stathis. 2003. *Does Literature Think? Literature as Theory for an Antimythical Era*. Stanford: Stanford University Press.

Graham, Billy. 1995. "Remarks by President, Governor and Rev. Graham at Memorial Service." *New York Times*, April 24, B8.

Grange, Joseph. 1989. "Metaphysics, Semiotics, and Common Sense." Review of *Recovery of the Measure: Interpretation and Nature by Robert Cummings Neville*. Albany: State University of New York Press. In *Feature Reviews*, 43, *Philosophy East and West*. April 1, 1993, Electronic Library, 303.

Greenhouse, Linda. 1995. "Again, Bombs in the Land of the Free." *New York Times*, April 23, Section 4, 1.

Gutting, Gary, ed. 1980. *Paradigms and Revolutions: Appraisals and Applications of Thomas Kuhn's Philosophy of Science*. Notre Dame, IN: University of Notre Dame Press.

Harding, Wendy, and Jacky Martin. 1994. *A World of Difference: An Inter-Cultural Study of Toni Morrison's Novels*. Westport, CT: Greenwood Press.

Harrison, Barbara Grizzuti. 1980. "Joan Didion: Only Disconnect." Online at http://dept.English.upenn.edu/-afilreis/103/didion-per-harrison.html.

Hart, Jeffrey. 1984. *Reactionary Modernism: Technology, Culture, and Politics in Weimar and the Third Reich*. New York: Cambridge University Press.

Hartley, George. 2003. *The Abyss of Representation: Marxism and the Postmodern Sublime*. Durham, NC: Duke University Press.

Harvey, David. 1989. *The Condition of Postmodernity*. Oxford: Blackwell.

Hassan, Ihab. 1990. *Selves at Risk: Patterns of Quest in Contemporary American Letters*. Madison: University of Wisconsin Press.

Hayles, Katherine N., ed. 1984. *The Cosmic Web: Scientific Field Models and Literary Strategies in the Twentieth Century.* Ithaca: Cornell University Press.

———. 1991. *Chaos and Order: Complex Dynamics in Literature and Science.* Chicago: University of Chicago Press.

Heard, Alex. 1999. *Apocalypse Pretty Soon: Travels in End-Time America.* New York: Norton.

Heinze, Denise. 1993. *The Dilemma of "Double-Consciousness": Toni Morrison's Novels.* Athens: University of Georgia Press.

Henderson, Katherine Usher. 1980. *Joan Didion.* New York: Ungar.

Henneberger, Melinda. 1995. "Where Nothing Ever Happens, Terrorism Did." *New York Times,* April 21, A26.

———. 1995. "A By-the-Book Officer, 'Suspicious by Nature,' Spots Trouble and Acts Fast." *New York Times,* April 23, A32.

Higgins, George V. 1975. *The Friends of Richard Nixon.* Boston: Little, Brown.

Hirsch, David H. 1991. *The Deconstruction of Literature: Criticism after Auschwitz.* Hanover, NH: University Press of New England.

Hite, Molly. 1983. *Ideas of Order in the Novels of Thomas Pynchon.* Columbus: Ohio State University Press.

Hodder, Alan D. 1989. *Emerson's Rhetoric of Revolution: Nature, the Reader, and the Apocalypse Within.* University Park: Pennsylvania State University Press.

Hofstadter, Richard. 1963. *Anti-Intellectualism in American Life.* New York: Knopf.

———. 1963. *The Paranoid Style in American Politics and Other Essays.* Cambridge: Harvard University Press.

Holloway, Karla F. C., and Stephanie A. Demetrakopoulos. 1987. *New Dimensions of Spirituality: A Biracial and Bicultural Reading of the Novels of Toni Morrison.* New York: Greenwood Press.

Horvath, Brooke, and Irving Malin, eds. 2000. *Pynchon and* Mason & Dixon. Newark: University of Delaware Press.

Hume, Kathryn. 1987. *Pynchon's Mythography: An Approach to Gravity's Rainbow.* Carbondale: Southern Illinois University Press.

Hutcheon, Linda. 1988. *A Poetics of Postmodernism: History, Theory, Fiction.* New York: Routledge.

Ingebretsen, Edward J. 2001. *At Stake: Monsters and the Rhetoric of Fear in Public Culture.* Chicago: University of Chicago Press.

Isaacs, Susan. 1998. *Red, White and Blue.* New York: HarperCollins.

Iyasere, Solomon O., and Marla W. Iyasere. 2000. *Understanding Toni Morrison's Beloved and* Sula: *Selected Essays and Criticisms.* Troy, NY: Whitson Publishing Company.

Jameson, Fredric. 1991. *Postmodernism, or, The Cultural Logic of Late Capitalism.* Durham, NC: Duke University Press.

Janeway, Michael. 1999. *Republic of Denial: Press, Politics, and Public Life.* New Haven: Yale University Press.

Johnson, Steven. 2001. *Emergence: The Connected Lives of Ants, Brains, Cities, and Software.* New York: Scribner.

Johnston, John. 1998. *Information Multiplicity: American Fiction in the Age of Media Saturation.* Baltimore: Johns Hopkins University Press.

Jones, Bessie W., and Audrey Vinson. 1985. "An Interview with Toni Morrison." In *Conversations with Toni Morrison,* ed. Danille Taylor-Guthrie. Jackson: University Press of Mississippi, 1994, 171–87.

Kaminer, Wendy. 1999. *Sleeping with Extra-Terrestrials: The Rise of Irrationalism and Perils of Piety.* New York: Vintage.

Kaplan, Robert. 1998. *An Empire Wilderness: Travels into America's Future.* New York: Random House.

Karl, Frederick. 1983. *American Fictions: 1940–1980.* New York: Harper and Row.

Keenan. Sally. 1998. " 'Four Hundred Years of Silence': Myth, History, and Motherhood in Toni Morrison's *Beloved.*" In *Toni Morrison:* Beloved, ed. Carl Plasa. New York: Columbia University Press, 118–33.

Keesey, Douglas. 1993. *Don DeLillo.* New York. Twayne.

Kermode, Frank. 1967. *The Sense of an Ending: Studies in the Theory of Fiction.* London: Oxford University Press.

Kernan, Alvin. 1990. *The Death of Literature.* New Haven: Yale University Press.

Kifner, John. 1995. "At Least 21 Are Dead, Scores Are Missing after Car Bomb Attack in Oklahoma City Wrecks 9-Story Federal Office Building; 17 Victims Were Children in 2nd-Floor Day-Care Center." *New York Times,* April 20, A1, B9.

Kipen, David. 2001. "DeLillo's Bursts of Brilliance: New Novella Sings, but Only in Parts." Review of *The Body Artist. San Francisco Chronicle,* February 7. Online at http://www.sfgate.com/cgibin/article.cgi?file=/chronicle/archive/2001/02/07/DD186107.DTL&type=books.

Klinkowitz, Jerome. 1992. *Structuring the Void: The Struggle for Subject in Contemporary American Fiction.* Durham, NC: Duke University Press.

Knight, Peter. 2000. *Conspiracy Culture: From Kennedy to the X-Files.* London: Routledge.

———, ed. 2002. *Conspiracy Nation: The Politics of Paranoia in Postwar America.* New York: New York University Press.

Koenan, Anne. 1980. "The One Out of Sequence." In *Conversations with Toni Morrison,* ed. Danille Taylor-Guthrie. Jackson: University Press of Mississippi, 1994, 67–83.

Kramer, Jane. 2002. *Lone Patriot.* New York: Pantheon.

Kuehl, John. 1989. *Alternate Worlds: A Study of Postmodern Antirealistic American Fiction.* New York: New York University Press.

LeClair, Thomas. 1981. "The Language Must Not Sweat: A Conversation with Toni Morrison." In *Conversations with Toni Morrison,* ed. Danille Taylor-Guthrie. Jackson: University Press of Mississippi, 1994, 119–28.

———. 1989. *The Art of Excess: Mastery in Contemporary American Fiction.* Urbana: University of Illinois Press.

Lee, Rachel C. 2000. "Missing Peace in Toni Morrison's *Sula* and *Beloved.*" In *Understanding Toni Morrison's Beloved and Sula: Selected Essays and Criticism,* ed. Solomon O. and Marla W. Iyasere. Troy, NY: Whitson Publishing, 277–96.

Lehman, David. 1991. *Signs of the Times: Deconstruction and the Fall of Paul de Man.* New York: Poseidon Press.

Leitch, Vincent B. 1988. *American Literary Criticism from the 30s to the 80s.* New York: Columbia University Press.

Lentricchia, Frank. 1980. *After the New Criticism.* Chicago: University of Chicago Press.

Leonard, John. 2001. "The Hunger Artist." *New York Review of Books,* February 22, 14–17.

Levin, Murray M. 1971. *Political Hysteria: The Democratic Capacity for Repression.* New York: Basic Books.

Levine, George, and David Leverenz, eds. 1976. *Mindful Pleasures: Essays on Thomas Pynchon.* Boston: Little, Brown.

Levine, Robert S. 1989. *Conspiracy and Romance: Studies in Brockden Brown, Cooper, Hawthorne, and Melville.* Cambridge: Cambridge University Press.

Levitas, Daniel. 2002. *The Terrorist Next Door: The Militia Movement and the Radical Right.* New York: St. Martin's Press.

Lilla, Mark. 1998. "The Politics of Jacques Derrida." *New York Review of Books,* June 25, 36–41.

Lindsey, Hal. 1970. *The Late Great Planet Earth.* New York: Bantam Books.

Livio, Mario. 2000. *The Accelerating Universe: Infinite Expansion, the Cosmological Constant, and the Beauty of the Cosmos.* New York: John Wiley and Sons.

Lyotard, Jean-François. 1984. *The Postmodern Condition: A Report on Knowledge.* Minneapolis: University of Minnesota Press.

MacIntyre, Jeffrey. 2002. "Don DeLillo." *Salon.com.* Online at http://www.salon.com/people/bc/2001/10/23/delillo/?x.

Madsen, Deborah L. 1991. *The Postmodernist Allegories of Thomas Pynchon.* New York: St. Martin's Press.

Maltby, Paul. 1991. *Dissident Postmodernists: Barthelme, Coover, Pynchon.* Philadelphia: University of Pennsylvania Press.

Malti-Douglas, Fedwa. 2000. *The Starr Report Disrobed.* New York: Columbia University Press.

Marcus, George, ed. 1999. *Paranoia within Reason: A Casebook on Conspiracy as Explanation.* Chicago: University of Chicago Press.

Marrs, Jim. 2000. *Rule By Secrecy: The Hidden History That Connects the Trilateral Commission, the Freemasons, and the Great Pyramids.* New York: HarperCollins.

Marty, Martin E. 1997. *The One and the Many: America's Struggle for the Common Good.* Cambridge: Harvard University Press.

McCarthy, Mary. 1974. *The Mask of State: Watergate Portraits.* New York: Harcourt Brace Jovanovich.

McClure, John A. 1994. *Late Imperial Romance.* London: Verso.

McFadden, Robert D. 1995. "Visiting Suspect's Past: Could He Have Done IT?" *New York Times,* April 23, A1.

McHale, Brian. 1992. *Constructing Postmodernism.* London: Routledge.

McHoul, Alec, and David Wills. 1990. *Writing Pynchon: Strategies in Fictional Analysis.* Urbana: University of Illinois Press.

McKay, Nellie. 1983. "An Interview with Toni Morrison." In *Conversations with Toni Morrison,* ed. Danille Taylor-Guthrie. Jackson: University Press of Mississippi, 1994, 138–55.

Melley, Timothy. 2000. *Empire of Conspiracy: The Culture of Paranoia in Postwar America.* Ithaca: Cornell University Press.

Melville, Herman. 1956. *Moby-Dick.* Boston: Houghton Mifflin.

Menand, Louis. 2001. *The Metaphysical Club: A Story of Ideas in America.* New York: Farrar, Straus and Giroux.

Merkin, Daphne. 1998. "This Year in Jerusalem: Robert Stone Thrills to the Holy Land." *New Yorker,* April 13, 74–76.

Michael, John. 2000. *Anxious Intellects: Academic Professionals, Public Intellectuals, and Enlightenment Values.* Durham, NC: Duke University Press.

Michel, Lou, and Dan Herbeck. 2001. *American Terrorist: Timothy McVeigh and the Oklahoma City Bombing.* New York: HarperCollins.

Middleton, David L., ed. 1997. *Toni Morrison's Fiction: Contemporary Criticism.* New York: Garland.

Miller, Laura. 2001. "Eighteen Pages of Genius—Then Modernist Mandarinism." Review of *The Body Artist. New York Observer,* January 29, 20.

Miller, J. Hillis. 1992. *Illustration.* Cambridge: Harvard University Press.

Moore, Thomas. 1987. *The Style of Connectedness:* Gravity's Rainbow *and Thomas Pynchon.* Columbia: University of Missouri Press.

Morrison, Toni. 1987. *Beloved.* New York: Knopf.

———. 1992. *Jazz.* New York: Knopf.

———. 1992. *Playing in the Dark: Whiteness and the Literary Imagination.* Cambridge: Harvard University Press.

———. 1994. *The Nobel Lecture in Literature, 1993.* New York: Knopf.

———. 1998. *Paradise.* New York: Knopf.

Moses, Tai. 1996. "Fear of Meaning." *Metro,* November 21–27. Online at http://www.metroactive.com/papers/metro/11.21.96/books-9647.html.

Naylor, Gloria. 1985. "A Conversation: Gloria Naylor and Toni Morrison." In *Conversations with Toni Morrison,* ed. Danille Taylor-Guthrie. Jackson: University Press of Mississippi, 1994, 188–217.

Nealon, Jeffrey T. 1993. *Double Reading: Postmodernism after Deconstruction.* Ithaca: Cornell University Press.

New York Times Magazine. 1997. "Belief by the Numbers," compiled by Russell Short. In "God Decentralized." *New York Times Magazine,* December 7.

———. 2000. "What's Really on the Minds of Americans: The Way We Live Now Poll, A Nationwide Survey of America's Inner Life." *New York Times Magazine,* May 7, entire issue.

Newman, Charles. 1985. *The Post-Modern Aura: The Act of Fiction in an Age of Inflation.* Evanston, IL: Northwestern University Press.

Norris, Christopher. 1990. *What's Wrong with Postmodernism: Critical Theory and the Ends of Philosophy.* Baltimore: Johns Hopkins University Press.

———. 1997. *Against Relativism: Philosophy of Science, Deconstruction, and Critical Theory.* Oxford: Blackwell.

———. 2000. *Deconstruction and the "Unfinished Project of Modernity."* New York: Routledge.

———. 2000. *Quantum Theory and the Flight from Realism: Philosophical Responses to Quantum Mechanics.* London: Routledge.

O'Brien, Tim. 1980. *Going After Cacciato.* London: Triad/Granada.

———. 1991. "The Magic Show." In *Writers on Writing,* ed. Robert Pack and Jay Parini. Hanover, NH: Middlebury College Press / University Press of New England.

———. 1992. "Maybe So." In *Vietnam, We've All Been There: Interviews with American Writers,* ed. Eric James Schroeder. Westport, CT: Praeger.

———. 1994. *In the Lake of the Woods.* Boston: Houghton Mifflin.

O'Donnell, Patrick. 1986. *Passionate Doubts: Designs of Interpretation in Contemporary American Fiction.* Iowa City: University of Iowa Press.

———. 1991. *New Essays on* The Crying of Lot 49. Cambridge: Cambridge University Press.

———. 2000. *Latent Destinies: Cultural Paranoia and Contemporary United States Narrative.* Durham, NC: Duke University Press.

O'Leary, Stephen D. 1994. *Arguing the Apocalypse: A Theory of Millennial Rhetoric.* New York: Oxford University Press.

Osteen, Mark. 2000. *American Magic and Dread: Don DeLillo's Dialogue with Culture.* Philadelphia: University of Pennsylvania Press.

Page, Philip. 1995. *Dangerous Freedom: Fusion and Fragmentation in Toni Morrison's Novels.* Jackson: University Press of Mississippi.

Patell, Cyrus R. K. 2001. *Negative Liberties: Morrison, Pynchon, and the Problem of Liberal Ideology.* Durham, NC: Duke University Press.

Payne, Michael, and John Schad, eds. 2003. *Life After Theory.* London: Continuum.

Pearce, Richard. 1981. *Critical Essays on Thomas Pynchon.* Boston: G. K. Hall.

Peterson, Nancy J., ed. 1997. *Toni Morrison: Critical and Theoretical Approaches.* Baltimore: Johns Hopkins University Press.

Picknett, Lynn, and Clive Prince. 1997. *The Templar Revelation: Secret Guardians of the True Identity of Christ.* New York: Bantam.

Pillow, Kirk. 2000. *Sublime Understanding: Aesthetic Reflection in Kant and Hegel.* Cambridge: MIT Press.

Pipes, Daniel. 1997. *Conspiracy: How the Paranoid Style Flourishes and Where It Comes From.* New York: The Free Press.

Plasa, Carl, ed. 1998. *Toni Morrison:* Beloved. New York: Columbia University Press.

Poirier, Richard. 1987. *The Renewal of Literature: Emersonian Reflections.* New York: Random House.

———. 1999. *Trying It Out in America: Literary and Other Performances.* New York: Farrar, Straus and Giroux.

Popper, Karl. 1961. *The Poverty of Historicism.* New York: Harper and Row.

Porush, David. 1994. "'Purring into Transcendence': Pynchon's Puncutron Machine." In *The Vineland Papers: Critical Takes on Pynchon's Novel,* ed. Geoffrey Green, Donald Greiner, and Larry McCaffery. Normal, IL: Dalkey Archive Press.

Purdum, Todd S. 1995. "Army Veteran Held in Oklahoma Bombing; Toll Hits 65 as Hope for Survivors Fades; Three in Custody; Officials Suspect Links to Far-Right Militia Based in Michigan." *New York Times,* April 22, A1, A8.

Pynchon, Thomas. 1973. *Gravity's Rainbow.* New York: Viking.

———. 1990. *Vineland.* Boston: Little, Brown.

———. 1997. *Mason & Dixon.* New York: Henry Holt.

———. 1998. *Slow Learner: Early Stories.* Boston: Little, Brown.

———. 1999 [1966]. *The Crying of Lot 49.* New York: Perennial.

Rafferty, Terence. 1988. "Self-Watcher." *New Yorker,* September 26, 108–10.

Rapaport, Herman. 2001. *The Theory Mess: Deconstruction in Eclipse.* New York: Columbia University Press.

Reames, Kelly. 2001. *Toni Morrison's* Paradise: *A Reader's Guide.* New York: Continuum.

Remnick, David. 1997. "Exile on Main Street: Don DeLillo's Undisclosed Underworld." *New Yorker,* September 15, 42–48.

Ricoeur, Paul. 1985. *Time and Narrative,* 3rd ed. Chicago: University of Chicago Press.

Robinson, Douglas. 1985. *American Apocalypses: The Image of the End of the World in American Literature.* Baltimore: Johns Hopkins University Press.

Rody, Caroline. 2000. "Toni Morrison's *Beloved:* History, 'Rememory,' and a 'Clamor for a Kiss.'" In *Understanding Toni Morrison's* Beloved *and* Sula: *Selected Essays and Criticism,* ed. Solomon O. and Marla W. Iyasere. Troy: Whitson Publishing, 83–112.

Rose, Jacqueline. 1992. *The Case of Peter Pan, or, The Impossibility of Children's Fiction.* Philadelphia: University of Pennsylvania Press.

Rosenblatt, Louise M. 1978. *The Reader, The Text, The Poem: The Transactional Theory of Literary Work.* Carbondale: Southern Illinois University Press.

Roth, Philip. 1986. *The Counterlife.* New York: Penguin.

———. 2000. *The Human Stain.* Boston: Houghton Mifflin.

Rothstein, Edward. 2001. "Attacks on U.S. Challenge the Perspectives of Postmodern True Believers." *New York Times,* September 22, A17.

———. 2001. "Exploring the Flaws in the Notion of the 'Root Causes' of Terror," *New York Times,* November 17, A23.

———. 2002. "Moral Relativity Is a Hot Topic? True. Absolutely." *New York Times,* July 13, AL 1,15.

Ruas, Charles. 1981. "Toni Morrison." In *Conversations with Toni Morrison,* ed. Danille Taylor-Guthrie. Jackson: University Press of Mississippi, 1994, 93–118.

Rushdie, Salman. 2002. *Step Across This Line: Collected Nonfiction, 1992–2002.* New York: Random House.

Sack, Kevin. 2001. "Apocalyptic Theology Revitalized By Attacks: Calling 9/11 a Harbinger of the End Times." *New York Times,* November 23, A17.

Salamon, Julie. 2001. "A Stark Explanation for Mankind from an Unlikely Rebel." Review of PBS' "Evolution." *New York Times,* September 24, E5.

Sargent, Lyman Tower, ed. 1995. *Extremism in America.* New York: New York University Press.

Saul, John. 1992. *Shadows.* New York: Bantam.

Scanlan, Margaret. 2001. *Plotting Terror: Novelists and Terrorists in Contemporary Fiction.* Charlottesville: University Press of Virginia.

Schaub, Thomas H. 2000. "Plot, Ideology, and Compassion in *Mason & Dixon.*" In *Pynchon and* Mason & Dixon, ed. Brooke Horvath and Irving Malin. Newark: University of Delaware Press, 189–202.

Schell, Jonathan. 1975. *The Time of Illusion: An Historical and Reflective Account of the Nixon Era.* New York: Vintage.

———. 1989. *Observing The Nixon Years.* New York: Pantheon.

Scholes, Robert. n.d. "'Because of the Angels': Getting Serious about Reading." Unpublished essay. Published as "Sacred Reading: A Fundamental Problem." In *The Crafty Reader.* New Haven: Yale University Press, 2001, 212–239.

———. 1985. *Textual Power: Literary Theory and the Teaching of English.* New Haven: Yale University Press.

———. 1989. *Protocols of Reading.* New Haven: Yale University Press.

———. 1998. *The Rise and Fall of English.* New Haven: Yale University Press.

Schopp, Andrew. 2000. "Narrative Control and Subjectivity: Dismantling Safety in Toni Morrison's *Beloved.*" In *Understanding Toni Morrison's* Beloved *and* Sula: *Selected Essays and Criticism,* ed. Solomon O. and Marla W. Iyasere. Troy, NY: Whitson Publishing, 204–30.

Schudson, Michael. 1992. *Watergate in American Memory: How We Remember, Forget, and Reconstruct the Past.* New York: HarperCollins.

Schwartz, Hans. 1995. *Evil: A Historical and Theological Perspective.* Minneapolis: Fortress Press.

Schwartz, Regina M. 1997. *The Curse of Cain: The Violent Legacy of Monotheism.* Chicago: University of Chicago Press.

Selden, Raman, and Peter Widdowson. 1993. *A Reader's Guide to Contemporary Literary Theory.* Lexington: University Press of Kentucky.

Serrano, Richard A. 1998. *One of Ours: Timothy McVeigh and the Oklahoma City Bombing.* New York: Norton.

Siegel, Mark Richard. 1978. *Pynchon: Creative Paranoia in* Gravity's Rainbow. Port Washington, NY: Kennikat Press.

Sim, Stuart. 1992. *Beyond Aesthetics: Confrontations with Poststructuralism and Postmodernism.* Toronto: University of Toronto Press.

Simpson, David. 1995. *The Academic Postmodern and the Rule of Literature: A Report on Half-Knowledge.* Chicago: University of Chicago Press.

Sitchin, Zecharia. 1998. *The Cosmic Code: Book VI of the Earth Chronicles.* New York: Avon.

Slethaug, Gordon E. 2000. *Beautiful Chaos: Chaos Theory and Metachaotics in Recent American Fiction.* Albany: State University of New York Press.

Sokal, Alan, and Jean Bricmont. 1998. *Fashionable Nonsense: Postmodern Intellectuals' Abuse of Science.* New York: Picador.

Stanford, Peter. 1996. *The Devil: A Biography.* New York: Henry Holt.

Starr, Kenneth. 1998. *The Starr Report.* New York: Public Affairs.

Steiner, George. 1989. *Real Presences.* Chicago: University of Chicago Press.

Steiner, Wendy. 1995. *The Scandal of Pleasure.* Chicago: University of Chicago Press.

Stepto, Robert. 1976. "Intimate Things in Place: A Conversation with Toni Morrison." In *Conversations with Toni Morrison,* ed. Danille Taylor-Guthrie. Jackson: University Press of Mississippi, 1994, 10–29.

Stewart, Kathleen. 1999. "Conspiracy Theory's World." In *Paranoia within Reason,* ed. George E. Marcus. Chicago: University of Chicago Press, 13–19.

Stickney, Brandon M. 1996. *"All-American Monster": The Unauthorized Biography of Timothy McVeigh.* Amherst, NY: Prometheus Books.

Stone, Robert. 1981. *A Flag for Sunrise.* New York: Picador.

———. 1986. *Children of Light.* New York: Ballantine.

———. 1997 [1973]. *Dog Soldiers.* Boston: Houghton Mifflin.

———. 1998. *Damascus Gate.* Boston: Houghton Mifflin.

Storey, John. 1998. *An Introduction to Cultural Theory and Popular Culture.* Athens: University of Georgia Press.

Strandberg, Victor. 2000. "Dimming the Enlightenment: Thomas Pynchon's *Mason & Dixon.*" In *Pynchon and* Mason & Dixon, ed. Brooke Horvath and Irving Malin. Newark: University of Delaware Press.

Strehle, Susan. 1992. *Fiction in the Quantum Universe.* Chapel Hill: University of North Carolina Press.

Strozier, Charles, and Michael Flynn, eds. 1997. *The Year 2000: Essays at the End.* New York: New York University Press.

Sypher, Wylie. 1960. *Rococo to Cubism in Art and Literature.* New York: Vintage.

Tabbi, Joseph. 1995. *Postmodern Sublime: Technology and American Writing from Mailer to Cyberpunk.* Ithaca: Cornell University Press.

Tabor, James D., and Eugene V. Gallagher. 1995. *Why Waco? Cults and the Battle for Religious Freedom in America*. Berkeley: University of California Press.

Tate, Claudia. 1983. "Toni Morrison." In *Conversations with Toni Morrison*, ed. Danille Taylor-Guthrie. Jackson: University Press of Mississippi, 1994, 156–70.

Taylor-Guthrie, Danille, ed. 1994. *Conversations with Toni Morrison*. Jackson: University Press of Mississippi.

Thomas, Jo. 1998. "Behind a Seamless Façade; The Fractures of Discontent; Small Kansas Town Known for Right-Wing Links." *New York Times*, November 12, A16.

Thompson, William Irwin. 1996. *Coming into Being: Artifacts and Texts in the Evolution of Consciousness*. New York: St. Martin's Press.

Timehost. 2001. In Kelly Reames, *Toni Morrison's Paradise: A Reader's Guide*. New York: Continuum, 61. Online at http://www.time.com/time/community/transcripts/Chattro12198.html.

Tolstoy, Leo. 1982. *War and Peace*. New York: Penguin.

Toobin, Jeffrey. 1998. "The Plot Thins: The Oklahoma City Conspiracy That Wasn't." *New Yorker*, January 12, 8–9.

———. 1999. *A Vast Conspiracy: The Real Story of the Sex Scandal That Nearly Brought Down a President*. New York: Simon and Schuster.

Weber, Eugen. 1999. *Apocalypses: Prophecies, Cults, and Millennial Beliefs through the Ages*. Cambridge: Harvard University Press.

Weisenburger, Steven. 1988. *A Gravity's Rainbow Companion: Sources and Contexts for Pynchon's Novel*. Athens: University of Georgia Press.

White, Theodore H. 1975. *Breach of Faith: The Fall of Richard Nixon*. New York: Atheneum.

Whittier, Stephen. Unpublished letter to the author.

Wilentz, Gay. 1997. "Civilizations Underneath: African Heritage as Cultural Discourse in Toni Morrison's *Song of Solomon*." In *Toni Morrison's Fiction: Contemporary Criticism*, ed. David L. Middleton. New York: Garland, 109–33.

Wills, Garry. 1990. *Under God: Religion and American Politics*. New York: Simon and Schuster.

———. 1999. *A Necessary Evil: A History of American Distrust of Government*. New York: Simon and Schuster.

Wilson, Edward O. 2002. *The Future of Life*. New York: Knopf.

Wilson, Judith. 1981. "A Conversation with Toni Morrison." In *Conversations with Toni Morrison*, ed. Danille Taylor-Guthrie. Jackson: University Press of Mississippi, 1994, 129–37.

Wójcik, Daniel. 1997. *The End of the World as We Know It: Faith, Fatalism, and Apocalypse in America*. New York: New York University Press.

Wolfe, Alan. 2000. "The Opening of the Evangelical Mind." *Atlantic Monthly*, October, 55–76.

———. 2000. "The Pursuit of Autonomy." *New York Times Magazine*, May, 53–56, 67.

Wood, James. 1999. *The Broken Estate: Essays on Literature and Belief.* New York: Random House.

Woodward, Bob, Carl Bernstein, Haynes Johnson, Lawrence Meyer, and the staff of the *Washington Post.* 1974. *The Presidential Transcripts.* New York: Dell.

Wright, Stuart A., ed. 1995. *Armageddon in Waco: Critical Perspectives on the Branch Davidian Conflict.* Chicago: University of Chicago Press.

Wyatt, Jean. 1993. "Giving Body to the Word: The Maternal Symbolic in Toni Morrison's *Beloved.*" *PMLA* 108, no. 3 (May): 474–88.

Yardley, Jim. 2001. "Execution on TV Brings Little Solace." *New York Times,* June 12, A19.

Zavarzadeh, Mas'ud, and Donald Morton. 1994. *Theory as Resistance: Politics and Culture after (Post)structuralism.* New York: The Guilford Press.

Zernike, Kate. 2002. "Assigned Reading on Koran in Chapel Hill Raises Hackles." *New York Times,* August 20, A1.

———. 2002. "Georgia School Board Requires Balance of Evolution and Bible." *New York Times,* August 23, A8.

Index